A Psychoanalytic Exploration of Female to Male Transition

Drawing on theory from a range of schools of psychoanalytic thought, this timely book addresses and explores the phenomenon of the increasing number of people who were assigned female at birth and now identity as male, and what might underly the cultural pull to remove femaleness from self and body.

In *A Psychoanalytic Exploration of Female to Male Transition*, Serena Heller considers how early recognition of the difference between the sexes might evoke a melancholic attitude towards one's anatomy, as being one sex and not the other. She considers the ramifications of the developing sexual bodies of young women at a time when they are having great difficulty accepting them, addressing the complexity of female sexual development in relation to sexual aim and object, and how manifestations of early bisexuality can resurface during puberty. Focusing solely on the experience of female-to-male transition, rather than making broad assumptions of a universal trans experience, Heller provides a depth of theoretical analysis of biological and psychic aspects of female sexuality, and trans gender identifications.

Empathic in its approach and thorough in its conceptualisation, this volume is a vital resource for psychodynamic and psychoanalytic psychotherapists working directly with trans patients, and with those experiencing gender dysphoria and issues of sexual identity. The book assumes no prior expertise in analytic thought, and is designed to help mental health practitioners, students and researchers engaged in queer studies, gender studies and the intersection of psychoanalytic thought and gender identity.

Serena Heller, PhD, is a psychoanalytic psychotherapist in private practice in London, UK. She supervises, teaches and is a training therapist for child and adolescent, and adult trainings.

A Psychoanalytic Exploration of Female to Male Transition

Serena Heller

Routledge
Taylor & Francis Group

LONDON AND NEW YORK

Designed cover image: Vassily Kandinsky: Figurinen zu Bild XV1. Kiew. (1928) (C) Centre Pompidou, MNAMCCI, Dist. GrandPalaisRmn/Georges Meguerditchian

First published 2025
by Routledge
4 Park Square, Milton Park, Abingdon, Oxon OX14 4RN

and by Routledge
605 Third Avenue, New York, NY 10158

Routledge is an imprint of the Taylor & Francis Group, an informa business

British Library Cataloguing-in-Publication Data
A catalogue record for this book is available from the British Library

ISBN: 978-1-032-71857-6 (hbk)
ISBN: 978-1-032-60342-1 (pbk)
ISBN: 978-1-032-71861-3 (ebk)

DOI: 10.4324/9781032718613

Typeset in Times New Roman
by KnowledgeWorks Global Ltd.

Contents

Acknowledgements

I'd like to thank the trans men I interviewed for their participation.

Thanks also to Lionel Bailly, Mignon Nixon, Poul Rohleder, Sham Bailly and Heather Wood for their encouragement. And a huge thank you to Peter for his support, help and extraordinary patience.

Chapter 3 reworks some elements of an article I wrote for the BJP: Heller, S. (2023). Matriarchy, matricide & mourning. *British Journal of Psychotherapy*, *39*(1), 50–68. John Wiley & Sons Ltd and The British Psychotherapy Foundation.

Introduction

I approach the highly charged, complex and sensitive subject of gender identity by looking at trans men. My stance is psychoanalytic, which might make me an un-invited guest from the 'out set'. The explorations are intended to contribute to the understanding of how an experience of bodily incongruence might emerge from relational dimensions, which are necessarily underpinned by unconscious drives and instincts, usually the unrepresentable area of the mind. As humans we are driven by disruptive forces that can feel alien and impossible to navigate; these forces often locate in sexuality and gender manifestations. A feeling of alienation from one's body, markedly during adolescence, can compound alienation from one's external environment thereby complicating social belonging and access to help. My focus on trans men, as a specific aspect within the wider context of gender identity that has become a central, vexed and controversial aspect of identity politics in the 21st century, makes the subject of this book both topical and divisive culturally, socially, politically and academically.

There is a large and continually growing body of literature on gender transitioning that spans different disciplines: psychoanalytic, relational, psychosocial, sociological, medical, queer theory and trans studies. Although I traverse these disciplines, my approach is mainly psychoanalytic. Psychoanalysis is liminal in that it inhabits the uncertain terrain between where you have been and where you are going, physically emotionally and metaphorically. It finds a space "between phantasy and reality, between primary and secondary process thinking, between theory and experience, between conceptualization and intuition, between 'Now' and 'Elsewhere' ... It thus involves a temporal 'gap', the gap necessary for trans-formation" (Birksted-Breen, 2016: 27). The unconscious can make retroactive decisions that might take time to be recognised (Gozlan, 2018: 3–6). Although I refer to protest and rebellion as one of the elements through which to understand the proliferation of referrals for female to male transition, I concur with the description of transness as "a particular trajectory through which a subject comes to reckon with sexual and gender instability and find a more adequate means of inhabiting their body" (Osserman, 2024: 8).

I revisit well-trodden psychoanalytic formulations such as the registration of the primal scene, sexual difference, mourning, phantasy, reality and symbolisation.

DOI: 10.4324/9781032718613-1

I hope to shed some new light on these concepts and their application to gender identity, without weighted presumptions, reductivity or projections. Interpretations of the origins of gender incongruence might alight too easily on explanatory frameworks of early trauma, imprisonment in the 'wrong' body or hatred towards one's natal sex, albeit through the lens of conscious and unconscious reasoning. But perhaps it is more helpful to consider the level of the symbolic organisation (Amir, 2018: 42) that can underly this reasoning.

In recent decades there has been a proliferation of young people who were assigned female at birth (AFB) but now identify as trans masculine or trans men. I explore possible unconscious elements that might underly aspects of this proliferation that include a flight from womanhood and a move away from female homosexuality. There has been a substantial growth[1] in referrals to Gender Identity Clinics amongst AFB children and adolescents in the United Kingdom in recent years. There have been complex consequences to this overload that I mention later on, but significantly the GIDS (Gender Identity Development Service) at the Tavistock was closed in March 2024. By analysing this phenomenon, I look at how psychoanalysis as a discipline can better understand gender identity, paying particular attention to the underlying structures in the registration of sexual difference and the movement from femininity to masculinity and femaleness to maleness. The body, at the centre of experiences of gender disharmony, can in some instances become the site for protest. I look at the possible meaning and timing of this from an individual and social perspective. The sexual revolution in the 1960s has morphed into a gender revolution. Although the struggles embedded within a trans identity are by no means a new phenomenon, they have shifted to centre stage politically and ethically in recent decades.

How clinicians approach the fragile territory of gender variance also merits consideration. Clinicians can reside on a spectrum that stretches from 'trans-receptivity' (Lemma, 2023a: 813) to 'trans-prejudice'. Lemma introduces this receptive position as one that requires "an uncommitted position to what a transgender identification means so that we can be truly receptive to the idiosyncratic meanings and functions it has for a given person" (2023a: 813). Gender can stir up primitive forms of anxiety in patients and practitioners alike. Practitioners can find themselves caught up in, on the one hand, a form of rigidity or denial that might be antagonistic towards their patient's wishes, and on the other hand an unquestioning affirmative receptivity that can foreclose the potential for insight. Clinical approaches towards trans patients require a democratisation and 'unstraightening' (by this I mean a relinquishing of antiquated and heteronormative approaches) of the psychoanalytic therapeutic process, removed from a projection of pathology into a patient and towards gender as a subject for exploration for patient and therapist alike:

> … there needs to be constant challenge to a priori, bedrock notions about the natal body, the natal mind, and neutrality. The actually proper analytic attitude is anti-destiny – in relation to mind *and* body – and thus as open as possible to a future that cannot be known in advance.
>
> (Kloppenberg, 2022: 543)

Early recognition of the difference between the sexes might evoke a melancholic attitude towards one's anatomy, as being one sex and not the other. This disillusionment may have its origins in earlier experiences of infancy. The body of the infant and early stages of the developing mental apparatus are *orientational* and *relational*, there is a reaching towards another from the beginning of life through sound, smell and touch. Need is biologically driven; the baby's screams are bodily and the earliest form of protest. It is later that need converts to desire which incorporates the body and the mind sexually. Proprioception and perception precede a sense of identity, gradually weaving a pathway towards a sense of belonging. Belonging in my skin and body, namely embodiment, constructs who and how I am in the world.

During puberty a wish in individuals who were AFB,[2] to take flight from femaleness and femininity, can at times intensify; I consider the ramifications of the developing sexual bodies of trans men pre-transition, at a time when they are having great difficulty accepting them. I address the complexity of female sexual development in relation to sexual object and sexual aim, and how manifestations of early bisexuality can resurface during puberty. When the tie between mother and daughter is markedly ambivalent, early forms of aggression can also resurface onto and into the female body.

Spizzirri (2021) found in their study on Brazil, that the estimated proportion of gender diverse individuals varies between 0.1% and 2% of the population, indicating a wide range of possibilities. Figures will depend on the inclusion criteria and locations where studies were held. Most of the epidemiological studies were conducted on individuals already treated or referred for treatment at gender affirming healthcare centres. This means that available data may exclude large numbers who simply do not or are reluctant to seek help, and this seems to be the case not only in Brazil.

In the United Kingdom, questions on gender identity first appeared on the Census form in 2021, indicating a recognition of the growing importance of this data for public health policies. This Census (of England and Wales) was apparently the first in the world to collate information from an entire population, on gender identity (Biggs, 2023: 2). As both the 2021 UK Census, and electronic medical record systems in the United States now include gender identity questions within their data intake fields, more data is becoming available to researchers. The two clear trends that most studies reveal according to Nolan, Kuhner, and Giolani (2019), are the growth in the proportion of Transgender and Non-Binary[3] (TGNB) self-identifying individuals over time, and a higher proportion of TGNB amongst the younger generations.

An estimate by the UK Government Equalities Office (2018) suggested that there could be between 200,000 and 500,000 people who identify as transgender across the United Kingdom as a whole. In the 2021 UK Census, 262,000 people aged 16 and over from England and Wales said that their gender identity was different to their birth sex, 0.5% of the population (ONS, 2021), which seems to be broadly in line with the 2018 estimate, and also the Williams Institute research.

However, Biggs (2023) suggests that the Census might significantly overstate the number of trans individuals. The Census question, "Is the gender you identify with the same as your sex registered at birth?", assumes that people are familiar with the idea of making a distinction between sex and gender, which might not be the case in all sections of society and age groups, and many languages do not have separate words for sex and gender (Biggs, 2023).

The Williams Institute's research (Herman, Flores, & O'Neill, 2022) found that a growing number of population-based surveys in the United States and internationally ask questions to identify transgender people; that includes surveys by the US federal government. In their findings, based on survey data from 43 states of the United States, around 1.3 million adults (aged 18 and older) identify as transgender, of whom 38.5% are transgender women, 35.9% are transgender men, and 25.6% reported they are gender nonconforming.

Additionally, 300,000, 13 to 17-year-olds identify as transgender in the United States, which is 1.4% of those in that age bracket. Within the adult population, identification as transgender in those aged 18 to 24 was 1.3%, in those aged 25 to 64 it was 0.5% and in those aged 65 or older it was 0.3%, making an overall figure of 0.5% of the adult population.

The survey found that 13 to 17-year-olds comprised 18% of the transgender-identified population compared to their estimate of 10% in 2017 2018 (2022: 1), thus showing that the proportion of transgender individuals in younger age groups is very much higher than in older ones.

This raises the question of whether the greatly higher proportion of transgender individuals in the 13 to 17 age range (nearly three times the adult figure) will transfer to the adult population, or whether the identifications of this group will ultimately tend towards the adult average. The study also finds a regional divide amongst 13 to 17-year-olds: whilst in New York 3% of this age group identify as transgender, in Wyoming the figure is 0.6%.

Puberty suppression[4] for gender dysphoric adolescents, in the form of hormones, was first introduced in Amsterdam in The Netherlands in 1994 (Cohen-Kettenis & Van Goozen, 1998); there has subsequently been provision in Northern America (United States and Canada), in some countries in Europe, and in Australia/New Zealand. This has occurred despite reluctance due to lack of data on the long-term physical outcome. At what age and whether puberty should be medically controlled stimulates much debate and conflict (Biggs, 2019; Giordano, 2020); not least in the outcome of the 2020 UK Judicial Review (Bell-v-Tavistock, 2020) in which it was decided that it is highly unlikely that a child aged 13 or under would be competent to give such consent and doubtful that a child aged 14 to 15 could understand and weigh the long-term risks and consequences. With those aged 16 and over the presumption is that they have the ability to consent, but given that the treatment is as yet innovative and experimental, clinicians may seek the authorisation of the court prior to commencing clinical treatment. This was upheld in (September) 2021, following an Appeal (Bell-v-Tavistock, 2021). The outcome of the Court of Appeal stated that the decisions on competence to consent to receiving puberty blockers were for clinicians rather than the court to decide upon.

De Graaf and Carmichael (2019) verify that gender diverse individuals are contesting, owning and refining the language of gender. There is an emphasis towards de-pathologising in healthcare, that includes self-definition and self-determination. As an example, the preferred definition for 'biological sex' became *natal gender* and then *birth-assigned gender* (2019: 357). To my mind this language slippage *from sex to gender* as a defining category is highly symbolic, and epitomises a cultural shift from objectivity, essentialism and rationality to subjectivity and social constructivism. Sex, in this context, can morph into gender, which blurs their difference.

As part of previous research, I interviewed seven trans men aged between 18 and 30 years in 2019. I used the Psychoanalytic Research Interview method as advocated by Cartwright (2004), which recognises the use of psychoanalysis as a valid research method. I conducted these interviews as a researcher rather than as a psychotherapist and the subject was an interviewee and not a patient; but I used my psychoanalytic knowledge and experience to analyse the material. I then conducted some follow-up interviews in 2024. I include excerpts and discussion from some of these interviews throughout this book. I also include material from experiences of trans men that I have found in the literature and online. Trans men are a varied group like all other individuals, and it is therefore important not to reduce or generalise. In discussing trans men from a psychoanalytic stance, I may be at risk of accusations of transphobia. This brings in the conflict of accommodating unconscious processes, that diverge from the purely conscious approach that predominates. My material provides a particular analysis, based on interview material and psychoanalytic texts, which cannot and should not be generalised to all transgender identities. My thinking about trans men has continued to develop, and I can now see that in my previous writing some of my psychoanalytically based ideas or approaches leaned too heavily on presumptions and projections. An open psychoanalytic stance necessarily requires the freedom to explore the 'why' and 'how' in a non-pathologising or prejudiced manner. The historical prejudices (towards homosexuality) within psychoanalysis have hindered its reputation, but need not limit its potential as a rich resource for the understanding and exploration of sexuality and gender, particularly in relation to unconscious processes.

The trans-world is subjected to much prejudice, Young-Bruehl (1996) has written extensively about the derivatives of obsessional or hysterical forms of prejudice. Within these extreme forms of prejudice groups of people can be unconsciously ascribed a representation and embodiment of repressed and disavowed illicit sexual and aggressive desires. She applied this to racism, as did Fanon (1961) in his writing about the projection of 'animality' from white racists onto black African men and women. Young-Bruehl (1996: 108–109) discusses racism (via other theorists) as a prejudice representing or symbolising genital power or sexual prowess (Rohleder, 2024). These extreme and often irrational kind of projections can be transposed onto trans individuals in the form of transphobia. There can also be strong projection from within the trans community outwards. This leads to a situation of "prejudice against prejudice" (Hinshelwood, 2017: 206) which can lead to an endless cycle of confrontation, as well as impasse.

Psychoanalytic clinicians working with trans individuals can be pulled into extreme positions of acceptance or rejection. These pulls are partly driven by differing clinical positions in how gender is approached, but can also be understood as part of the (sometimes transphobic) countertransference[5]. The clinician's position is also challenged by the fact that gender transitioning cannot be placed in a preexisting familiar category, as it is "… its own singular phenomenon" that has the potential for new and open ways of thinking, less steeped in psychoanalytic rigour (Kloppenberg, 2022: 543). In writing about trans individuals, I too, subject myself to projections but hope that my writing will be taken as a contribution that can open up thinking rather than foreclose it.

Freud's seminal *Three Essays on the Theory of Sexuality* (1905) casts a new light on what is meant by a sexual instinct, and on whether we are inherently object-relating or not. The contradiction or conflict between these two positions is central to psychoanalytic theory. Freud did not conclude on this issue, perhaps deliberately as a way to draw the reader into this universal dilemma between instinct and object. Freud's statement that "What is essential and constant in the sexual instinct is *something else*" (my italics) (1905: 149), implies that Freud did not want to reduce sexuality either to relations or to object related interpretations.[6]

There has emerged what might be termed a growing 'gender impulse' or impulsion towards gender adjustment and transition in recent decades, as the possibilities of gender identity have become increasingly pliable. The difference between instinct and object applies to the vicissitudes of transgender identity: an *instinct* towards male or female identity in oneself and the sexual *object* of choice in the other can become entangled. In attempting to comprehend transgender identity our minds are put to work as it falls outside more traditional gender categories; for some it is counter-instinctual as we try to grasp that *natal sex no longer denotes gender*. The nuances in gender identity require nuanced thinking on the part of psychoanalytic clinicians who are faced with patients presenting with potentially life changing modifications to their bodies.

This requires a shift towards asking 'how' from asking 'why'; albeit 'why' ought not to be prohibited from meaningful exploration. Optimally clinicians will adopt and adapt to an openly enquiring stance open to gender variation, and a move away from an orthodoxy that might wish to pathologise unorthodox presentations of gender identity. The clinician's stance in relation to gender is on a spectrum of acceptance, scepticism or disavowal. It requires thoughtful flexibility, a Janus like capacity to keep an eye looking back at history as well as one looking forwards in relation to bodily consequences, with the bifocal ability to see close up (the present) and also into the far distance (the future).

Bi-ocularity is advocated as an important function of the analytic setting in order to foster symbolic thinking. This requires the psychic process of reverie alongside 'analysing', in the psychoanalytic setting. It has the function of "fostering ambiguity of the different times and spaces without collapsing them into the clear, logical and explanatory". It facilitates a space which is 'other', not just here and now, or you and me. (Birksted-Breen, 2016: 25). I suggest that this other space or dual vision is highly applicable to clinicians in relation to gender variance and transition.

Freud (1905) placed what he termed the (sexual) perversions on a continuum with normality. At the beginning of his work on the theory of sexuality, the sexual perversions as part of human sexuality were being subjected to a systematic study by Krafft-Ebing (1886) and Havelock-Ellis (1897), part of a group known as sexologists who were establishing sexology as a scientific discipline, so it was a topical area of investigation. It also has resonance and remains topical one hundred years on, but more in relation to gender identity than sexuality. Freud's approach was to throw open the more traditional definition of sexuality by using perversion as a yardstick. He found that the general disposition to (sexual) perversion was not unusual and this led him to the notion of polymorphous perversion in pregenital infantile sexuality.[7] This idea enabled Freud to then view adult perversion as a persistence or re-emergence of a component part of sexuality. The words perversion and normality are historically and culturally specific and therefore need to be used in context. The insight that perversion was equally applicable to us all, albeit propelled unconsciously, is valid and useful in contemporary clinical work. Freud enabled mysterious sexual symptoms to be understood psychically, and hence independently from biology; access to the psychic realm was via phantasy and psychic reality.

Whereas Freud described a continuum, my interviewees and many trans individuals refer to a spectrum of identities amongst which they locate their gender identity. The breadth of the spectrum facilitates multiple options for gender identification, which denotes a creative plethora of gender possibilities. Some aspects of gender freedom carry a defiant stance. This lends gender an air of rebellion or protest, which opens up poignant questions: *what is the 'gender protest' rebelling against*? Are the loosened boundaries of gender and the rapid access of gender identity empowering or disempowering for the young person in search of identity? There is (or has been) a risk that gender is latched onto as an explanatory framework that can subsume or cover up other psychological struggles that include depression, anxiety, anorexia, self-harm amongst others, and in that sense can be coexistent with other struggles and hence comorbid.

The concept of protest requires context. It can be linked to survival, and situations in which the personal becomes political and vice versa. Pilgrim (2020) usefully reminds us that the first cry of protest is the cry of the baby whose need is unmet. The social world into which we are born predates us. As Pilgrim puts it:

… we are born into a world in which social structures, norms and mores are *already present* and are not to do with our construal of them. Social structures are an intransitive aspect of reality, even if in human affairs the blurring of the boundary between transitive and intransitive aspects of reality needs constant attention … When we are born, we are thrown into a particular world that is structured physically by nature, psychologically by those immediate to us and socially by our species as a whole to date. However, we have the power as human agents individually and collectively to either preserve the *status quo* or to endeavour to alter it.

(2020: 117)

He goes on to discuss the psychosocial choices of protest and acquiescence. Trans individuals might well feel a sense of social injustice when they have to fight for their rights as citizens. Inevitably the challenge is in finding a position between the poles of protest and acquiescence without militancy, submission or social exclusion.

In usual circumstances, from birth onwards the infant is in their parent's hands, and more often than not in their mother's hands at the early stages of development. This of course would not be so definitive or binary with single parenting, gay male or female couples, transgender couples or combinations of these. I place the mother's or primary carer's very early forms of relating and handling of the infant's body as highly significant and influential. The child both absorbs and tries to make sense of what the mother or parents transmit consciously or unconsciously; this is what Laplanche (1997, 2007) termed enigmatic signifiers or the transmission of 'the sexual'.[8]

Puberty affirms the body's development along sexual and gender lines and it is often during puberty that gender conflicts for trans men come to the fore via unwanted secondary sex characteristics. The (then) female body with developing breasts and menstruation is confirmed as reproductive and thereby like mother's body. I discuss how this realisation and identification impacts on a body for which femaleness and femininity are felt as incongruent, and can evolve into "gender non-contendedness".[9] I also look at the movement of and within sexuality during gender transition.

The subject I am researching is currently in the public eye. Gender identity once was not, and now very much is woven into the fabric of everyday life in some parts of society and less so in others. For many young people under 30 it is unquestioned, uncontroversial and just 'is', whereas for other people across all ages it can be troubling and incomprehensible. Not only on widely used social media forums like Facebook, and YouTube but also in the recent UK Census, gender identity 'affiliation' is broken down into detail, confirming that it is now socially and culturally important to document it. This enhances the relevance of projects that aim to further our understanding of the subject, that includes follow-up research on the long-term consequences of transition and detransition.

The Chapters

In Chapter 1, I look at the melancholic aspect of knowing that one is born as one sex and not the other, and how this can trigger an early form of depression and entry into the reality of limits. I consider the different forms that this melancholic recognition can take, and how it can develop into a protest of femininity and femaleness as aligned with motherhood and an identification with mother's body. I consider how early awareness of difference between the sexes and contrast between phantasy and reality can trigger conflict that encompasses depression and denial. When this is unmanageable it can instigate a protest, and a schism between body and mind.

This chapter explores this early recognition and how it introduces a reality principle, that requires a rudimentary capacity to register and mourn *that which one is not*. It moves away from the earlier omnipotence of the option to have all options. I refer to Freud and Klein on mourning, and to Klein's Depressive Position (1935). I also include theoretical positions on when recognition of the sexed body can be registered and mentalised developmentally.

I expand Freud's dictum that "anatomy is destiny", to contemporary experiences of a psychically gendered anatomy. The body that is held in mind, rather than in one's anatomy, is destiny. This creates a tension between psychic and physical anatomy that is central to many aspects of gender identity conflicts, not only for the trans individual but also for clinicians (whether medical or psychological), siblings, parents and teachers.

The female anatomy, particularly from menstruation onwards, can be perceived as being tantamount to pregnancy and childbirth and evoke terror about this fated or expected female trajectory. This can compound the (unwanted) awareness of being one sex and not the other. I suggest that this melancholic realisation can at times, and in many differing ways, transform itself into a wish to undo femaleness.

I look at and discuss the concepts body schema, sexual schema, unconscious body image and the mind's image of itself as a way into further understanding the body and mind as registers.

In Chapter 2, I consider guilt, housed in the body early in life, as a manifestation of persecutory anxiety that can then resurface during adolescence in the form of aggressive impulses. I suggest that these can be ignited by pronounced ambivalence between a mother and daughter, at times leading to a wish in the daughter to excise femaleness from her body. This drive might also stem from an early registration of rejection in the body, as not being that which mother desires.

I explore how early manifestations of guilt might take root in the body before a capacity to symbolise or mentalise has developed. It can be hard to disentangle guilt from early forms of persecutory anxiety that are bound up with the infant's rudimentary drive to survive. This drive is experienced in the body via sensations of repletion and depletion. I discuss manifestations of guilt through clinical and interview material.

In Chapter 3, I introduce the idea of matricide that can bypass the mother and land instead in the daughter's body, or against her female body. In this way actual murderous feelings, whether conscious or unconscious, from a daughter towards her mother are redirected, as the female body becomes the antagonist. In this chapter I discuss incidents of matricide via Orestes and Zeus, as well as Athena's so-called motherless state.

Matricide for a daughter has potency, not unlike Oedipal patricide for a son. If the Oedipus complex cannot be lived, an alternative complex might manifest in daughters: that of killing femininity or femaleness, in which 'a mother is being beaten'. I suggest that when the tie between mother and daughter is markedly ambivalent, early forms of aggression can resurface onto and into the female body which can then become the site for enacted matricidal wishes. The female body becomes the enemy that is vulnerable to attack, rather than the mother, whether in phantasy or reality. Identification with femaleness in relation to one's mother is rejected and unwanted, and her symbolic structuring power is thus denuded. I include incidents of matricide in Greek mythology such as Orestes' murder of Clytemnestra, and Athena's so-called motherless state as symbolic in its erasure of Metis.

In Chapter 4, I describe the bespoke nature of masculinity for some trans men as non genital, in that it does not necessitate a penis. The body can be used as a symbol for the realisation of a wish, which creates equivalence between the psychic and physical terrain.

Non genital masculinity is not based on being born male. It differs from 'female masculinity' or 'masculine femininity'. It is a gender identity I wish to consider specifically in relation to trans men. The body may or may not be altered hormonally or surgically to corroborate the gender *as felt and seen in the mind's eye.*

Lacan dislodged the anatomical penis from the biological to the symbolic, bringing to light a momentous shift from body to symbol, a severance from 'anatomy is destiny'. I describe different forms of concrete and symbolic masculinity that include: hegemonic, seminal, medicalised, pharmacological and après-coup. I discuss the phallus in its Freudian, Lacanian, Lesbian and Feminist forms that traverse aspects of Queer Theory. The notions of non-phallic and non-genital masculinity, the trans phallus and après-coup masculinity are introduced as part of my exploration.

In Chapter 5, I look at the unique or bespoke temporality that aspects of trans identity can inhabit when the present informs the past: 'I am therefore I was'. The temporality of gender has specific meaning when 'psychic gender' does not correspond with natal gender, as identity is retrospectively attributed, thus reversing après-coup into 'what is now was then'. The term après-coup is a well-recognised psychoanalytic term that reformats, challenges and introduces a non-linear timeline for development of sex, sexuality and gender; it questions causal links that shape personal history. This temporality can unbind chronology as historical or linear and is antithetical to the usual psychoanalytic discourse. It disturbs the vertical generational links between mothers and daughters or fathers and daughters or horizontal links between brothers and sisters or between sisters.

An understanding of trans identity might require the therapist to develop what the Botellas (2005: 10–12) describe as a particular capacity for retrogressive movement in order to enter into the patient's non-representability so that a perception of the void can be grasped and then become representable. This could manifest as countertransference that necessitates deep empathic identification. The retrogressive movement would also require an entry into trans-temporality, that restructures linear development.

I refer to the distinction that Scarfone (2014) makes between the sequential developmental line of maturational infantile sexuality and the infantile sexual that remains as the unconscious centre of adult sexuality and precludes evolution and maturity (2014: 335). The notion that time is not rooted in chronology is pertinent to some experiences of trans individuals who might not welcome the historicising of their experience. It is as if, in some cases, the experience of transgender identity exists somewhere outside linear time, in a more unconscious than conscious suspended space, that cancels developmental time. Past time can be set up against present time in what can become a negation of origin that includes conception.

In Chapter 6, I look at detransitioning, and the painful aspect of mourning a prior wish or quest that was not realised. This aspect of gender identity can be more invisible. Sometimes the reality of the transitioned body does not live up to prior wishes or desires, although in many instances it does bring relief to much prior discomfort. When post-transition relief is not experienced, it can bring about a more melancholic aspect of gender identity as once desired and not achieved. The disappointment of having to live with irreversible changes to the body, via hormones or surgery, that were once actively and determinedly sought, is a painful process and requires a capacity to revisit and mourn earlier wishes and look back at a younger and driven self. This throws light on the difficulty of a sometimes concrete or physical solution for a psychic difficulty that is complex and might require in-depth exploration. Whereas once the contention was about the age of consent for sex, it has now become about the age of consent for puberty blockers. In question also is the individual capacity for intra-psychic consent, agreeing with the part of the self that identifies with and as one gender rather than another. I look at ethical considerations in relation to aspects of the decision-making process for clinicians working with trans individuals.

My initial interest in gender identity was born out of curiosity and a genuine wish to understand more, Klein's (1931) epistemophilic impulse or instinct (*Wissentrieb*), through expanding my knowledge in the field. I have not focussed on the politics of gender, or on transgender as a movement, although these cannot be entirely side-lined. One cannot take politics out of gender-ethics, or gender-ethics out of politics. Gender politics have been, are and will continue to be a lively and divisive subject area. A live component has been the outcome of the judicial review (2020) about how and when puberty blockers can be prescribed, the subsequent appeal against this outcome, that was upheld (2021), and the closure of GIDS at the Tavistock in March 2024, and more recently the Cass Review of gender identity services for children and young people (April 2024). Ethical principles of authority and decision-making comingle with autonomy, well-being, best interests, 'life chances'[10] and a child's right to an 'open future'[11]; that all require careful consideration.

There can be a temptation in the field of gender and sexuality to reduce concepts to binaries, and positing femininity against masculinity or vice versa achieves very little. Benjamin is lucid on this:

> If sex and gender as we know them are oriented to the pull of opposing poles, then these poles are not masculinity and femininity. Rather gender dimorphism itself represents only one pole, the other pole being the polymorphism of the psyche.
>
> (Benjamin, 1995: 140)

It is a challenge to write about gender identity whilst taking into account unconscious processes; although these are at the heart of psychoanalytic ways of thinking, there is much scepticism outside of the field. Gender is continually under construction internally and unconsciously and cannot be divorced from more conscious external forces: whether economic, medical, political, familial, regulatory and governmental. How these internal and external factors combine and evolve will shape one's gender identity. The impact of social forces cannot be underestimated, and neither can the less accessible influence of the unconscious. Important too is how gender becomes symbolised via phantasy, into a wish that can be realised in the body. The construction of gendered identity is inherently and ubiquitously unstable, recruits a vast complexity of processes and, as Freud (1925) pointed out, leans on the psychic conundrum of sexual difference that cannot be limited to genital difference alone.

Gender identity is situated within the larger construct of identity. As Lemma puts it, we inhabit an *identity economy* (2023b). Gender identity, although not a new phenomenon, has become a central component of identity politics within the cultural zeitgeist of the 21st century. In many academic disciplines, that include most of the humanities and social sciences, identity has become a substantial field of study. The focus on identity has developed from the quest to achieve a coherent sense of self following a social move towards individuation and individualising (Rustin, 2023). Social and economic changes have brought about the need for identities to present differently in different work situations (Goffman, 1956). The promotion of self via identity takes place in a hugely competitive world both culturally and socially. As Rustin states: "It is evident that assertions of identities that are based on biologically or socially defined categories as race, ethnicity, religion, gender, sexuality, and nationality (among others) have become central to many individuals' and groups' understanding of themselves" (2023: 451). The group allegiance can function to strengthen or redress experiences of disadvantage and provides a collective voice. My exploration of gender identity is necessarily situated within this broader context of identity. Although I am introducing themes that might relate to trans men as a group, I am equally aware of the importance of not letting the group subsume the individual.

Notes

1 An increase in referrals of 40 natal females in 2009/2010 to 929 in 2015/16, Gender Identity Development Service statistics. Between 2011 and 2017 natal female and male referrals to GIDS had risen approximately tenfold (Butler et al., 2018); in 2021/22 to number of referrals rose to 3585 (GIDS, 2023).
2 The term Assigned Female at Birth, is used to indicate natal femaleness although this may not be the individual's current gender identity.
3 A gender identity that does not subscribe to the binary of male or female, regardless of natal sex.
4 GnRHa, gonadotropin-releasing hormone agonist. Also referred to as 'puberty blockers', or 'puberty delaying medication'.

5 Countertransference is a term that describes an unconscious reaction in the therapist to what can be 'transferred' unconsciously from a patient. It can be helpful to the therapist in discerning what emotional reaction this might stir up in relation to their patient. A therapist needs to acquire the ongoing capacity to disentangle their own internal emotional responses from what might be a projection, and what the patient might be recreating in the therapeutic dynamic.

6 This aspect of the *Three Essays* is discussed by Blass (2016).

7 In Freud's (1905) understanding of pregenital infantile sexuality component instincts are interlinked with the diversity of erotogenic zones.

8 The Sexual (in translation) or le sexual as opposed to the more standard French term le sexuel, is a neologism of Laplanche (2007). By *sexual* Laplanche is encompassing Freud's more expanded idea of sexuality.

9 Rawee, P., Rosmalen, J. G. M., Kalverdijk, L., & Burke, S. M. (2024). Development of gender non-contendedness during adolescence and early adulthood. *Archives of Sexual Behaviour, 53*(5): 1813–1825.

10 Spade, D. (2011). The term 'life chances' is used by Spade to describe the neoliberal and capitalist conditions of unequal distribution, and their disproportionate impact on trans people.

11 Feinberg, J. (1992).

Bibliography

Amir, D. (2018). The two sleeps of Orlando: Transsexuality as caesura or cut. In O. Gozlan (Ed.), *Current critical debates in the field of transsexual studies* (Chapter 2, pp. 36–47). London & New York: Routledge.

Bell-v-Tavistock. (December 1, 2020). Judicial review. Retrieved July 29, 2020, from https://www.judiciary.uk/wp-content/uploads/2020/12/Bell-v-Tavistock-Judgment.pdf

Bell-v-Tavistock. (2021). Retrieved April 15, 2024, from https://www.judiciary.uk/wp-content/uploads/2022/07/Bell-v-Tavistock-summary-170921.pdf

Benjamin, J. (1995). Sameness and difference: Toward an 'Overinclusive' model of gender development. *Psychoanalytic Inquiry, 15*(1), 125–142.

Biggs, M. (July 29, 2019). *The Tavistock's Experiment with Puberty Blockers*, version 1.0.1. Retrieved July 29, 2021, from https://users.ox.ac.uk/~sfos0060/Biggs_ExperimentPuberty Blockers.pdf

Biggs, M. (2023). Gender Identity in the 2021 Census of England and Wales: What Went Wrong? Retrieved April 15, 2024, from https://www.sociology.ox.ac.uk/publication/1327667/crossref.

Birksted-Breen, D. (2016). Bi-ocularity, the functioning mind of the psychoanalyst. *The International Journal of Psychoanalysis, 97*(1), 25–40.

Blass, R. (2016). Understanding Freud's conflicted view of the object-relatedness of sexuality and its implications for contemporary psychoanalysis: A re-examination of three essays on the theory of sexuality. *International Journal of Psychoanalysis, 97*(3), 591–613.

Botella, C., & Botella, S. (2005). *The work of psychic figurability* (pp. 1–13). London and New York: Routledge.

Butler, G., De Graaf, N., Wren, B., Carmichael, P., Adu-Gyamfi, K., Brain, C., Goedhart, C., Kleczewski, S., Perkins, E., Roberts, A., Alvi, s, Avatpalle, B., Carruthers, P., Mushtaq, T., Walker, J., Abid, N., & Shaikh, G. (2018). Assessment and support of children and adolescents with gender dysphoria. *Archives of Disease in Childhood, 103*(7), 631–636. Published online April 12, 2018.

Cartwright, D. (2004). The psychoanalytic research interview: Preliminary suggestions. *Journal of the American Psychoanalytic Association, 52*(1), 209–242.

Cohen-Kettenis, P. T., & Van Goozen, S. (1998). Pubertal delay as an aid in diagnosis and treatment of a transsexual adolescent. *European Child & Adolescent Psychiatry*, *7*, 246–248.

De Graaf, N. M., & Carmichael, P. (2019). Reflections on emerging trends in clinical work with gender diverse children and adolescents. *Clinical Child Psychology & Psychiatry*, *24*(2), 353–364.

Fanon, F. (1961, 2001). *The wretched of the earth*. C. Farrington (trans), Penguin Classics.

Feinberg, J. (1992). *The child's right to an open future*. Princeton: Princeton University Press.

Freud, S. (1905). Three essays on the theory of sexuality. In *Standard Edition* (Vol. 7, pp. 125–243). London: Hogarth Press.

Freud, S. (1925). Some psychical consequences of the anatomical distinction between the sexes. In *Standard Edition* (Vol. 19, 241–258). London: Hogarth Press.

GIDS. (2020). Gender Identity Development Service, Referrals to GIDS, Financial Years 2015–2016 to 2019–2020. http://gids.nhs.uk/number-referrals, accessed September 16, 2023, site inactive September 11, 2024.

GIDS. (2023). Number of Referrals to GIDS [WWW Document] Gender Identity Development Service. https://gids.nhs.uk/about-us/number-of-referrals/, accessed September 2, 2023, site inactive on September 11, 2024.

Giordano, S. (2020). Is puberty delaying treatment 'experimental treatment'? *International Journal of Transgender Health 21*(2), 113–121.

Goffman, E. (1956). *The presentation of self in everyday life*. New York: Doubleday.

Government Equalities Office. (2018). Trans People in the UK, GEO-LGBT factsheet. Retrieved April 17, 2024, from https://assets.publishing.service.gov.uk/media/5b3a478240f0b64603fc181b/GEO-LGBT-factsheet.pdf.

Gozlan, O. (2018). Introduction. In O. Gozlan (Ed.), *Current critical debates in the field of transsexual studies* (pp. 1–12). London & New York: Routledge.

Havelock-Ellis, H. (1897–1928). *Studies in the psychology of sex*. F.A. Davis.

Herman, J. L., Flores, A. R., & O'Neill, K. K. (2022). How Many Adults and Youth Identify as Transgender in the United States? *The Williams Institute, UCLA School of Law*.

Hinshelwood, R. D. (2017). On not thinking straight: Comments on a conceptual marriage. In N. Giffney & E. Watson (Eds.), *Clinical encounters in sexuality* (pp. 197–210). Earth, Milky Way: Punctum Books.

Klein, M. (1931). A contribution to the theory of intellectual inhibition. *International Journal of Psychoanalysis*, *12*, 206–218.

Klein, M. (1935). A contribution to the psychogenesis of manic-depressive states. *International Journal of Psychoanalysis*, *16*, 145–174.

Kloppenberg, B. (2022). What happens when a trans patient happens? *Journal of the American Psychoanalytic Association*, *70*, 525–546.

Krafft-Ebing, R. (1886/1965). *Psychopathia sexualis*. New York: Putnam's Sons.

Laplanche, J. (1997). The theory of seduction and the problem of the other. *International Journal of Psychoanalysis*, *78*, 653–666.

Laplanche, J. (2007). Gender, sex, and the sexual. *Studies in Gender and Sexuality*, *8*(2), 201–219.

Lemma, A. (2023a). The missing: Exploring the use of photographs in "Working Through" the Natal body with Transgender youth. *International Journal of Psychoanalysis*, *104*(5), 809–828.

Lemma, A. (2023b). The seductions of identity: Thinking about identity and transgender. *Psychoanalytic Quarterly*, *92*, 407–434.

Nolan, I. T., Kuhner, J., & Giolani, W. D. (2019). Demographic and temporal trends in transgender identities and gender confirming surgery. *Translational Andrology and Urology*, *8*(3), 184–190.

Office for National Statistics (ONS). (2021). Retrieved April 17, 2024, from https://www.ons.gov.uk/peoplepopulationandcommunity/culturalidentity/genderidentity/bulletins/genderidentityenglandandwales/census2021.

Osserman, J. (2024). Psychoanalysis and trans, a study of two psychosocial scenes. In S. Frosh et al. (Eds.), *The Palgrave handbook of psychosocial studies*. Springer Nature, Cham, Switzerland: Palgrave Macmillan.

Pilgrim, D. (2020). Why do we protest (sometimes)? In *Critical realism for psychologists* (Chapter 9, pp. 111–128). London and New York: Routledge.

Rohleder, P. (2024). Homophobia and the psychic life of LGBTQ people. In S. Frosh et al. (Eds.), *The palgrave handbook of psychosocial studies*. Springer Nature, Cham, Switzerland: Palgrave Macmillan.

Rustin, M. (2023). Identity or identification? Why the difference between these concepts matters. *Psychoanalytic Quarterly*, *92*, 11–25.

Scarfone, D. (2014). The three essays and the meaning of the sexual in psychoanalysis. *The Psychoanalytic Quarterly*, *83*(2), 327–344.

Spade, D. (2011). As cited by Hughes, L. in Wronging the right-body narrative: On the universality of gender uncertainty, O. Gozlan (2018) (Ed.), *Current critical debates in the field of transsexual studies* (Chapter 13, pp. 181–193) London & New York: Routledge.

Spizzirri, G. (January 26, 2021). Proportions of people identified as transgender and non-binary gender in Brazil, Pub. Scientific Reports II, Article no. 2240.

The Cass Review. (2024). Independent review of gender identity services for children and young people. Final report. April 2024. Retrieved April 18, 2024, from cass.independent-review.uk/home/publications/final-report/

Young-Bruehl, E. (1996). The prejudice that is not one. *The anatomy of prejudices* (Chapter 4, pp. 104–136). Cambridge, Massachusetts: Harvard University Press.

Chapter 1

The Melancholy of Anatomy

For as the distraction of the mind, **amongst** other outward causes & perturbations, alters the temperature of the body, so the distraction & distemper of the body will cause a distemperature of the soul and 'tis hard to decide which of these two do more harm to the other.

(Burton, 2021/1621: 367)

At a certain point relatively early on in life we who are born female notice that our body is not the same as other bodies around us, whether it is the body of a brother, friend or father, and initially mother's developed female body is also different. The question that Alice Neel's mother asks highlights a pronounced demarcation of the sexes in the past: "I don't know what you expect to do in the world, Alice? You're only a girl".[1] The roots of the word 'girl' are apposite in relation to my enquiry, as the first appearance of it in the written record comes from a poem around the year 1300, which describes 'gurles and men', the gurles referring to either children or boys, and 'men' referring to adults, lending this word *girl* a gender-neutral meaning. For a number of centuries after 1300, the word 'girl' could mean a child of either sex (Nuttall, 2023: 190). The early awareness of the difference *of* and *between* the sexes and generations might be thought of as an early demarcation into differentiating groups: that I belong to, do not belong to, wish to acquire and do not wish to acquire. The realisation requires a shift from a more omnipotent position in which I can be all things, all ages and any sex or gender. This recognition of omnipotence introduces a demarcation that ushers in an awareness of limits within which there may not be an option to have or be all options. This momentary or gradual awareness can land in many different ways and is highly individual. Freud referred to this as the Reality Principle, separate and different to the Pleasure Principle (1920).

This early introduction of reality requires a rudimentary capacity to register, renunciate and mourn *that which I am not*. It can also prompt curiosity, puzzlement and rage about why I am different anatomically to my brother, friend or father, who have an externally visible part to their anatomy; and to my mother who has breasts and bodily hair. A female infant might start to notice, in a rudimentary way, and wonder what she has and what she does not have. This early registration precedes

DOI: 10.4324/9781032718613-2

the capacity for mental processing. Coming to terms with external reality breaks into what is held in phantasy, and ushers in conflict, disillusionment and protest, but also the capacity to imagine and create.

The psychoanalytic stance on this demarcation, from Freud onwards, has tended to concentrate on the *experience of a lack*, rather than the *experience of difference*, in spite of these concepts in some respects being bound together with one another. Although much psychoanalytic clinical observation has supported the experience in women of this lack or variations on this theme, it was an obstinate vision and obstructive to other ways of thinking about the difference between the sexes.

The awareness of the difference between the sexes, gradually and by no means coherently or definitively, moves into a sense of identity that has gendered aspects. This can be over the course of a few years or a lifetime. Gender to a certain extent has replaced (biological) sex as a category of identity. I mean this more schematically than categorically. This slippage from sex to gender has become a contentious issue in the field of gender identity. Although Freud referred to sexual impulses, there has been an increase in what might be termed 'gender impulsivity' in recent decades.

A sense of gender identity cannot be divorced from a constellation of parents and siblings, who either preceded one's existence, made it happen or might have been present from or before birth. Freud (1918/1914) referred to 'the primal scene' as the actual act of our conception and the multiplicity of phantasies that it can generate in our unconscious. The reality of the pre-existence of conception, in whichever form it might have taken, is an immutable fact. We are not self-created or self-produced; there were progenitors who preceded us.

The complex struggle to locate one's gender has been referred to as "the trauma of gender" by Gozlan (2008), who links the challenges of gender to the challenges of making sense of one's own desire, as that which rests between its signifiers and as something in constant movement. In his writing, he shows how the archaic nature of gender "...pushes for settlement, forcing a choice (to be a man or a woman) as a way to settle the traumatic nature of the self for which desire is not finite and where nothing can be settled once and for all" (2008: 541). He sees the psychoanalytic clinic as a place to help reconcile gender as an unconscious registration of trauma.

There are differing schools of thought on when a small child is capable of recognising and knowing that they are one sex and not another. There are gendered projections from parents, carers or siblings towards a child, that are absorbed consciously and unconsciously. These projections fall into a wide range from the concreteness of the colour of a bedroom, clothing, toys, to more complex projections from parents' unconscious expectations, hopes, experiences and phantasies. Laplanche referred to these as enigmatic signifiers (Laplanche, 1997, 2007). A mother might want her daughter to look feminine, wear nice dresses, have long hair, wear only boyish clothes, or decide that her child will be raised as 'gender neutral'. The last one can be thought of as eradication or bypassing of the reality of having conceived a female or male child, a neutralisation of difference.

In some respects the influences of parental expectations and projections are ever-present in shaping the infant and toddler's gendering, or gendered projections. Fausto-Sterling (2012) puts it well:

> The environmental trappings of gender, from the voices, faces, modes of holding and touching, dress, hair, and grooming, to the colours in the room, the toys offered and the baby clothing used, are ever present. From birth or before an infant absorbs them, commits them to memory, develops expectations about them, and receives bodily messages about their own sex and gender.
>
> (2012: 14)

Edgcumbe and Burgner (1975), British child and adult psychologists and psychoanalysts, discuss the early development of body representation and identifications in girls. They claim that it is only after the attainment of a clearly defined self-representation, that is achieved due to developing ego capacities, that a girl can start to make comparisons between her own body and the male body. They see the capacity for a girl to come to terms with her body and the boy's body as reliant on her narcissistic organisation, extent of ego development as well as interactions with significant 'objects'[2] or others in her environment. All of these contribute to her gradual acceptance of her female body, and it is not until adolescence that this process is completed, *if it is completed at all* (1975: 174).

The subjective experience of being masculine or feminine is gradual, developmental and not a biological feat for Fast (1984: 4–21), a professor of Clinical Psychology at the University of Michigan, who wrote about gender identity. She advocated the existence of an 'undifferentiated and overinclusive early matrix of gender development' that precedes the dawning awareness of gender differences. To my mind, this is a good description of a 'pre-gendered' state. For Fast, it is not until the second half of the second year that the child can identify maleness or femaleness in relation to both self and other. For her, awareness of the difference between the sexes takes place when the limitations of one's own gender are fully recognised. She believes that children initially take in a broad array of characteristics from people in their surrounding environment to the extent that no attribute is left out. It is not until actual awareness of the differences between the sexes becomes established that the prior notion of unlimited possibilities has to be relinquished.

I am particularly interested in the manifestations of this dawning reality or renunciation and how it affects gender identity. There are varying views on how and when the awareness of what one is, and what one is not and cannot be, emerges developmentally. I suggest that the capacity to bear the reality of the limitations of one's gender is pivotal, whether this capacity registers consciously or unconsciously. The psychological nature of this registration is also pivotal. It is hard to place this capacity in a definitive timeframe, as there is no consensus on when exactly this occurs. The conscious and unconscious logging of this experience can stretch out from early childhood to adolescence and adulthood, and is subject to much variation in how and where it is managed psychically. It may be part of a wider network of perceptual experiences, simultaneously acknowledged and denied that all become part of an individual archive of sensory and bodily registrations that form sexual and gender identity. A small child can behave and pretend that there is no difference between the sexes until an actual social experience breaks up this belief.

Pre-Oedipal Representation

It is important and difficult to establish at what age or stage of development a child can register the difference between the sexes. This recognition requires a capacity to mentalize difference, beyond the all-inclusive undifferentiated phase that Fast (1984) refers to for both girls and boys. It is not until the second half of the second year that the child can identify maleness or femaleness in relation to both self and other.

Whereas Freud postulated that boys and girls believed themselves to be initially male and masculine, Fast dissents from this and believes that children initially take in a broad array of characteristics from people in their surrounding environment to the extent that no attribute is left out. Awareness of the difference between the sexes takes place when the limitations of one's natal sex are fully recognised and the prior notion of unlimited possibilities has to be relinquished.

Fonagy and Target (1996) introduced 'psychic equivalent' and 'pretend mode', two forms that differ in the assumed relationship between internal and external realities, in a small child. They maintained that the subjective sense of oneness between what is internal and external in the development of children is a universal phase. For the small child, inner experience is equivalent to and hence mirrors external reality, and this extends to feeling that others have the same experience that he (or she) does; and that the very young child does not yet have the capacity for the merely representational nature of ideas and feelings (pp. 217–219).

It follows that there is no exact consensus on the age at which the recognition of difference between the sexes is established, and that these can occur on a spectrum of 'capacity to mentalize', from rudimentary registration to a more sophisticated awareness.

I conducted a series of interviews with trans men aged between 18 and 30 with some follow-up interviews four years later with some of the interviewees. I will discuss aspects of these interviews[3] throughout this book. I will refer to all of the trans men as 'he', as this is how they identified at the time of the interviews.

I asked Milo (aged 20 at time of interview) how he related to his body.

He responded:

So initially when I started feeling that I was in the wrong body was when puberty hit because I think that everybody's kind of really similar when you are kids, so I just didn't think about it. ... there was a time when I was convinced that I wasn't going to get a menstrual cycle for whatever reason. I don't remember what my child rationale was for that but I was really proud of that, but then that was not the case. I guess a lot of it had to do for me with my internal anatomy, having a uterus and the idea of being pregnant just freaked me out…

(Milo, 2020)

Milo explained that he grew up in a gender-neutral home so was not really conscious of gender until puberty. The difference between the sexes is ironed out in the house of Milo's mother's mind in which gender is neutralised. This is transmitted to her daughter who is then confused by this 'enigmatic signifier' and by the social reality of the difference between the sexes. Until then, he presented androgynously, and aspects of puberty like menstruation and breast growth were disliked and deeply uncomfortable. He described that his body was not developing in the way that he'd thought it would be; and that when he dreamed, he'd be in a man's body, indicating a strong unconscious alliance with maleness.

It seemed that Milo was frightened and alienated by the physicality of a female internal anatomy. His unconscious anatomy and identity were male. His menstruating female body and the male body in his dreams were at odds, and this disjunction was hard to bear.

Milo developed an eating disorder as one way to stem having menstrual cycles. Milo did not wish his body to be like his mother's or sister's and wanted to be like his dad. His eating disorder can be read as his determined attempt to control or starve his 'femaleness' from developing in the body and an early signal of body dysphoria. He found a way to try and control the unwanted reality of having a female body with an orifice that could both menstruate, be penetrated and lead to pregnancy. As Milo had an aversion to his female genitals or the idea of penetration, his mouth became the orifice that he was closing off symbolically. Williams has written about 'the no-entry system of defences' in relation to adolescent eating disorders whereby the defence has been installed as a protection from projections that can often be experienced as persecutory foreign bodies (Williams, 1997: 121).

Joe, a trans man, aged 19, spoke about a kind of discomfort he'd experienced ever since the approach of puberty and that he did not quite know why that discomfort was there. It became noticeable when his developing female body expressed itself more obviously to both himself and to the world.

When I was younger, I used to hang out with the boys a lot more, and then when I started becoming more feminine physically, I started feeling uncomfortable around the boys and I started making more friendships with the girls. And that's still how it is now. If I do make friendships with the boys, it turns out that they're actually on the LGBT spectrum.

(Joe, 2020)

Joe describes an allegiance with maleness earlier on in life:

… when I was very young between a toddler and ten, where my hair was really short and obviously with kids you can't tell a boy voice from a girl voice because they all sound the same, and my chest wasn't growing yet and I would always get the question: "are you a boy or a girl"? And I felt annoyed to say that I was a girl, I kind of wanted to be a boy and hang out with the boys … play football and do all that stuff.

(Joe, 2020)

For Joe, it was during puberty that his female body became a source of extreme discomfort, and led him to question his gender identity. He initially identified as a gay woman and then questioned his attraction to women, as likely to be emanating from his masculinity and maleness. He came to the realisation that he did not like being a woman, and wondered if there was something more to him than just liking women.

I am interested in this point of departure from that of remaining a gay woman, attracted to other women, towards the move away from this identity to another one that wishes to sever a more overtly homosexual sexuality. I think that embedded in this drive is the wish to get away from having and acknowledging a female anatomy, which would include an orientation from this body towards another female body, and from another female body towards him. Joe, I surmised, needed to cement something more male for himself, as that was how he experienced himself.

Understandably, Joe did not like to be "misgendered", once he identified as a trans man. But it seems that what was perhaps most depressing for him, was being confronted physically and psychologically by his own female body. The reality of his female anatomy breaks up the wish and lived experience of presenting to the world, or passing[4] as male.

Penis-less: The Philosophy of Lack

The earliest manifestation of the renunciation for girls is coming to terms with not having a penis, and for boys it is not being able to bear children, which includes not having breasts that are both sexual and feeding.

Karen Horney was a psychoanalyst and a contemporary of Freud's. She practiced at the Berlin Psychoanalytic Society until 1932, and then moved to the United States. She held a strong belief in socio-cultural factors as important influences on lifelong development. She adopted Freud's notions of penis envy and castration anxiety, although she questioned the conflation of these notions (Mitchell, 1975: 125) with what might be thought of as a dissenting feminist approach. She struggled to accept the way in which women were defined in relation to men, and understood penis envy as a woman's wish to have a similar status to a man *culturally* rather than a wish to actually possess a penis. Horney wrote about womb envy in men as a parallel loss that fuelled a drive to succeed. She wrote several papers between 1922 and 1937 on feminine psychology, a field in which she is regarded as a pioneer. Her insight in relation to the difference between men and women, at a time when patriarchy was so dominant, stands out.

It was the inherently masculine foundation from which ideas or long familiar 'facts' emanated that Horney questioned, especially in relation to the development of women; this was also questioned by Stoller[5] later on (Stoller, 1964, 1968, 1985).

Horney was interested in aspects of difference between the sexes that went beyond anatomical differences (1926: 327), such as a woman's reproductive capacities. She posits Ferenczi's idea (1924) that the act of penetration for a man is linked to a desire to return to the mother's womb. Horney cites the existence of masculine envy of pregnancy, childbirth and motherhood, but sees it as more easily sublimated than the girl's penis envy.

The small girl's plight named by Freud (1925) as 'penis envy' (*penisneid*) is relevant and resonant to some extent, as is the *being* non-male or non-masculine beyond the having or not having a penis. For some trans men, it can often be the male social rather than sexual function that is wanted. Many trans men, for various reasons do not necessarily pursue phalloplasty surgery. I return to this in chapter 4.

Freud's ideas about masculinity and femininity emanated from phantasies of the trauma of castration. It was the notion of lack, for him, that structured identity – either in the fear of castration (for boys) or in the already castrated (for girls).

> For Freud it is not the perception of sexual difference in itself that is meaningful, but the primal fantasy of castration which gives meaning to the perception and propels development along masculine and feminine lines.
>
> (Birksted-Breen, 1996: 121)

Within the realm of unconscious phantasy, the lack is more symbolic and less concrete, and for Freud it manifested in either the wish for the penis or the fear of losing it. Having it is associated with potency and masculinity, and losing it is associated with the female plight and emasculation. What it might mean psychoanalytically to desire it, have it and fear losing it can have a multitude of meanings. One of the embedded complexities is *what it means to desire and how the nature of desire takes shape in relation to femininity and masculinity.*

Kubie (1974) makes the poignant observation in his paper 'The Drive to Become Both Sexes' that the drive exists in all of us and the challenge is not so much to give up the other gender but to find unconscious ways of incorporating the other gender alongside our birth gender in a complimentary fashion so that we do end up as both.

Whilst Freud registered the envy that can be engendered by the privileged place of the penis and the way that this can form mental structures, Klein's focus was more on envy towards the maternal breast and womb and fantasies[6] about their contents (Birksted-Breen, 1996: 121). This division between Freud and Klein's theoretical thinking about the direction of envy, in itself forms an interesting gender divide between Freud as a man and Klein as a woman, although this observation might reduce their difference too concretely.

Money-Kyrle, a British psychoanalyst (1968: 691–698; 1971: 103–106), referred to the 'facts of life' that centre on recognition of differences that we all struggle to accept. These are: the goodness of the breast, the difference between the sexes, recognition of parental intercourse as a creative act, the difference between the generations and the reality of the passage of time. The hatred of these facts comes from the envy they can provoke and the threat to omnipotence. As a way to avert and deny these 'facts' a mythology is invented, which functions to avoid facing our mortality and dependence on others (Steiner, 2018). I suggest that gender (identity) has become one way to manage these 'facts of life' as it is sometimes deployed to override psychic struggles with these unmanageable realities.

Lemma (2022) discusses the reality of the body:

> The body is a basic fact of life that supports all other psychic functions. In the best of circumstances, it provides an anchor in reality, not least the reality of the parental couple who gives us birth and hence acts as a reminder, imprinted on the 'given body', of the reality of difference and insufficiency that have to be borne rather than omnipotently denied. Being-in-a-body entails acknowledgement of the time of the couple – a time 'before' the body and hence before the body was given life.
>
> (Lemma, 2022: 37)

The 'facts of life' as they are in a more contemporary context, writing in 2023–2024, are very different as genders traverse an expansive range with 100 options on tumblr (2020). These include gender fluid, gender neutral, gender non-conforming, non-binary, pangender to name a few of many. There is a move away from biological origins that supports the proclamation that 'my genes are not my gender'. The approach stems more from a constructivist realm, as biological essentialism can be a source of provocation. This raises interesting cultural, philosophical and ethical questions about reality as a target for protest. If reality is in question, we can feel unmoored and ungrounded, as the new territory has new ground rules and parameters. Reality becomes elastic and slides from objectivity to subjectivity. The question of who has the authority or autonomy to make decisions about changes to the body and identity recognition all form part of a new reality and ethical framework. What is felt as real psychically can transport itself to the physical body, albeit not in a complete sense. For a trans man, the historical female body cannot be completely eradicated, whether consciously or unconsciously. A modified body always contains within it a history, albeit with much variance in how this history is located and thought about. The 'facts of life' now might require a more nuanced approach from clinicians towards aspects of gender variance, away from pathologising and towards non-judgemental curiosity. An additional fact of life is proposed by Lemma: the inescapable fact of our embodied nature (2023: 811).

Abraham (1877–1925), a contemporary of Freud's, was a psychoanalyst who wrote prolifically in his relatively short life. His contribution to the field can sometimes be underestimated; his untimely death at 48 sadly halted his career and potential. In his writing about the "Female Castration Complex" (1920), he says:

> Many women are often quite conscious of the fact that certain phenomena of their mental life arise from an intense dislike of being a woman; but on the other hand, many of them are quite in the dark as regards the motives of such an aversion.
>
> (1920/1953: 338–339)

His analysis of the plight of female identity in relation to the awareness of a lacking organ followed Freud. Amongst Abraham's ideas about the psychical trajectory of how to conceptualise the lack of a penis, I am interested in the idea of what I am calling an *unconscious phantasy of retrieval*. By this I mean: I had something once, it was taken from me, I want it back and I will get it back. Abraham describes girls in their narcissistic period of development as watching over their possessions and those of others with jealousy. "It wants to keep what it has and to get what it sees" (1953: 340). Abraham uses language in relation to the plight of girls that is of its time: she "has a lifelong defect", "has a wound", "has been robbed", "… is inferior". It is interesting that much psychoanalytic theory and clinical observation was attuned to these culturally embedded ideas. Perhaps what has changed in the culture is that now we are more inclined to speak about difference, without assigning a higher or lower level to the difference between the sexes, the moral imperative is not so loaded up with cultural weight, which is not to say that it has disappeared. In the time of Freud and Abraham, the cultural and social differences were indescribably more marked in relation to the limited status for girls or women, which was taken as a fact of life then and in many respects was a fact of life then.

In his paper on 'The Female Castration Complex' (1920) Abraham describes an observation of a little girl of two who went to a box of cigars and brought one to her father, she then went back and brought one to her mother. She then returned to the cigar box and took a third one out and positioned it in front of the lower part of her body. After this her mother placed the three cigars back into their box. After waiting a little while, the child repeated the game (1953: 341). The symbolic aspect of this game is very apparent. It also bears some resemblance to Freud's description of the Fort Da game (1920). Freud gave this name to a game played by his eighteen-month-old grandson, Ernst, in which the boy repeatedly threw a cotton reel out of his cot, with the exclamation 'Oo' that made his mother retrieve it for him, at which he exclaimed 'Ah'. Freud interpreted these noises to mean 'gone' (fort) and 'there' (da). Freud discusses the significance of this game as the child's symbolic way of managing loss by repeatedly reversing the unhappy loss into a happy reappearance. The game and Freud's interpretation of it show a small child's creative solution at retrieval of what has been lost.

The child in the cigar-sharing scenario not only wishes for equality between mother and father, but includes herself in the triangle so that she is not excluded. This symbolic act restores parity between her parents, and between herself in relation to them and attempts to create what has been called a "deadly equal triangle" (Mattinson, 1981). This term was used in relation to the supervisory constellation of patient/therapist/supervisor.

Abraham describes the lasting impact on women of what he calls 'the castration complex', whether this impact is conscious or unconscious. He sees it potentially transplanted onto or into children by their mothers and having influence on the psychosexual development of daughters. This can be done through a disparagement of female sexuality as conveyed to their daughters or through an aversion to men that is displayed more unconsciously. This kind of aversion and disparagement can also be passed onto sons, but in this book my focus is more on daughters.

Other female contemporaries of Freud's who were writing about female castration anxieties and the female Oedipus complex were Horney (as mentioned), Deutsch, Lampl de Groot, Mack Brunswick, Bonaparte, Muller and Klein. Ernest Jones, a male contemporary of Freud's, made significant contributions in his writing about female sexuality that dissented from Freud's views, whilst acknowledging 'the master' at the same time.

The writings of Karen Horney (1924, 1926,1933, 1967) stand out in particular, as she had the confidence to challenge some of Freud's ideas, particular in relation to female sexual identity and development. She questioned Freud's thinking about the vagina as undiscovered by the small female infant, and hypothesised that: "behind the 'failure to discover' the vagina is a denial of its existence" (Horney, 1933: 69). Horney was unconvinced by the theories of her time about female masochism, which she felt were too readily assigned to women (mostly by men) without sufficient evidence.

In her attempt to understand the differences in sexual development for boys/men and girls/women, she delves into the phenomenon of the male 'dread of women', and what the origins of this are. She understands this more as dread of the female genital, and does not think that this is sufficiently explained by a boy's castration anxiety transferred onto women, to whom he might imagine this has already happened. She sees the boy's dread of his father as more tangible than the uncanny dread of "the existence of the sinister female genital" (1967: 138). Horney describes the small boy's desire to penetrate (in games, wishes and dreams) as deriving from phallic impulses, but also a genital that is immature initially (compared to fathers or to what he might imagine that mother desires). This wish might propel him to find an opening in the female body that he lacks, but has some intuitive sense of: "... for the one sex always seeks in the other that which is complementary to it or of a nature different from its own" (1967: 140).

I am interested in the parallel 'dread of women' that stems from small girls, who might *share these phantasies that are assigned to small boys about the female body* in relation to their mothers and themselves. It is as if the small girl is at a certain stage of development so identified with the small boy, or so unkeen to know herself as female-bodied, that she experiences *the same dread as the small boy*. It is not clear whether this is via identification (both conscious and unconscious), or whether as has been suggested by Horney (albeit in relation to women, not small girls) in the following quote, the masculinity is taken into herself concretely.

I picture their origin as follows: when the woman takes refuge in the fictitious male role her feminine genital anxiety is to some extent *translated into male terms* - the fear of vaginal injury becomes a phantasy of castration. The girl gains by this conversion, for she exchanges the uncertainty of her expectation of punishment (an uncertainty conditioned by her anatomical formation) for a concrete idea.

(my italics) (1926: 336)

What is of interest here is how long the small girl's identification with a small boy continues for, what the intensity of the identification is, and how it might manifest. As mentioned earlier, Fast suggested an all-inclusive undifferentiated phase of development in which the cognition of sexual difference is not yet there. This is also referred to as omnipotence and understood to be a usual part of child development that can emerge in all phases of development: oral, anal, phallic, oedipal and genital. Omnipotence is generally thought, psychoanalytically, to be useful and helpful as a way to manage more difficult aspects of frustration and deprivation, which are embedded in all experiences of childhood development. It can be used positively as a defence against loss and depression, and can help maintain mental buoyancy in relation to early loss of the love object. The omnipotent state of mind is one in which there is complete control; Freud referred to 'His Majesty the Baby', an illusion of controlling one's own kingdom and a defence against loss that can feel too threatening.

Although manifestations of omnipotence can be beneficial in childhood, these manifestations can have the potential to be more problematic in adolescence and adulthood, as it is a state of mind that creates a defensive distance from the limitations of reality precisely because they are too much to bear. Whereas in infancy this state of mind can be recruited usefully, when it takes hold in adolescence or adulthood, it is more problematic and sometimes dangerous.

Adolescent Turmoil

Puberty is a phase of life that is extremely challenging. The body announces itself as sexual, and this opens up the risk of enactment for both girls and boys, who have to negotiate a new reality. Longings and incestuous wishes that were safer during infancy and the latency phase of childhood are now present in a different register. For adolescent girls, menstruation declares the body as one that bears the possibility of pregnancy. For adolescent boys, their genitals are mature enough for sexual intercourse, whether homosexual or heterosexual. The emotional weight of the maturing sexual body opens up new vistas of anxiety, excitement, stimulation, prohibition and acting out.

I will focus on the female body. If an adolescent girl has been ambivalent about her femaleness, puberty can shatter the wish or phantasy to 'not be female'. Menstruation delivers a clear bodily message about internal organs and their function. The adolescent girl is now more symmetrically aligned with her mother physically as she too can become pregnant and give birth. The demarcation between the generations remains but is altered.

The female anatomy, particularly from menstruation onwards, can be perceived as being tantamount to pregnancy and childbirth and evoke terror about this fated or expected female trajectory. This has been referred to as 'the bikini vision of biology'[7] (Bigg, 2023) which can compound the (unwanted) awareness of being one sex and not the other. I suggest that this melancholic realisation can at times transform itself into a wish to undo femaleness. This so-called 'bikini-vision' has a correlation with Fletcher's description in his discussion of Laplanche and Freud, that "the sexual drives are ultimately integrated by Freud into a normative developmental sequence that has reproduction as its preordained goal" (Fletcher, 2007: 1250).

For Milo and Joe, discussed earlier, puberty burst into their 'gender-neutral' lives, shattering the omnipotent belief that a strong wish to be male could materialise there and then. There is no stronger signifier of femaleness and femininity than the onset of menstruation and the growth of breasts. This powerful anatomical reality threw both Milo and Joe into an emotional turmoil, one that brought conflict into the schism between the natal physical body and the psychical wished for body. The challenge for us all as Lemma puts it is "how to transform the body one has into the body one is" (Lemma, 2022: 37). When the bodily gender is at odds with the body in mind, this is a particularly painful conflict to resolve.

Although the natal body is beyond personal choice, the mind has the flexibility to re-present the body. These representations of the body image are shaped by phantasies that are, in turn, shaped by individual developmental experience. These phantasies are central to the formation of a psychoanalytic understanding of unconscious processes. Lemma refers to these as *body imaginings* (2010, 2022):

> Body imaginings grow out of the earliest internal bodily experiences, for example, of pain and pleasure, in relation to others and colour the individual's experience of their body-self. ... It is built on projective and introjective mechanisms. Importantly, the body representation is fundamentally a function of libidinal cathexes.
>
> (2022: 41)

Mourning

Freud (1917) contributed to the understanding of mourning and the psychical work that it requires in order to, in time, let go of the death internally, or kill it off through gradual decathexis. He pointed out pathological variants of mourning in which either ambivalence predominates (depressive), or the ego identifies with the dead object (melancholic). Klein expanded on Freud's ideas on mourning, ambivalence and unconscious guilt, particularly from her work with children. She connected depression in children with their aggression and guilt, and similarly to Freud she comprehended that losing an ambivalently loved object was linked to guilt and depression. These ideas evolved into her formulation of the Depressive Position in 1935, in which the significance moved from projection (in prior paranoid states) to introjection and phantasy, whole objects, reparation and love (Klein, 1935).

The capacity to mourn plays a central part in the psychoanalytic understanding of psychic growth that includes the development of sexual and gender identity. This capacity is closely tied up with experiences of separation, frustration, aggression and love. A small boy has to mourn what he is not, and a small girl likewise has to let go of the phantasy of being both sexes. My use of the term 'to mourn' traverses a range of developmental and cognitive capacities. How this 'giving up' is managed ties in with the capacity or lack of capacity to mourn and bear guilt, which Klein understood as working through feelings of hostility towards others. During puberty, when the sexual body becomes central, I suggest that earlier hostilities can at times be re-activated and locate themselves in the sexual and gender arena.

This notion of mourning which invokes sadness about loss does not blend easily with the notion that gender is socially constructed rather than biologically given. My discussion here is not about whether gender is the former or the latter. The capacity to mourn what one is not is, in my view, part of the capacity to bear reality with all the limitations that it bestows on us as human beings. If a loss is not mourned, it becomes denied, displaced, disavowed or repressed and does not disappear. Where a psychological working through of the loss might have been, a concrete solution in the form of renewal, replacement or a manic solution can at times take hold.

A child's capacity to mentalize[8] has ramifications for how and when the difference between the sexes can be represented as a reality that invokes loss. Psychological and physical pain are equated in instances of psychic equivalence (Fonagy & Target, 1996), so that psychological pain is experienced as bodily pain. This throws up the likelihood that the difference between the sexes is initially registered *in the body*, and is mentalized later on. I think that this does not preclude the early registration of difference, but at a more primitive somatic level.

Klein (1935) conceptualised the Depressive Position as the capacity for remorse for hostile attacks on the object,[9] usually in the form of mother's body. It is an infantile state similar to the clinical state of depression. I speculate on the idea that accepting the limitations of reality, which include the sex I was born as, might require the capacity for Depressive Position functioning. Klein proposed that throughout life we all fluctuate between the two positions that she termed: Paranoid Schizoid and Depressive Position.

It appears to be crucial how the awareness of what sex one is, and what one is not and cannot be, varies developmentally. I see aspects of the capacity to bear this reality of limitations, even if this is at a very primitive level, as pivotal.

In some cases of gender transition, the capacity to mourn the loss of one's natal sex is only possible post transition. Lemma (2012, 2015) points out that although the new body for transsexual (sic) individuals can bring immense relief, the historical body cannot be wiped out, and the state of mind that is held in relation to what can be delivered by the surgery is vital for future relationships (2012: 276). She stresses the psychic importance, and painful work of recognizing the 'original' body (2015: 97). Lemma refers to the biological function of the 'original' genital, and cites Mitchell's statement that "we are sexed around reproduction". Managing the loss of reproductive parts of the body, Lemma goes on to say, requires the process of mourning (Mitchell, 2004 as cited in Lemma, 2015: 101).

In a different sense gender transition can, in and of itself, be thought of as reproductive. One is reproducing oneself as different to the natal sex that one was born
into. This reproduction, however, is not generational, parental, or sexual; it is self-
produced. And in this sense might incorporate a negation of origins that necessarily
involves parental input.

Freud made the salient observation that the ego is first and foremost a bodily ego
(1923). Life begins with a body and bodily sensations of repletion and depletion
that do not yet have resonance in the mind or in language. I suggest that coming
to terms with one's anatomy, can invoke a melancholic reaction, whether this is
registered unconsciously or consciously. I'd include this melancholic registration
in what Money-Kyrle referred to as "the facts of life", within which he included the
difference between the sexes.

I will expand Freud's dictum that "anatomy is destiny", to contemporary experiences of a psychically gendered anatomy. The body that is held in mind, rather than
in one's anatomy, is destiny. This creates a tension between psychic and physical
anatomy that is central to many aspects of gender identity conflicts.

Freud's differentiation between mourning and melancholia is relevant here. In
melancholia or melancholic mourning, there is a difficulty with letting go of the
lost object that becomes internally lodged. I suggest that there can be an early
response to being female that bears similar melancholic characteristics, which can
become lodged in different ways. I will expand on these in the following chapters.

If the capacity to mourn 'what or who one is or is not' is impaired, the loss of the
wish for a different reality can at times and in some instances ignite a protest. This
protest can either lodge itself psychically and remain psychological, or steer itself
towards action that recruits physical change. There are cultural aspects to this, as
in the last decades the possibilities (internet access, social media, hormonal and
surgical) for gender transition have expanded.

The notion of a protest connotes an objection to *something that came before*,
which must be contested or eradicated. The gender protest might be thought of as
ubiquitous, as something embedded in the unconscious for us all. We cannot be
what we are not, or have that which came before we were born, determine who we
are conceived by, born to or born as. Protest is born out of a sense of injustice, and
its earliest form is in the baby's cry.

The Body Schema, Sexual Schema, Unconscious Body Image & the Mind's Image of Itself

It can be assumed within psychoanalytic thinking that the body has a presence that
is readily perceived by the mind or felt in the mind that habituates and affirms its
reality. The materiality of the body, embodiment, can be taken for granted, rather
than questioned and examined as a more tenuous presence, that is open to exploration. Psychoanalysis addresses how the subject comes to know him or herself,
how the self becomes formed and reformed in relation to others, whether actual
others or internalised versions of others. In this sense there is always a historical

and relational dimension that shapes desire, expressed by Salamon as "… my history shapes my desire" (2010: 45). Reality is an all-encompassing concept or state of being in the world, which is necessary, anchoring, and can be taken for granted in relation to the gendering and materiality of a body as felt in the mind. These assumptions are explored by Salamon (2010) through the work of phenomenological thinkers, Schilder (1950) and Merleau-Ponty (1962).

Salamon points out that *container metaphors* are often recruited within psychoanalysis. She gives the example of Anzieu who wrote extensively about skin in *The Skin Ego* (1989), through the images of envelope and kernel. I expand on the skin ego in Chapter 2. Understanding the body as an envelope that houses the psyche as an internal 'core' (Anzieu) is questionable for Salamon. As I understand Salamon, this delineation of inside and outside is too simplistic. For Anzieu, the skin ego is that which the child utilises in early developmental phases to represent itself as an ego that contains psychical contents (1989: 40). Salamon translates this as an outside of 'matter' that contains a non-material psychic depth inside. She contends that this can reduce the importance of the 'outside' skin, the social envelope.

It is true that container metaphors are prevalent within psychoanalysis, and in many ways these metaphors are taken for granted, but in my view, this is for good reason. Psychoanalysis is per force the analysis of the psyche/soma, usually practiced in a clinical setting in which the psychoanalytic practitioner absorbs the patient through a psychical exchange. From birth and pre-birth (inside the womb) humans ingest in order to survive, whether this is oxygen, air, or fluids. From the beginning there is a necessity to take in from the other and digest their milk, presence, projections, attunement, or rebuffals. The containing or anti-containing metaphor fits well with this, notably by Bion's concept "container contained" (1962).

Rey's (1994) description of the psychoanalytic process affirms the metaphor:

> What part of the subject, situated where in space and time, is doing what to what part of the object, situated where in space and time and with what motivations and with what consequences for the subject and object?
>
> (1994: 7)

A metaphor emanates from a physical experience, as Freeman Sharpe (1940/1978) points out, which consolidates the recruitment of containing metaphors in psychoanalysis. She maintains that the use of metaphor in language is psycho–physical. She cites Grindon (1879) who states that "No word … is metaphysical without its first having been physical". Freeman Sharpe's theory is that it is only after the control of bodily orifices (in my understanding this means an inside, outside, retention, emission) that metaphor can evolve in language or the arts. Early experiences of infant life are expressed through metaphor, thus converting the material to the immaterial (1940: 202).

In most instances of psychoanalytic treatment there is a psychotherapist/psychoanalyst and a patient. The nature of containment informs this dynamic: what is projected or transferred, whether consciously or unconsciously, from the patient, how the projection or transference is received and translated via interpretation, is experienced by both. This movement is at the heart of psychoanalytic work. There is a large body of literature on these aspects of psychoanalysis, which are beyond the subject of this book.

A contemporary of Freud with a background in medicine and philosophy, Schilder (1950) conceived of the body schema as countering the idea that the body envelopes the psyche or that the skin is an envelope for the body. His notion conceptualises the body and psyche as *labile* rather than containing; the body can exceed the skin confines. I quote Salamon's succinct summary of his argument:

> We only have recourse to our bodies through a body image, a psychic representation of the body that is constructed over time. The body image is multiple (any person always has more than one), it is flexible (its configuration changes over time), it arises from our relations with other people, and its contours are only rarely identical to the contours of the body as it is perceived from the outside.
>
> (2010: 29)

Salamon endorses Schilder's capacity to connect up the disciplines of psychoanalysis, phenomenology and neurology in relation to embodiment, which encompasses Freud's bodily ego. The term "body image" has been attributed to Schilder (2010: 196). He accentuates the body as situated in a social world which gives context to the body's constructedness. This has the flavour of a work in progress, removed from anything fixed or certain, always under construction. In Schilder's words "It is not a shape ... but the production of a shape" (113). He alternates the terms 'postural model', 'body image' and 'body schema'. Touch is integral to the postural model of the body, the kind of interest from others towards various parts of the body libidinally. This verifies the body from its inception or conception as relational. It is neither a representation or a perception, and cannot be reduced to pictures, which he thought simplified the facts. The body schema always in flux, has a temporal dimenson, attributed to Head (1920).

In Schilder's work that I am reading with Salamon's help, the body schema's origins are relational. The image of the body cannot be structured without the relation to the world; its social dimension. It cannot be "... an entirely voluntaristic project" (126, in 2010: 31). The description in Schilder's writing, which takes from Head's definition of bodily schemata, has at its core a relational dimension: incoming sensory impulses that rise into consciousness in a recognisable way are already charged with a relation to something that has happened before.

This description captures the psychoanalytic temporality of après-coup, in which present feelings are re-enlivened by past occurrences. To my mind it describes the force of the unconscious, although it is not named as such. For Schilder the materiality of the body has to contend with the complicated apparatus of the body schema, its physiological basis is uncertain. As the accessibility of the body's materiality is compromised, the body schema questions how bodies signify beyond their material contours, and how this body is lived and understood? These questions have relevance to all bodies, but are helpful and resonate in relation to trans bodies, in which the materiality of the body is unfixed, questioned, and not rooted in certainty that can be taken for granted.

In the work of Merleau-Ponty (1962) sexuality is (helpfully) ambiguous. Its temporality invokes both past and future, the future that is always shaped by past experiences is propelled via the sensations within desire. The future is shaped by the past sexual history, which is alive in the motivations of the sexual self. He is inquisitive about desire and love and how this brings us into being, how the body is shaped by desire. He moves away from the boundary or fixity of separateness or physical confirmation that makes the body distinct from other bodies. Sexuality is centred on the body's capacity to sense. A sexual physiognomy is delivered to the body by the sexual schema, similarly to how the body schema (Schilder) delivers a body morphology. The body is initially defined vaguely, followed by the underlying sexual schema and after that he portrays the sexual regions of the body. Gender comes into view after this last portrayal of the sexual regions driven by desire. Merleau-Ponty describes desire as being in or from the body, rather than sexuality in or from the genitals; it is not the erotogenic zones that define sexuality, but the intentional movement towards others in the world. In relation to the acquisition of masculinity, it is cited as gestural, mimetic and informed by the sexual schema that is highly individual.

Desire is at the centre of sexuality and described as an ambiguous atmosphere spreading forth from a particular part of the body like an odour or sound. He mentions 'unspoken transposition' embedded within sexuality that directs specific experience from the body outwards towards that which I desire. He sees sexuality as coextensive with life and places ambiguity at the centre of human existence, perhaps affirming his approach as phenomenological and divorced from materiality. The object's meaning is received through perception, which in my understanding acts as a mediator, enabling me to relate outwards and receive inwards, which curiously invokes a container metaphor. The ambiguity that is central to Merleau-Ponty's depictions moves us away from concepts like 'reality', often deployed in attitudes towards gender ambiguity. For Salamon many of these descriptions, which are by no means exhaustive here, fit well with an understanding of trans gendered embodiment as an identity that is not defined by the body's materiality.

Dolto, a French psychoanalyst influenced by Lacan, but not one of his disciples, constructed her own theory based on terminology and concepts such as desire, the desiring subject, the Real, Symbolic and Imaginary. She trained and began to practice in the 1930s and 1940s. She is known for the sensitivity and originality of her work with children, who she respected as intelligent, curious and able to make meaning from her intuitive and skilfully delivered communications with them. She was eager to help very small children and their parents in order to prevent the emergence of psychological disturbances.

Her interest lay in the process of the construction of identity by following the thread of the desiring subject. Like the phenomenologists cited above, she saw the significance of the perceptual apparatus as that through which meaning could be received and filtered, particularly, in Dolto's case, for the small child. She set out her own theory of how the human psyche develops alongside body development, especially for children.

She devised the concept of "The Unconscious Body Image" (UBI), which she differentiates from the bodily schema. She gives the UBI many definitions, leaving it hard to be succinct with its meaning. I'll quote from some of her definitions, as translated by Bailly, S. (2023a, 2023b):

> The bodily schema is partly unconscious but also preconscious and conscious, while the body image is eminently unconscious; it can become partly preconscious only when it is associated with conscious language, which uses metaphors and metonymy referring to the body image, as much in facial as in verbal expressions.
>
> The body image is the living synthesis of our emotional experiences: interhuman, repetitively experienced through elective erogenous sensations, archaic or current. It can be considered as *the unconscious symbolic embodiment of the desiring subject.*
>
> (Bailly, S. 2023a, in Dolto, 2023: 2)

Sharmini Bailly, who translated Dolto's book *The Unconscious Body Image* (2023a), is very helpful at clarifying Dolto's often obscure concepts and terms. Bailly (UCL conference paper, 2023b) breaks down her understanding of the UBI as a psychic representation of bodily experiences that are stored within the central nervous system. It is via those bodily parts and functions that cathect with libido that it is created, through interactions with the object; it forms the basis of thought and subjectivity when it is linked with further perceptual and higher order representations. Bailly (2023b) draws a link with both Klein's (1923, 1932) and Isaacs' (1948) concept of Unconscious Phantasy; both Dolto, Klein and Isaacs attempt to decode the unconscious meaning of images, words, actions by listening and observing children closely.

It is the total experience that is recorded, initially by the baby in relation to its mother, endorsing the relational aspect that Schilder and Merleau-Ponty emphasise. Isaacs (1948) writes about unconscious phantasy in her eponymous paper, and Brierley (1942) describes phantasy as a "ticker-tape that records happenings on the mental stock exchange. But the observer has to infer from the figures whether the market is rising or falling, and this inference is, in effect, a generalization from the specific figures recorded" (1942: 110). Dolto's word is "engrammed", and she describes newborns as engrammed with "magnetic tape, somewhere in their cortex, these first expressions". Bailly points out that both Brierley and Dolto turn to the technology of their time for these metaphors.

Dolto's bodily schema is based on the French *schema corporel*, which is the neurological map of the body, showing sections of the body as exaggerated in relation to their usage. She expands the more neurological template to include perception and bodily response. In that the unconscious body image is a representation or sensory registration of an interaction, it appears to be similar to both Schilder's body image and body schema, and to Merleau-Ponty's sexual schema. All of these have tentacles in Freud's *Three Essays on the Theory of Sexuality*, although he is not always referenced.

The concept of unconscious phantasy covers a wide psychoanalytic terrain, and is mostly attributed to Klein's developments of Freud's work, through her initial work with children. As Bell (2017) points out, the term captures and traverses different phenomenologies. I wish to home in on one aspect, Freud's term of "endopsychic perceptions", which are the mind's perceptions of its own mental activities. Freud places mental activities in unconscious bodily phantasy. He sees the capacity for judgement as residing in primitive bodily activity: swallowing, vomiting, retaining and defecating. These physical activities are the means by which thoughts are allowed in or expelled, staining and illuminating 'the mind's image of itself' (Wollheim, 1969) via the archaic bodily theory of the mind (Bell, 2017). Wollheim's exploration of what it is to be a person, although philosophical utilises psychoanalysis and especially Klein's work. He divides mental life into mental states, mental dispositions and mental activities. The mental dispositions are unconscious, can be lived as phantasies and triggered by mental states that bring them more into consciousness.

I quote Bell on Wollheim:

And if it is dispositions that carry our history, and if these dispositions are in the large part phantasies, then it is phantasy that carries the mark of our history, that install us within the narrative of our own lived lives ...

(2017: 793)

Unusually Wollheim, as a philosopher, sees memory as conjoined with phantasy. It is the living out of the phantasy that preserves it and the event that initiated it is maintained by the causal link to it. Bell sees the representation through which desire is fulfilled as inhabiting the most primitive phantasies. Klein (1957: 179) described the earliest phantasies as "memories in feeling". These descriptions of unconscious phantasy appear to tally with the work of Schilder, Merleau-Ponty and Dolto, who all tried to capture the recording and registration of experiences in the mental apparatus and body. Bion (1962) developed this further with his attention on mental functions particularly the function of thinking. Bion's early work was mainly phenomenological and epistemological. He explored how mental processes are used in getting to know aspects of one's objects in the inner world, and the relations between these and elements of the external object world.

My interest in including all of these concepts is their resonance with trans bodies and how unconscious registration can manifest in the body in relation to gender and sexuality. Important too is the concept of desire, instead of need, the former inhabiting the psychic realm and the latter belonging more to the biological. Desire (as different to need that is more linked to survival) propels the body towards another, and affirms us as relational and orientational. Dolto's linkage of desire with the Unconscious Body Image "provides one mechanism whereby drive cathected within a network of representation spreads outwards from it" (Bailly, 2023a: 6). This spreading of desire requires both language and what Dolto refers to as castration, a limit that can push development forwards. I expand on this term in Chapter 6.

In *Project for a Scientific Psychology* (1895/1950), Freud explored the beginning of a mind formed by the relationship to the primary object of need and satisfaction in order to render pain bearable. This drive that is propelled by need necessitates possible changes in the mental apparatus via reliable repetitions of experience that enable the introjection of the object, establishing it in the psyche of the infant. The links that form in these repeated experiences become signals. Freud, as discussed by Mawson (2012), referred to affects, the residues of pain and satisfaction mingled with wishful states that anticipate the object. He saw these as extremely significant "because they leave behind psychological motives which compel attraction towards objects, initially towards their recorded images" (Mawson, 2012. 6).

There are cross-overs evident in the works of Schilder, Merleau-Ponty and Dolto as well as aspects of Freud, Klein and Bion; reading sections of their material with the aid of Salamon, Bailly, Bell and Mawson bring to light many recurring themes and concepts that are helpful in my attempt to write about how and in what form the mind registers and represents the body. The key concepts that are helpful are the uncertainty of the body's materiality from a phenomenological stance, the early registration of another (usually a mother) in the forming of the mental and physical apparatus and in what form this registration occurs, the central role of desire that emanates from early sensations in the self and towards the object that inform sexuality, and the necessity of 'castrations' as an aid to growth and development that includes separation and independence. All of these complex moves or states of mind and body are necessarily melancholic; the body or anatomy has material limits. The material limits of the body are relevant for trans bodies. Desire or the frustration of it emanate from a drive towards another in the social world (sometimes satisfied and sometimes not). My exploration affirms the notion that gender has a relational origin.

Notes

1 Alice Neel (1900–1984), American painter, remembered her mother's words. Barbican exhibition, Feb-May 2023, Alice Neel: Hot Off the Griddle.
2 The word object is used psychoanalytically as a component in the mental representation of an instinct. That which is represented in unconscious phantasy is a relationship between the self and an object, in which the object is imbued with good or bad impulses. More simply, it is a person or persons as internalised, and entirely distinct from external physical objects.
3 Names of interviewees have been changed to preserve confidentiality.
4 The term passing is used to indicate that a person is identifying and being perceived as their desired and lived gender.
5 Stoller, R. (1924–1991) was a professor of psychiatry at UCLA who published his theories on the development of gender identity widely. He is credited with having coined the term "gender identity" and introducing the concept of gender through his writing and research.

6 The spelling of 'fantasies' can also be 'phantasies', the latter spelling has become associated with Melanie Klein, or Kleinian approaches, but also as a way to mark out unconscious processes. According to Isaacs, the English translators of Freud adopted the *ph* spelling to differentiate the psychoanalytic significance of the term, as predominantly unconscious (Isaacs, 1948: 80). I have used this latter spelling unless it has been used differently by the author I am referring to.

7 Bigg, M. L. (2023) The idea that everything beyond the reproductive organs is the same across genders is attributed to Bart Fauser, Professor of Reproductive Medicine and Gynaecology, University of Utrecht.

8 Mentalisation refers to the capacity to understand, infer, recognise and access one's own behaviour and state of mind as well as that of another. It is a mostly imaginative mental activity, that helps self-organisation and affect regulation (Fonagy & Allison, 2012).

9 Klein, M. (1946) understood infants as having aggressive impulses and phantasies (unconscious) that were directed towards the mother, she saw these projections as part of the infant's way of managing and discharging unmanageable primitive emotions.

Bibliography

Abraham, K. (1920/1953). Manifestations of the female castration complex. In *Selected papers of Karl Abraham* (1953, pp. 338–369). New York: Basic Books.

Anzieu, D. (1989). *The skin ego* (C. Turner, Trans.). New Haven: Yale University Press.

Bailly, S. (2023a). *The unconscious body image* (S. Bailly, Trans.). London and New York: Routledge.

Bailly, S. (2023b). The Role of the Unconscious Body Image in the formation of the desiring subject, and their links with the British Object Relations tradition, *paper presented at UCL conference on the work of Françoise Dolto*, 14.10.2023.

Bell, D. (2017) Unconscious phantasy: some historical and conceptual dimensions, *International Journal of Psychoanalysis*, *98*, 785–798.

Bigg, M. L. (2023). *This won't hurt, how medicine fails women*. Great Britain: Hodder & Strouton.

Bion, W. R. (1962/1984). Chapter 9: A theory of thinking. In *Second Thoughts* (pp. 110–119). London: H. Karnac (Books).

Birksted-Breen, D. (1996). Unconscious representation of femininity. *Journal of the American Psychoanalytic Association*, *44S*(Supplement), 119–132.

Brierley, M. (1942). 'Internal objects' and theory. *International Journal of Psychoanalysis*, *23*, 107–112.

Burton, R. (2021/1621). Continent, inward, antecedent, next causes, and how the body works on the mind, memb. 5. Subsect. 1. In *The anatomy of melancholy* (pp. 367–369). London, UK: Penguin Random House.

Dolto, F. (2023). *The unconscious body image* (Sharmini Bailly, Trans.). London and New York: Routledge.

Edgecumbe, R., & Burgner, M. (1975). The phallic-narcissistic phase – a differentiation between preoedipal and oedipal aspects of phallic development. *Psychoanalytic Study of the Child*, *30*, 161–180.

Fast, I. (1984). *Gender identity a differentiation model*. University of Michigan: The Analytic Press.

Fausto-Sterling, A. (2012). The dynamic development of gender variability. *Journal of Homosexuality*, *59*, 398–421.

Ferenczi, S. (1924/2011) *Thalassa: A theory of genitality*. London: Karnac Books. (Original work published 1924).

Fletcher, J. (2007). Seduction and the vicissitudes of translation: The work of Jean Laplanche. *Psychoanalytic Quarterly*, *76*(4), 1241–1291.

Fonagy, P., & Allison, E. (2012). What is mentalization? The concept and its foundations in developmental research and social-cognitive neuroscience. In N. Midgeley & I. Vrouva (Eds.), *Minding the child: Keeping children in mind: Mentalization-based interventions with children, young people and their families*. Hove, East Sussex & New York: Routledge.

Fonagy, P., & Target, M. (1996). Playing with reality: 1. Theory of mind and the normal development of psychic reality. *International Journal of Psychoanalysis, 77*, 217–233.

Freeman Sharpe, E. (1940/1978). Mechanisms of dream formation. In *Dream analysis* (pp. 40–65). London: The Hogarth Press and The Institute of Psychoanalysis (Chapter 2).

Freud, S. (1895/1950). Project for a scientific psychology (1900a). In *Standard Edition* (Vol. 1). London: Hogarth Press.

Freud, S. (1908). On the sexual theories of children. In *Standard Edition* (Vol. 9, pp. 205–226). London: Hogarth Press.

Freud, S. (1917/1915). Mourning and melancholia. In *Standard Edition* (Vol. 14, pp. 237–258). London: Hogarth Press.

Freud, S. (1918/1914). From the history of an infantile neurosis (The 'Wolf-man'). In *Standard Edition* (Vol. 17, pp. 1 122). London: Hogarth Press.

Freud, S. (1920). Beyond the pleasure principle. In *Standard Edition* (Vol. 18, pp. 1–64). London: Hogarth Press.

Freud, S. (1923). The ego and the id. In *Standard Edition* (Vol. 19, pp. 1–59). London: Hogarth Press.

Freud, S. (1925). Some psychical consequences of the anatomical distinction between the sexes. In *Standard Edition* (Vol. 19, pp. 241–258). London: Hogarth Press.

Gozlan, O. (2008). The accident of gender. *Psychoanalytic Review, 95*, 541–570.

Grindon, L. H. (1879). *Figurative language: Its origin and constitution*. London: James Speirs (as cited in Sharpe, E. F. (1940).

Head, H. (1920). *Studies in neurology* (Vol. 2). London: Frowde Hodder and Stroughton.

Horney, K. (1924). On the genesis of the castration complex in women. *International Journal of Psychoanalysis, 5*, 50–65.

Horney, K. (1926). The flight from womanhood: The masculinity-complex in women, as viewed by men and by women. *International Journal of Psychoanalysis, 7*, 324–339.

Horney, K. (1933). The denial of the vagina – A contribution to the problem of the genital anxieties specific to women. *International Journal of Psychoanalysis, 14*, 57–70.

Horney, K. (1967, orig. 1932). The dread of woman. In H. Kelman (Ed.), *Feminine psychology* (pp. 133–146). New York and London: W.W. Norton & Company.

Isaacs, S. (1948) The nature and function of phantasy, *International Journal of Psychoanalysis, 29*: 73–97.

Joe (2020) Interview (anonymised).

Klein, M. (1923). The role of the school in the libidinal development of the child. *International Journal of Psychoanalysis, 5*, 312–331.

Klein, M. (1932). *The psychoanalysis of children*. London: The Hogarth Press.

Klein, M. (1935). A contribution to the psychogenesis of manic-depressive states. *International Journal of Psychoanalysis, 16*, 145–174.

Klein, M. (1946). Notes on some schizoid mechanisms. *International Journal of Psychoanalysis, 27*, 99–110.

Klein, M. (1957). Envy and Gratitude. In *Envy and gratitude and other works 1946–1963*. London: Virago Press (Chapter 10).

Kubie, L. S. (1974). The drive to become both sexes. *Psychoanalytic Quarterly, 43*, 349–426.

Laplanche, J. (1997). The theory of seduction and the problem of the other. *International Journal of Psychoanalysis, 78*, 653–666.

Laplanche, J. (2007). Gender, sex, and the sexual. *Studies in Gender and Sexuality, 8*(2), 201–219.

Lemma, A. (2010). *Under the skin: A psychoanalytic study of body modification*. London: Routledge.

Lemma, A. (2012). Research off the couch: Re-visiting the transsexual conundrum. *Psychoanalytic Psychotherapy, 26*(4), 263–281.

Lemma, A. (2015). The body one has and the body one is: The transsexual's need to be seen. In *Minding the body: The body in psychoanalysis and beyond* (pp. 88–101). London and New York: Routledge (Chapter 5).

Lemma, A. (2022). Arriving at the body. In *Transgender identities, a contemporary introduction* (pp. 36–60). London and New York: Routledge (Chapter 3).

Lemma, A. (2023). The missing: Exploring the use of photographs in "working through" the natal body with transgender youth. *International Journal of Psychoanalysis, 104*(5), 809–828.

Mattinson, J. (1981). The deadly equal triangle. In *Change and renewal in psychodynamic social work: British and American developments in practice and education for services to families and children*. London: Group for the Advancement of Psychotherapy in Social Work.

Mawson, C. (2012). *Reading Bion*, papers for members of CAPS seminars on The Work of Bion, May 2012, Institute of Psychoanalysis, Unpublished.

Merleau-Ponty, M. (1962). *Phenomenology of perception* (Colin Smith, Trans.). London: Routledge.

Milo (2020). Interview (anonymised).

Mitchell, J. (1975). *Psychoanalysis and feminism*. Penguin Books (Pelican edition). Middlesex, England: Harmondsworth.

Mitchell, J. (2004). The difference between gender and sexual difference. In I. Mathis (Ed.), *Dialogues on sexuality, gender and psychoanalysis*. London: Karnac.

Money-Kyrle, R. (1968). On cognitive development. *International Journal of Psychoanalysis, 49*, 691–698.

Money-Kyrle, R. (1971). The aim of psychoanalysis. *International Journal Psycho-Analysis, 52*, 103–106.

Nuttall, J. (2023). Ghyles and hags, words for ages and stages. In *Mother Tongue: The surprising history of women's words* (pp. 188–213). London: Virago Press (Chapter 7).

Rey, J. H. (1994). *Universals of psychoanalysis in the treatment of psychotic and borderline States*. London: Free Association Books.

Salamon, G. (2010). The bodily ego and the contested domain of the material. In *Assuming a body: Transgender and rhetorics of materiality* (pp. 13–65). New York: Columbia University Press.

Schilder, P. (1950). *The image and appearance of the human body: Studies in the constructive energies of the psyche*. New York: International Universities Press.

Steiner, J. (2018). Time and the Garden of Eden illusion. *International Journal of Psychoanalysis, 99*(6), 1274–1287.

Stoller, R. J. (1964). *A contribution to the study of gender identity. International Journal of Psychoanalysis, 45*, 220–226.

Stoller, R. J. (1968). *Sex & gender* (pp. 3–348). New York: Science House.

Stoller, R. J. (1985). A primer for gender identity. In *Presentations of gender* (pp. 10–24). New Haven and London: Yale University Press (Chapter 2).

tumblr (2020). *Common non-binary genders*. https://genderfluidsupport.tumblr.com/gender

Williams, G. (1997). The no-entry system of defences. *Internal landscapes and foreign bodies, The Tavistock Clinic Series* (pp. 115–122). London and New York: Karnac (Chapter 2).

Wollheim, R. (1969). The mind and the mind's image of itself. *International Journal of Psychoanalysis, 50*, 209–220.

Chapter 2

Body of Guilt

Murderous phantasies, wishes and actions form a kind of psychic blood sport. In this chapter, I'll be writing about blood relations that can invoke murderous wishes, the configurations that can underpin such wishes and where these wishes might land. I explore how early manifestations of guilt might take root in the body before a capacity to symbolise or mentalise has developed. It can be hard to disentangle guilt from early forms of persecutory anxiety that are bound up with the infant's rudimentary drive to survive. This drive to survive is experienced in the body via sensations of repletion and depletion, fullness and emptiness.

Guilt can be applied to ordinary individual aspects of female development and also to the much broader development of theories of femininity within the psychoanalytic canon. There have been objections to theories that invoke the female plight as emanating from a lack, as if femaleness can only ever be interpreted as 'not maleness', the sex that is without. There have also been objections (Moi, 2004) to the focus on femininity and castration as representing, or synonymous with, sexual difference.

Separations and early experiences of need can feel persecutory. Fears associated with the primitive need to survive and total reliance on the feeding parent (usually mother) can evoke aggression that leads to guilt. Terms such as guilt or aggression are multi-faceted and overlay the pre-verbal primitive raw terror of need and survival early on in life. Psychoanalytically, we identify that *need drives fear, fear drives aggression and aggression drives guilt*. Klein expanded our understanding of this with her writing on envious attacks into and onto the mother's body through her work with children and her insight into their inner worlds.

I wish to discuss how this chain of need, fear, aggression and guilt takes hold in infancy and then re-emerges in the developed sexual body; how that body might then be used as a symbol for the realisation of an unconscious wish. Might a daughter kill off her femininity as one way of bypassing the guilt that can arise from a harsh superego, one that commands the erasure of mother or motherhood? In this way, the body can both house the guilt *and* become the site of brutality. This scenario can stem from early and unresolved aggressive impulses, which can be thought of as the precursors of psychic guilt that resurface in adolescence or young adulthood.

DOI: 10.4324/9781032718613-3

Unconscious guilt is perhaps built into all separations from birth onwards. When the tie between mother and daughter is complicated by pronounced ambivalence, aggression and guilt can assume particular resonance. Infantile and then adolescent forms of aggression that emanate from guilt might impact on a daughter's relationship to femaleness in her mother and her bodily self.

The daughter's detachment and dis-identification from her mother is a necessary and challenging developmental step. This separation can be thought of as a traumatic severance. In some situations, which could have implications for aspects of gender identity, the unconscious matricidal wish can take the form of a drive towards *separation from femaleness and femininity in the body*. Guilt can also stem from an early sense of rejection by a daughter of her homoerotic desires towards her mother, as not being the object of mother's desire (Elise, 2002). This too might stimulate a drive towards undoing femaleness in oneself that includes being on the receiving end of female desire or the object that the desire is directed from. The archaic and unconscious maternal rejection might be embedded in a way that might contaminate female-to-female desire. For trans men, the orientation from or towards a female anatomy can understandably be experienced as incongruent.

Freud named the part of the mind that is prone to harshness and criticism, sometimes to a debilitating and extreme degree, the superego (1923). This formed part of his second topographical model of the mind consisting of the ego, superego and id. His original structural theory proposed a division into unconscious, preconscious and conscious. The two structural theory proposals complement one another with the later one of ego, id and superego being both conscious and unconscious.

The maternal and paternal aspects of the superego are not precisely delineated by actual parental figures or genders, but these underlying unconscious structures might contribute to the complexity of maternal and paternal identifications. The quality of the maternal object that shapes the superego can be compounded by experience of an actual deprived and depriving mother, particularly when this experience is imbued with an infant's own aggression and phantasies. If the paternal object has been either remote or idealised, this can lead to split or confused identifications. I delineate elements of these difficulties through clinical and interview material.

From the time that Freud put forward his version of the daughter's navigation from 'mother to father to other', it has been questioned and contested. Freud laid down his theory more assuredly in relation to boys' patricidal wishes. I suggest an equivalent conceptualisation to the son's act of patricide, in the form of matricide, as a prototype of the female version of the Oedipus Complex. I expand on this concept in Chapter 3.

Skin as a Vulnerable Boundary

Initially, rudimentary experiences are inscribed in the body. Guilt emanates from these bodily sensations: in the awareness of a feeding or needing mother who offers and withdraws her breast, and in the primitive greed or grace of the biting baby, or the baby that can wait. I link guilt to these unconscious phantasies of *taking, receiving and not having*, as well as the wish for (unconscious) retrieval. Feeling full or robbed of feeling full can lead to frustration, resentment and at times murderous rage. The infant is not a passive or invariant entity, and the dynamic between an infant and feeding adult is bi-directional, albeit with unequal power.

Bick (1968) developed the concept of a 'second skin', an imaginary hide or coating that evolves as a defensive measure against loss. An infant might have to compensate for an emotional lack through the use of his or her body or muscularity. The body can make up for or house what cannot be borne in mind. This form of physical compensation is functional but might be at the cost of developing a capacity to bear mental pain.

Bick saw the skin as having the function of binding together parts of the personality that were not yet differentiated from parts of the body. At a primitive and very early phase of life, the skin functions as a boundary. The capacity to hold parts of the self together is initially reliant on the introjection of an external object (usually the mother) experienced as able to fulfil this function. This enables the infant to move from an unintegrated state of helplessness to one in which there can be a phantasy of internal and external space.

Femaleness aligns a daughter to her mother's body through symmetrical identification. Identification with (maternal) femininity appeared to be unwanted for Joe, a trans man and one of my interviewees, who was more at ease when younger with a masculinised identification and presentation. This form of identification might have conjured up the yearned for and absent father, in the form of a presence he could, in phantasy inhabit. Identification with his mother might have been experienced as less safe.

The creation of or identification with maleness might have provided a defence against or compensation for a missing parent. For Joe, there was no actual father to fill this void, leaving him only with phantasies of this part of his identity. Children will often blame themselves for the departure of a parent, and this feeling can endure. It can also displace anger towards the remaining parent.

His father could leave, but his mother once pregnant had to stay, perhaps in Joe's eyes leaving motherhood, femaleness and femininity as betrayed, abandoned and undesirable. He might also have had the phantasy or belief that if he'd been born a boy, things would have been very different. The identification with father might be seen as enacted via a wish to acquire masculine attributes. This might be through a phallic identification in phantasy or through making alterations in the actual physical body.

At the age of 19, in relation to chest growth at puberty, Joe explained:

> I didn't feel any desire to make them look bigger like the other girls would. … I have felt some kind of discomfort ever since puberty started approaching, but I obviously didn't know why that discomfort was there until I turned fifteen and I gave it some thought.
>
> (Joe, 2020)

Joe was unsure how masculinity was going to manifest in him physically, as he had no external image of his father. Would he be able to grow a beard and would his hairline recede?

> Yeah, so just shooting into the dark really. But at the same time, it's kind of exciting because it's always a surprise. I mean a very slowly forming surprise.
>
> (Joe, 2020)

I was struck by the phrase "shooting into the dark" as in some respects never having met his father Joe had been shot into the dark, without his father's physical materialisation. More unconsciously, Joe might have felt that his mother had kept him in the dark, as no surprises about his father were forthcoming. His mother might have had to manage the guilt of a pregnancy with no father for her child. This is what Laplanche (1997, 2007) referred to as an enigmatic message, transmitted unconsciously, from parent to child, leaving the child to translate the enigma.

At a follow-up interview four years on from the first interview, Joe, now 23, had been on testosterone for a year and a half. He felt more at ease physically, both within himself and in the external world. He spoke about his attempt to connect to his cultural roots, and mainly his father's culture, through physical characteristics such as his hair. Whereas his mother wanted him to have long hair whilst younger as it was pretty, he did not like having longer hair when younger. Now he felt he could have a "connection to my hair that's not fixated on femininity" (Joe, 2020). There was something more comfortable for Joe in his masculine alignment with his father's culture, manifesting in his own appearance. This was also a move away from his mother's wishes for her (then) daughter. He was pleased with his voice that sounded masculine, which he said made him speak more, whereas previously he was inclined to listen more and speak less. It was a relief for Joe to find his own voice and hear it spoken.

The discussion of clinical material that follows is written as a composite from a number of patients and supervisees seen several years ago and is not based on an individual patient. Although I refer to Romi, she represents this composite of clinical material. The material shows how guilt, often manifesting defensively as aggression, can shape maternal and paternal objects, the figurations that form or inform the superego, the master of guilt. I will discuss Romi, and later on in the chapter, refer to material from other interviewees.

Romi's father was mostly an absent figure and her mother fluctuated in her moods. Father became the idealised and never present object, whilst mother for a long time garnered all bad attributes. This kept her actual father removed from reality. He became the ideal or redeemed father that never was.

Identification with (maternal) femininity appeared to be threatening for Romi, who was more at ease with a masculinised identification and presentation. This form of identification felt safer as it was removed from a depressed, unstable and threatening maternal object and conjured up the yearned for and absent father, in the form of a presence she could, in phantasy, have all to herself and also 'on demand'.

The identification with maleness provided a defence against an experience of helplessness. This was felt when faced with both her own identification with a dangerous or broken mother part of her as well as the helplessness of a young daughter who could not keep father there. Romi's parents became starkly split into good and bad. Guilt was internalised or indeed embodied, with the function of protecting her actual parents.

Klein understood the early development of the superego as partly emanating from parental figures infused by or even fused with infantile aggression that has been projected onto them, who can then, in phantasy, become externalised and feared as terrifying objects felt to exist in the outer world. Romi feared being aligned with her mother via aggression towards her own children that would then leave her with unbearable guilt. I am suggesting that this persecutory scenario arose from her matricidal feelings and wishes – a hybrid of her own murderous wishes towards her mother and the helpless child in herself that was at the mercy of mother's erratic violence. She was anxious about the possibility of unconscious repetition.

This raises various issues as to how we work clinically with a patient who has such a complex relationship to her own aggression, an aggression that can become more overt as a superego with harsh maternal qualities, behind which a superego with harsh paternal qualities might reside in a more concealed fashion.

Romi can be thought of as an infant, described by Esther Bick (1968), who, spurred on by mother's needs into pseudo-independence, develops a "second skin" constructed as a muscular type of self-containment. Bick described a mother who stimulated her child into making aggressive displays, which she both provoked and admired, referring to her six-and-a-half-month-old aggressive little girl as "a boxer". Similarly, I felt that Romi had this kind of defensive muscularity, and 'boxing gloves' were, so to speak, often close to hand. However, when a patient comes to recognise their aggression and can start to see its defensive quality, it can stimulate feelings of depressive guilt. Over time, she was able to relinquish aspects of her second skin mode of functioning.

In Romi's case, she did need to defend herself from her mother. Much more unconsciously, I suggest, there was also a defence against the father that neither she nor her mother could keep. The father's unnamed and unrepresented hostility had to be hidden and protected; what came to the fore was a feared identification with a hostile maternal object and with femininity or womanhood. The identification with father is enacted via a wish to acquire masculine attributes. This might be through making alterations in the actual physical body or in phantasy via a phallic identification. Masculinity served as an anchor for her, imagined as safer than being moored to a dangerous or disintegrated mother. The quality of the maternal object that shapes the superego can be compounded by experience of an actual deprived and depriving mother, particularly when this experience is imbued with an infant's own aggression and phantasies. If the paternal object has been remote or idealised, this can lead to split or confused identifications.

For Romi, perhaps someone somewhere has to be beaten. Cruel objects are the more accessible ones for her, and if she beats herself up, this functions as a matricidal wish once removed and possibly a patricidal wish twice removed. The phantasy of herself as a persecuted or murderous son to her father might be buried beneath more overt matricidal wishes. I discuss this further on in this chapter in relation to Anna Freud and also in Chapter 3. I have suggested a constellation of internal maternal and paternal objects that mould the ego and superego. If these objects are at war, this can propel universal conflicts of identity and identifications. I expand on the concept of matricide in the next chapter.

The primitive body of an infant can be likened to a membrane that holds everything: we are somatic beings in the beginning, as the mind has not yet developed the capacity to mentalise or process feelings in the form of thoughts. Bodily sensations precede a thinking mind. I am suggesting that in some instances of gender identity, a disturbance in the primitive maternal object relationship can render femaleness and femininity as hostile pursuits and a threat to identity. Unconscious murderous (matricidal) wishes can then become sublimated and sometimes manifest in a drive towards maleness and masculinity as a safer domain. I think that the motivation to move away from femaleness and femininity can sometimes be stronger than the motivation or wish to land in maleness. I expand on this in Chapter 4.

The quality of the maternal object that shapes the superego can be compounded by experience of an actual deprived and depriving mother, particularly when this experience is imbued with an infant's own aggression and phantasies. If the paternal object has been remote or idealised, this can lead to split or confused identifications.

Daughter/Mother

Some of the trans men I interviewed described their mothers' past wishes towards them. These wishes were for a particular kind of femininity (in their then daughters), perhaps a femininity that was not easily experienced by their mothers. This might have been a wish for a daughter to have long hair, wear feminine dresses or have a stereotyped feminine body. One interviewee, Ray, whose mother had herself had surgery to enhance the size of her breasts, was concerned that her (then) daughter would not experience the same disappointment and discomfort with her body. The daughter's (now trans man's) disappointment or dysmorphia went beyond the size of breasts to a wish not to have breasts at all, curiously resembling mother's pre-surgery more androgenous body. These maternal wishes, very much located in the mother's mind, might leave a daughter feeling guilt about not fulfilling the concrete (physical) desires of her mother, and more unconsciously not being the ideal love object for mother. Ray had hoped that puberty might be a time of mother/daughter bonding, but this was not borne out (Ray 2020).

Ray described femininity as something that felt unattainable in his (then) female self and perhaps was experienced as only attainable in another. Through female relationships, Ray can attend to femininity in the object, safely removed from himself whilst identifying as a gay woman or a trans man. Perelberg discusses the well-known accounts of Freud's patients (Anna O, Lucy R, Elizabeth Von R and Dora) as all bearing disappointment towards their fathers. She links this disappointment with the longing for another woman who personifies unattainable femininity. She asks whether this pursuit is out of a fear of being left only with mother as an internal imago (Perelberg, 2018: 4).

In the case of my interviewees, the move away from femininity manifested in a wish to transition away from mother's notions of a feminine daughter into a masculine identity, perhaps as a way of invoking a boundary or statement of a separate body unlike that of mother's. This separation from mother's desires might have felt safer than the experience of having one's body taken over or colonised. The thread of guilt is transferred both consciously and unconsciously between mother and daughter in what might be referred to as the projection (mother to daughter) and re-projection (daughter to mother) of gender. My conjectures might well be countered with the argument that maleness was omnipresent, and did not emanate from a flight from femininity, but that the pre-existing sense of maleness made femininity or femaleness difficult or impossible to manage.

Soma/Psyche

The movement between soma and psyche connects to a number of psychoanalytic ideas. Firstly, Freud's proclamation that the ego was "first and foremost a body-ego; it is not merely a surface entity, but it is itself the projection of a surface" (1923: 26). This shows Freud's early understanding of the body as that which initially holds and moulds the rudimentary forming of the ego via projected and introjected sensory experience. Secondly, it connects to Ferrari, an Italian psychoanalyst's concept of 'The Concrete Original Object'[1] (1992). By this, he meant the initial location and source from which mental phenomena are generated. He respects the sensory functioning of analysands, as if what he is seeing is the newly born baby on the couch struggling with oscillations between bodily manifestations that assume mental characteristics. He allows manifestations of concreteness to aid his analytic understanding. Thirdly Anzieu, a French Psychoanalyst (1923–1999), developed an imaginative and sophisticated theory in his attempt to bind regions of the mind to regions of the skin.

My exploration of trans male identity necessarily looks at how the body is housed in its skin, and how so much discomfort can be experienced by the feeling of being housed in the wrong kind of skin, that encases the body. The skin envelopes the body, as the mind envelopes thoughts and feelings. The mind is housed in the body and has to manage a psychic relationship to it. When surgical alterations are made to the body, it is the skin that bears the incisions and scars. With female to male hormonal changes (testosterone), the surface of the skin is changed via hair growth. Hormones can also alter the mind. One interviewee, Joe, said he felt more resilient after taking testosterone, less inclined to get upset as he might have done previously. He said he did not experience "roid-rage", which is sometimes attributed to changes in mood following the steroid testosterone (Joe, 2024).

As a child, Anzieu felt he was smothered physically by excessive layers of clothing which he called the envelopes of care, concern and warmth. He felt that he carried these layers with him when he left home and that his vitality was hidden under several layers of 'outer coverings'. At the age of 50, he became fully aware of this and developed the notion of psychic envelopes in his 1974 article on the skin ego (Anzieu, 1990: 3). He uses the metaphor that the skin of the psyche is like the skin of an onion (Anzieu, 1989: 215). He understands the senses of sound, smell, taste and sight to be interlocked with the sense of touch to form the skin of the psyche. Although the skin-ego is a distinct concept, it is enriched by the concept of psychic envelope that moves more to a way of thinking about the experience of the senses that are always interacting with one another.

The term 'skin ego' refers to an infant's mental representation that forms out of the experience of the surface of its body; it can also be used by the infant, albeit in a rudimentary fashion, to have a sense of itself as a vessel of mental contents. It is a structure that is "potentially present from birth" and is "realised as the relationship between the baby and its primary environment unfolds" (Anzieu, 1985: 102). It develops when the psychic ego differentiates itself from the body ego in practical terms whilst remaining indistinguishable from it in the imagination. The term sits in an intermediate place between metaphor and concept, not unlike Winnicott's concept of transitional phenomena (1951, 1987). It was introduced by Anzieu in 1974; he was interested in the skin's impact upon the mind.

Anzieu states that no orifice can be perceived without a sensation, however vague, *of surface* and *volume*. The infant begins to experience their skin as a surface at the same time or from the experience of the contact his body has with that of mother's body and within the framework of a secure attachment to her. So, the infant develops the notion of a boundary between inside and outside, interior and exterior, at the same time as developing the confidence to progressively master the orifices. This necessitates a basic feeling that affirms the integrity of the infant's bodily envelope. This is similar to Bion's notion of a psychic container, and the dangers of depersonalisation that go hand in hand with a sense of a perforated envelope in states of acute anxiety – a flowing away of vital substances through holes. This is an anxiety based on a sense of something being emptied out.

The skin ego develops as a response to a need for a narcissistic envelope and provides the psyche with a continuous sense of basic well-being. By skin ego, Anzieu means a mental image that the child's ego can make use of during early phases of development, on the basis of its experience of the surface of the body.

Anzieu's thinking about functions of the skin is based on Freud's idea that "every psychical function develops by supporting itself upon a bodily function whose workings it transposes on to the mental plane" (Anzieu, 1985: 96).

The concept of psychic envelope has emerged out of an attempt to create a theory about the actual analytic experience: a patient projects their psychic-envelope onto the setting of the session. Through the use of transference and countertransference, the therapist perceives the complex structure of the individual patient's particular psychic envelope from the inside out. "It involves being sensitive to the most intimate aspects of our experience of the skin and endeavouring to elaborate this experience mentally" (Houzel, 1990: 43). Skin here is meant in a metaphorical sense rather than anatomical sense. The psychic envelope is a dynamic concept that both delimits spaces and is permeable. It can be likened to a field of force that spreads around a magnet. It is a shape that is being moulded by the forces at work within and around it, like a valley that attracts a flow of water (Houzel, 1990: 44).

In Aeschylus' trilogy *The Oresteia* (Aeschylus, 2009), Orestes kills his mother Clytemnestra in order to avenge her killing of his father Agamemnon. Orestes is caught up in an Oedipal conundrum between trying to escape his father's curse and "the hounding furies of a mother's curse" (Britton, 2024: 59). He is damned if he does and damned if he doesn't. Following the act of matricide, Orestes' fate is described by Britton as "relentless persecution of the flesh" (Britton, 2024: 59), thereby locating guilt back into the body.

Was it their father that Orestes and Romi felt more murderous towards? This has a bearing on how we think that guilt forms, how it might shape the underlying unconscious structure of the maternal or paternal objects that structure the superego, and how in turn these might stimulate murderous wishes towards one parent who might stand in for the other. My suggestion is that Romi started life with a mother who had serious struggles with her own needs, fears and aggression and this beginning of life was and continued to be registered in Romi's body, a body of guilt.

Use of the Body as a Symbol

The relationship between bodies and symbols varies between differing psychoanalytic schools in relation to women and femininity. Whilst much has been written on the (Freud driven) theories of lack, the questioning of this opens up larger questions about the centrality of the Oedipal configuration as both providing and feeding the theoretical understandings that spring from it, or back to it, could this be termed 'the Oedipal Spring'? Although I appreciate the centrality and usefulness of the Oedipal drama to psychoanalytic academic and clinical thinking, it also has the potential to limit exploration, as so many streams of thought flow back to it as a somewhat immovable dogma. Oedipus, a tragic hero in Greek mythology, was the subject of Sophocles' tragedy *Oedipus Rex*. The wish of Oedipus to kill his father and marry his mother resonated for Freud in his self-analysis. Although the Oedipal myth is all about triangles, it was in Freud's singular, one to one analysis of himself (albeit linked to his own unconscious) that he uncovered the richness of it in relation to human dynamics. There have been objections to the heteronormative essence of the Oedipus complex, and it is not my intention to reinforce that, although it is important to acknowledge. It is also a versatile cornerstone of psychoanalytic theory, and I do not wish to diminish it as that which bestows psychoanalysis with its shibboleth (Blass, 2001).

My focus in this chapter is on manifestations of guilt in a female body and femininity, and how this body might be configured consciously, unconsciously and relationally.

Toril Moi, a professor in Gender, Sexuality and Feminist Studies at Duke University, explores the link between castration or sexual difference and femininity. She asks why it is that femininity is the culprit, so to speak, of the psychoanalytic explorations into sexual difference by both Freud and Lacan. She questions the need for a theory of femininity and not a theory of masculinity. Why is it that women have to be explained and men do not? Moi makes it clear that she is not in pursuit of an equality theory but rejects "theories that *equate* femininity and sexual difference, as if women were the only bearers of sex" (2004: 97). She sees Lacan and Freud as equally culpable in an overvaluation of masculinity and the phallus, although coming at the issue from a different means of understanding in relation to the body: Freud more taken up with the concrete phenomenological body and Lacan approaching it much more as an abstract and idealist concept. (107).

Moi objects to femininity (and hence women) always being placed at the centre of castration, as that which demarcates the difference between the sexes. She questions this placement and finds it sexist, not least as men too fear castration and have fears about the sex that they are. She does not see why 'that which is castrated' is (always) relegated to the feminine, especially for Lacan, where body parts are not part of the comprehension or theory. She thinks it is precisely because women do not have a penis that they are relegated to this group of the feminine and hence the castrated.

Moi states, "For Freud, to speak of sexual difference is to speak of femininity and *vice versa.* Men are human beings, women are sexed; masculinity is universal, femininity particular" (Moi, 2004: 102).

Returning to Freud's 'Analysis Terminable and Interminable' (1937) in which Freud expands on *penis envy* in women and the *masculine protest* in men, Moi can see that in Freud's mind castration is violently opposed in both sexes. The difference, in her reading of Freud's paper, is that whereas men fear castration, women are dismayed to find that it has already occurred. She draws from this that "Repudiation of femininity is repudiation of castration, and this is a biologically based attitude in both sexes" (118). She does not see why the repudiation of femininity cannot or could not have been expressed as a reluctance to accept our human condition? This loops back to the notion of accepting reality, accepting limits, and foregoing a more omnipotent stance that I have referred to previously.

Moi brings in Mitchell (1986) who was succinct on this subject of loss, the loss of having to belong to one sex only:

> But because human subjectivity cannot ultimately exist outside a division into one of the two sexes, then it is castration that finally comes to symbolize this split. The feminine comes to stand over the point of disappearance, the loss.
>
> (Mitchell, 1986: 393)

The need for a psychoanalytic theory that does not seek to explain the difference between the sexes via a theory of femininity or castration appears to be Moi's quest, but she can see that this theory would need to acknowledge that male and female bodies are different. Moi cites McDougall as advocating this kind of theory.

The title of Moi's essay is 'From femininity to finitude: Freud, Lacan, and feminism, again'. She ends it with a stress on the universal human struggle to accept finitude. This is one of the universal challenges elaborated from McDougall's definition of psychoanalysis as a form of thought that seeks to understand the psychic consequences of three universal traumas. These are the fact that there are others, the fact of sexual difference and the fact of death. I found it curious that Money-Kyrle was not acknowledged here, as he wrote about these (1971) as the facts of life and is often referenced.

It might be a leap to suggest that perhaps the difficulty to accept femininity resided more in the male psyches of Freud and Lacan than in individual women. Is it men who struggle to accept the female body rather than women, because in order to imagine a female body, a man would have to imagine a kind of castration? In their identification with it, what stands out is the lack (of a penis or phallus) and theories can and have been built up from this notion. Although this is a concrete approach, the body and our relationship to it is to a certain and undeniable extent concrete. I am not questioning the reality for Freud's female patients in terms of their cultural suppression. And clearly there are many young women in the culture of recent decades who would rather not be and feel themselves not to be female.

In my interviews with trans men, I noticed that in the material, their mothers were at times missing or vaguely referred to. Fathers were not necessarily positively portrayed, but a male social function was preferred to the more ambivalent daughter/mother, maternal identification. Femaleness and femininity were felt to be incongruent, and a male or masculine embodiment was both sought and felt using the body as a symbol for the realisation of this wish. I suggest that the body can be used as a symbol even if the wish might at times be seen as concrete.

One of my interviewees Milo elected to have a hysterectomy, as he did not want a reproductive body. This surgery, that brought much relief, might also be thought of as a castration of femininity, the womb representative of that which is quintessentially female. Perhaps to have or not have a womb captures something of the trans man's dilemma in relation to their current and past embodiment. For Milo, this wish was driven by certainty, and I suggest by a phantasy of pregnancy that felt untenable. I return to this in Chapter 3.

Elise (1998) suggests that for girls, the relational void in giving up the mother may be represented genitally. The symbolic withholding of the penis (by father), through his relational distance, can then be schematised by a body that is empty of something. The emptiness can manifest in the vagina or its mental representation. The object's hunger (for the paternal penis) lies behind vaginal repression or an inhibition of the role of the vagina in sexual desire (1998: 413). Elise posits that the relational void left by giving up the mother as a love object can leave an internal self-representation as a 'hole' to be filled, not unlike the function of the pacifier, when the nipple is unavailable (1998: 421).

There is also the blatant vulnerability of a female body, one that can be penetrated *and* impregnated that is specific to the female anatomy. Having a vagina can invoke anxieties about an internal space that is open to invasion (Barnett, 1966;

Bernstein, 1990; Horney, 1933). This might be exacerbated in instances of an intrusive mother, who might struggle with boundaries between herself and her daughter.

Toby, a 29-year-old interviewee, described his relationship to his gender as fluid but also strongly masculine from an early age. He described his mother as empathic to his early gender struggles. During puberty, she got him jeans with boxers attached to or enveloped inside them, as an aid to managing the inherent femaleness of menstruation. The boxers attached to the jeans might symbolise a form of adhesive masculinity, there is no genital differentiation: you can pretend to be male and I will assist you in this. Mother, in her attempt to help might have been colluding in or encouraging of a repudiation of femininity that might reveal her own stance on the masculine/feminine divide. His mother is well intentioned but might potentially be endorsing the experience of cutting off from the reality of the difference between the sexes.

Toby perceives his mother as being very co-operative with his wish to be masculine, which introduces the element of *her desire in his mind* as well as his perception of *her desire in her mind*. In this context, he might have tried to be the phallus for his mother (Lacan, 1958), not least as this time coincided with difficulties between his parents. Stoller (1975: 44–45) in his discussion about transsexual boys, which now reads as outdated, points to them having been the youngest child in the family for many years, five or more; and how mother can use this child to stem her loneliness and as part of her own body, namely female. Toby was the first daughter for his mother after a number of sons. I wondered if she might have inadvertently used her then daughter/now son as a phallus, leaving Toby with confused identifications about his body, sex and sexuality. She was keen to encourage maleness in him. This does not mean that parents should not support their children's struggles with gender identity, but in some circumstances, support can become collusion through identifications that might be unconscious (Toby, 2020).

It has been suggested (Abraham, 1982: 447) that Freud's picture of the Oedipal father *was in fact derived from his mother*. Freud's mother is described as difficult, self-centred, infantile and aggravating, whereas his father is described as amiable and somewhat ineffectual. In Freud's extensive correspondence, his mother is mentioned infrequently.

The Primal Scene

Primal scene phantasies are relevant here as they structure the child's unconscious archive and operate both pre-genitally and genitally during development. During the pre-genital phase, the phantasies can include oral devouring, bisexual confusions and the fear of losing the representation of one's body limits or sense of identity. If the individual's psychic reality is overloaded by these phantasies, sexual or love relations can become equated with castration, annihilation or death. The primal scene locates itself psychically in a complex network of phantasies in which confused or fused allegiances to mother, father, femininity and masculinity all play out. The capacity to hold in mind a benign link between one's parents, developed particularly in Britton's work (1989), is fundamental psychoanalytically. The attack on this link can have devastating consequences, not only is the link between the parents destroyed but also the link to the parents who excluded the subject from the primal scene.

There are differing schools of thought about the psychic incorporation of the primal scene. One angle of Klein's combined parent figure denotes aggression and hostility with both parents fused into one monstrous configuration; another angle is that of the parents in an "everlasting mutual gratification of an oral, anal and genital nature" (Klein, 1952: 55; Sodré, 2015). Britton has emphasised the missing link and the infant's exclusion from this act and their wish to 'get in on the act' (Britton, 1989, 1999). Mitchell, S. (1988) has stressed the reasons for the centrality of sexuality as deriving not from biological drives but from interactive and relational aspects of experience.

In Britton's paper 'Getting in on the Act: The Hysterical Solution', he suggests that: "... a central feature of hysteria is the use of projective identification by the subject to become in phantasy one or the other or both members of the primal couple". Britton suggests that "... in hysteria the patient, like some of Klein's children in the play-room, mounts the stage, to become one of the characters by a phantasy of projective identification"[2] (1999:3). This is demonstrated by a re-interpretation of Anna O's symptoms and psychopathology as they played out in her treatment by Breuer, who could not identify the erotic transference. He (Britton) discusses the 'other room' as the setting for the invisible primal scene of infancy. The consulting room during analysis can become a live version of this original space, particularly when a patient is unable to locate the other room in their imagination (1999: 8).

Aaron (1995) posits the poignant question of: *whom the child identifies with in the primal scene phantasy:*

> According to classical theory there are many reasons why the primal scene can be traumatic. One well-known cause is that, because of the child's immature cognition and because of the projection of jealous rage, the child imagines the sexual act as an aggressive one, as an aggressive and dangerous battle. Another explanation is that the primal scene is traumatic narcissistically because of the child's shame and humiliation at being excluded from the parental dyad. A less commonly recognized aspect of what can make the primal scene traumatic is that, *looking at the sexual scenario, the child does not know for the moment with whom to identify. Inasmuch as both partners to the scene are seen as in the pursuit of pleasure, it is plausible for the oedipal witness to be inclined to identify with both parties to the scene, male and female* (my italics).
>
> (Aaron, 1995: 205)

Aaron goes on to state that "according to classical theory" what emanates from this confusion is an intensification of castration anxiety and penis envy that moves onto the splitting or repression of bisexuality and the "extreme stereotyping of identity along gender lines" (Aaron, 1995: 206).

In his paper 'The Drive to Become Both Sexes', Kubie (1974) makes the poignant observation that this drive exists in all of us and the challenge is not so much to give up the other gender but to find unconscious ways of incorporating the other gender alongside our birth gender in a complementary fashion so that we do end up as both. It is interesting to think of how this can become sublimated in cultural aspects of everyday life. Kubie elaborates on the various manifestations of this drive: in art, literature, professional life, relationships and psychotic disturbances.

Guilt is usually invoked by the superego that can denote a structure of intrapsychic cruelty in which one part of the mind is attacking and demeaning another. Freud's paper 'A child is being beaten' (1919) is partly derived from his analysis of his daughter Anna, her daydreams and phantasies. Anna Freud's paper 'Beating Fantasies and Daydreams' (1922) lends rare access to her analysis, and the fantasies of a girl, in which a boy is being beaten by a man. Whereas for Anna, the guilt derived from *the shame* of masturbation, for Freud, the source of guilt was *the content* of these fantasies. This throws up an interesting body/mind distinction in relation to the source of guilt.

Maternal Desire & Infantile Guilt

Mother is generally (although not always) the first and central object of desire for the daughter in the early stage of mother-infant bonding. However, homoerotic desire towards her from a daughter might not always be validated by her. When it is not, it remains as unrecognised desire. This can leave the daughter with a sense that her desire is unrequited, that she does not have what mother wants or needs, whether this is genitally or emotionally. This lack of recognition by the mother can leave a daughter with a sense of guilt that might not be comprehensible and might register more unconsciously. Elise posits the idea of replacing the "negative oedipal complex" in girls, with "the primary maternal Oedipal situation" (2002: 209). Elise suggested that early homoerotic feelings between a mother and daughter can stir up ambivalent maternal desire (2002: 225). Her writing, in my view, corroborates the potential for complexity in female-to-female sexual desire and has some relevance to the move for some trans men away from female homosexuality.

For my interviewees, there was something that felt and was incongruent in identifying or remaining identified as lesbian. Prior to identifying as trans men, most of the interviewees identified as female and gay. But this identity, for all of them, was not one that they wished to retain for varying reasons. There appeared to be something too inherently female for them, not just in their embodiment but also in the orientation of the other towards them. To be perceived as a gay woman, is to be perceived as female, whatever one's presentation might be. The orienting *from* and *towards* a masculine position is important, whether bodily, psychically, socially or sexually. The masculine position for some trans men does not necessitate a biological penis. It is a form of non-genital masculinity.

Here is part of an interview with Joe (aged 19 at time of interview):

Me: …You said there was a phase in which you came out as gay initially and presumably there was a decision at some point that it wasn't quite right for you to be a gay woman … that there was a wish to be something else?

Joe: Yeah, a lot of trans men actually do start out as gay women because a lot of trans men are a lot more attracted to women than they are to men; so at first they would probably definitely come out as a gay woman and after that, they would probably think about the fact: they would think about why do I actually like dressing as, why do I like dressing masculine and why do I like women? And then they would start thinking like about their gender umm and usually after maybe coming out as trans they start exploring relationships with not just women umm but different genders as well. So, a lot of trans men that I know actually end up dating other trans men, women and men, so yeah it's a journey.

But I came out as a gay woman when I was fourteen, and that obviously then evolved into like the explanation of why I liked women and it turned out 'actually I don't even like being a woman', … and maybe there is more to me than just liking women, maybe there is something more hidden under that ….

(Joe, 2020)

Joe attempts to make sense of his attraction to women that goes beyond female-to-female attraction. He is trying to make sense of the orienting of his object choice from a masculine stance within himself. If he is attracted to women and feels himself to be masculine, then this must mean more than 'just' being gay. It is complex, as it denotes a difficulty with having *a masculinised desire from a female anatomy directed towards another*. It brings up the possibility that something in the midst of female homoerotic desire is wholly disconsonant. This might include unconscious aspects of the early mother/daughter relationship, particularly if the daughter's passion towards her first love object might have been left unrequited. This might leave the experience of female-to-female desire as a dangerous domain to revisit. This revisiting might also be complicated by a mother-daughter relationship that contains pronounced levels of friction.

My interpreting above might be an example of my projection of psychoanalytic thinking into an experience of bodily and gender incongruence. It might be that psychoanalytic clinicians including myself, really struggle to identify with a kind of gender incompatibility that feels so alien that it induces despair that can be suicidal.

In a self-narrated chapter about the struggles with being a trans man (Hertzmann & Newbigin, 2020), the narrator described being treated by an eating disorders team who'd suggested that 'she' was gay and didn't want to accept this. I quote from this narration:

> I tried reluctantly to believe this for many years, tying myself in knots of confusion and despair. I believe now that this was because I always knew I wasn't gay, but it was then impossible to explain my sexual attraction to heterosexual women ... In the safety of the therapy room with Dr C, it suddenly became obvious to me that my sexual attraction towards heterosexual women is because I am a heterosexual (possibly bisexual – all this has yet to be fully explored) *man*. I see and always have seen women through my male eyes, and my inner male self feels emotional, romantic, and sexual connections with women, which becomes lost in translation through my physical self.
>
> (2020: 269)

Magee and Miller (1992) explored psychoanalytic views of female homosexuality and pointed out that a lot of analytic thinking has been based on polarised categories such as activity/passivity, male/female, manifest/latent, homosexual/ heterosexual and secondary process/primary process (1992: 68). They imply that this kind of polarisation can limit a more nuanced understanding of female sexuality and relationships, and poignantly state that:

> To know that the patient is in homosexual relationships or identifies herself as homosexual is to know nothing about her specific developmental issues, the nature of her sexual experience, or her conflicts, nor about the quality of her external or internal object relations.
>
> (1992: 85)

As psychoanalytic theory moved on (from drive theory to ego psychology and object relations), it was Stoller (1985) and Marmor (1980) who emphasised the multi-determinant nature of any psychic phenomenon (1992: 71) away from the more pervasive phallocentric assumptions that Magee and Miller found through their literature review to have traversed theoretical orientations and informed formulations. More specifically relevant to my research is one of the phallocentric assumptions in the psychoanalytic literature that they pointed out: "*A woman who loves a woman must be a man, or be like a man, or must wish to be a man*" (1992: 72). This assumption reads as less phallocentric in relation to some trans men who wish to be men or feel that they are men. In the interviews, most of the interviewees identified as female and gay before moving to other gender identities that led onto and culminated in them identifying as trans men. There was a clear wish expressed by them not to remain identified (to themselves and others) as lesbians, which I comprehend as a repudiation of femininity, female sexuality and femaleness, understandably felt to be at odds with their trans male gender identification. Although Magee and Miller writing in 1992 read the assumption above as a typical and representative phallocentric assumption, in 2024 and in relation to trans men, it reads differently. The old-fashioned paradigm becomes re-modelled in relation to trans gender identity, which could be thought of as a way to accommodate deep-rooted sexual and gender incongruence.

I end this chapter with thoughts about the receptive nature of femaleness, symbolically, bodily and psychically. The female child, as this is my focus, is a receptor of projections from her parents, and usually more markedly from her mother, at least early on in life. Laplanche (1997, 2007) referred to these as enigmatic signifiers, the unconscious transmission of 'the sexual'[3] from parents to their children. Kristeva describes the origins of female sexuality via the child's erogenous zones that receive the imprints of these enigmatic signifiers from the mother's unconscious, as well as the erotic link she has with the father and his unconscious. It is the orifices that are the primitive receivers of these unconscious transmissions: "The child, who allows himself to be seduced and seduces with his skin and five senses, engages by the very fact of his orifices: mouth, anus and vagina for the little girl" (Kristeva, 2004: 42–43).

I'm interested in thinking about the representation of this transmission, as it becomes available for symbolisation. Does it necessarily take the form of a cavity that is filled or penetrated by another? And does this representation necessarily infiltrate psychosexual development in the form of an internal space for which an unconscious retrieval is sought of that former projection, intrusion or loss?

In 'object-relations theory' of human interactions, the mind is spatially organised as a receptor. Subject and object interact with one another, both being in different states at different times. These states depend on the object's situation and the subject's phantasy, and the recognition of the consequences of our actions in both phantasy and reality.

If one thinks about one's body as a part of the self that is treated like an object, it opens up the possibility of trying to explore the meaning of how the body is represented in the mind in relation to sexuality and gender identity. It necessarily becomes part of a network of relationships not least as the body originates in a mother's body which itself originated in a mother's body. Winnicott said that there is no such thing as an infant without thinking about the mother and infant couple, alluding to the infant's dependence on and link to maternal care (1960, 1965: 43). I suggest that there is also no such thing as a body that stands alone free of psychic projections into it, whether from one's own mind or that of another.

Guilt, which can be pared down to a persecutory bad feeling, and might be thought of as the antithesis of pleasure or satisfaction, is inextricably tied into all of the experiences and sensations that the body endures from within the womb onwards. The body and mind are not distinct initially; the body acts as a mind that can absorb sensations, prior to the development of language and thoughts. In the next chapter, I develop the idea of the female body as a site of brutality, one that can house matricidal wishes.

Notes

1 See also Lombardi, R. (2002).
2 This term is used to mean a projection felt to be intolerable, whether by an infant or patient, that is received and contained by a parent or therapist who can communicate this back to the child or patient. This can modify anxiety, as the projected intolerable feelings have been received, felt and returned in a modified form by the other.
3 Laplanche (2007) used the neologism le sexual, instead of le sexuel. He proposed that the sexual is the unconscious residue of the repression/symbolisation of gender by sex. He saw the sexual as multiple, polymorphous, Freud's fundamental discovery and the object of psychoanalysis.

Bibliography

Aaron, L. (1995). The internalized primal scene. *Psychoanalytic Dialogues*, *5*(2), 195–237.
Abraham, R. (1982). Freud's mother conflict and the formulation of the Oedipal father. *Psychoanalytic Review*, *69*(4), 441–453.
Aeschylus. (2009). *The Oresteia: Agamemnon, Libation-Bearers, Eumenides* (Alan H. Sommerstein, Ed. and Trans.). Harvard College: Loeb Classical Library.
Anzieu, D. (1974). Emboîtements. *Nouv. Rev. Psychoanal*, *9*, 57–71.
Anzieu, D. (1985, 1989). *The skin ego* (Dunod, Trans.). New Haven/London: Yale University Press, 1989.
Anzieu, D. (1990). *Psychic envelopes* (Didier Anzieu, Ed.). London: Karnac Books.
Barnett, M. C. (1966). Vaginal awareness in the infancy and childhood of girls. *Journal of American Psychoanalytic Association*, *14*, 129–140.
Bernstein, D. (1990). Female genital anxieties, conflicts and typical mastery modes. *International Journal of Psychoanalysis*, *71*, 151–165.
Bick, E. (1968). The experience of the skin in early object relations. *International Journal of Psychoanalysis*, *49*, 484–486.
Blass, R. (2001). On the teaching of the Oedipus complex: On making Freud meaningful to university students by unveiling his essential ideas on the human condition. *International Journal of Psychoanalysis*, *82*, 1105–1121.
Britton, R. (1989). The missing link: Parental sexuality in the Oedipus complex. In J. Steiner (Ed.), *The Oedipus complex today* (Chapter 2, pp. 83–101). London: Karnac Books.
Britton, R. (1999). Getting in on the act: The hysterical solution. *International Journal of Psychoanalysis*, *80*(1), 1–14.
Britton, R. (2024). Revenge or forgiveness: *The Oresteia*. In R. Britton & A. Novakovic (Eds.), *Psychoanalytic approaches to forgiveness and mental health* (Chapter 4, pp. 53–67). London & New York: Routledge.
Elise, D. (1998). The absence of the paternal penis. *Journal of the American Psychoanalytic Association*, *46*(2), 413–442.
Elise, D. (2002). The primary maternal Oedipal situation and female homoerotic desire. *Psychoanalytic Inquiry*, *22*(2), 209–228.
Ferrari, A. B. (1992). *L'eclissi del corpo [The Eclipse of the Body]*. Rome: Boria.
Freud, S. (1919). A child is being beaten. In *Standard Edition* (Vol. 17, pp. 177–204). London: Hogarth Press.
Freud, A. (1922). Beating fantasies and daydreams. *Writings*, *1*, 137–157.
Freud, S. (1923). The ego and the id. In *Standard Edition* (Vol. 19, pp. 1–59). London: Hogarth Press.
Freud, S. (1937). Analysis terminable and interminable. In *Standard Edition* (Vol. 23). London: Hogarth Press.

Hertzmann, L., & Newbigin, J. (2020). A person beyond gender: A first-hand account. In L. Hertzmann & J. Newbigin (Eds.), *Sexuality and gender now* (Chapter 11, pp. 256–287). London: Routledge.

Horney, K. (1933). The denial of the vagina – A contribution to the problem of the genital anxieties specific to women. *International Journal of Psychoanalysis*, *14*, 57–70.

Houzel, D. (1990). The concept of psychic envelope. In D. Anzieu (Ed.), *Psychic envelopes* (Chapter 2, pp. 27–58). London: Karnac Books.

Joe. (2020, 2024). Interview (anonymised).

Klein, M. (1952). Some theoretical conclusions regarding the emotional life of the infant. In *Envy and gratitude* (1975) (Chapter 6, pp. 61–93). London: Virago.

Kristeva, J. (2004). Some observations on female sexuality. In I. Matthis (Ed.), *Dialogues on sexuality, gender, and psychoanalysis* (Chapter 3, pp. 41–52). London & New York: Karnac Books.

Kubie, L. (1974). The drive to become both sexes. *Psychoanalytic Quarterly*, *43*, 349–426.

Lacan, J. (1958, 1982). The meaning of the phallus. In J. Mitchell & J. Rose (Eds.), *Feminine sexuality, Jacques Lacan and the école freudienne* (J. Rose, Trans.) (1982) (Chapter 2, pp. 74–85). New York & London: W.W. Norton and Panthean Books.

Laplanche, J. (1997). The theory of seduction and the problem of the other. *International Journal of Psychoanalysis*, *78*, 653–666.

Laplanche, J. (2007). Gender, sex, and the sexual. *Studies in Gender and Sexuality*, *8*(2), 201–219.

Lombardi, R. (2002). Primitive mental states and the body: A personal view of Armando B. Ferrari's concrete original object. *International Journal of Psychoanalysis*, *83*(2), 363–381.

Magee, M., & Miller, D. C. (1992). 'She Forswore her Womanhood': Psychoanalytic views of female homosexuality. *Clinical Social Work Journal*, *20*(1), 67–87.

Marmor, J. (1980). *Homosexual behaviour: Modern reappraisal.* New York: Basic Books; as cited in Magee, M., & Miller, D. C. (1992).

Mitchell, J. (1986). The question of femininity and the theory of psychoanalysis. In G. Kohon (Ed.), *The British school of psychoanalysis: The independent tradition* (1988) (pp. 381–398). London: Free Association Books.

Mitchell, S. (1988). *Relational concepts in psychoanalysis.* Cambridge: Harvard University Press.

Moi, T. (2004). From femininity to finitude: Freud, Lacan, and feminism, again. In I. Matthis (Ed.), *Dialogues on sexuality, gender and psychoanalysis* (Chapter 7, pp. 93–135). London & New York: Karnac Books.

Money-Kyrle, R. E. (1971). The aim of psychoanalysis. *International Journal of Psychoanalysis*, *52*, 103–106.

Perelberg, R. J. (Ed.) (2018). Introduction. In *Psychic bisexuality, a British-French dialogue* (pp. 1–57). London & New York: Routledge.

Ray. (2020). Interview (anonymised).

Sodré, I. (2015). The 'Perpetual Orgy': Hysterical phantasies, bisexuality and the question of bad faith. In P. Roth (Ed.), *Imaginary existences, a psychoanalytic exploration of phantasy, fiction, dreams and daydreams* (Chapter 14, pp. 216–231). London & New York: Routledge.

Sophocles. (1947). *The Theban plays* (trans) E.F. Watling, King Oedipus pp. 25–68, Harmondsworth, England: Penguin Classics.

Stoller, R. J. (1975). The transsexual boy: Mother's feminized phallus. In M. Masud & R. Khan (Eds.), *The transsexual experiment, volume two of sex and gender, The International Psycho-Analytic Library* (Chapter 3, pp. 38–55). London: The Hogarth Press & The Institute of Psychoanalysis.

Stoller, R. J. (1985). A primer for gender identity. In *Presentations of gender* (Chapter 2, pp. 10–24). New Haven & London: Yale University Press.

Toby. (2020). Interview (anonymised).

Winnicott, D. W. (1951, 1987). Transitional objects and transitional phenomena. In *Through paediatrics to psycho-analysis* (Chapter XVIII, pp. 229–242). London: The Hogarth Press.

Winnicott, D. W. (1965, 1960). The theory of the parent-infant relationship (1960). In *The maturational processes and the facilitating environment* (1965) (Chapter 3, pp. 37–55). London: The Hogarth Press.

Chapter 3

Matricide

Femininity Revoked

I suggest that Matricide is considered as an important counterpart to the traditional Oedipal manifestations of patricide. This chapter turns to 'The Oresteia' to examine its murderous protagonists and the meaning of the drive to eliminate mothers. A daughter may enact unconscious matricidal wishes in order to separate from an ambivalent tie to her mother, by excising femininity and femaleness in herself.

I explore early bisexual pulls that can emanate from primal scene identifications. The capacity to relinquish the option to have all options is brought in as a ubiquitous and painful developmental move away from having and being all sexes. There is no consensus on the age at which a child can register the difference between the sexes. Freud postulated that boys and girls initially believed themselves to be masculine; Fast (1984) suggested an all-inclusive undifferentiated phase for both boys and girls initially. The early awareness of a bifurcation into two sexes might register as a rudimentary sensory registration. This inevitably becomes more pronounced through childhood and adolescence. Bisexuality can sometimes pre-empt gender identity choice, perhaps indicative of a wish not to foreclose on (male or female) 'object-orientation'. A number of my interviewees identified as bisexual prior to identifying as trans men; some were surprised to have remained bisexual post their transitions; there was a belief that gender transition might alter or perhaps limit their bisexuality.

Father's role as crucial in the sexual development of daughters, including Freud's role in relation to his daughter Anna, will be considered and mourning is linked to Klein's Depressive Position. I include clinical material of two children from the literature and draw on interviews conducted with trans men to reflect on these struggles. The chapter explores early awareness of the difference between the sexes and argues that this can fuel a protest for daughters, sometimes manifesting as a 'no-mother' or matricidal state of mind. If these wishes or phantasies remain unmourned, they can at times, and for some individuals, lead to a concrete flight from femininity.

The Oedipus complex, as developed by Freud from his self-analysis and Sophocles' play, has at its centre a murder of a father by his son, namely an act of patricide. The much debated and contested daughter's version of navigating the (classical, straight and heteronormative) Oedipus complex is to manage the turns

DOI: 10.4324/9781032718613-4

from mother to father to other. I suggest that the move from mother or removal of mother psychically might require an equivalent to the son's act of patricide in the form of matricide. How a girl or daughter manages her detachment or dis-identification from her mother is no small psychological feat that can include a flight from femaleness and femininity. I see murderous impulses as universal.

This chapter aims to enhance rather than replace Freud's (female) Oedipus complex theory by suggesting a matricidal component. An unconscious desire to eliminate femininity is relevant to some aspects of gender emergence, and I explore how a psychoanalytic perspective can enrich understanding of this.

I consider how this might take shape psychologically and physically in the area of gender identity, particularly when a natal female might wish to 'kill off' or disavow her female body and identify as male. In some instances, I suggest that the development of antagonism towards the motivation to get rid of or the disavowal of one's female body and femininity may be linked to the psychic location of the mother in the girl or daughter's mind. So that, rather than killing the mother through the actual act of matricide, the daughter may opt to kill off her own female identity, which symbolically represents her mother within herself.

This bodily tie between mother and daughter is then ruptured: 'I am not the same as you, I never really was, I am un-female and I renounce my tie with the female body that gave birth to me. I am other than my mother psychically, physically and sexually'. As separations go, this is an extreme form of severance from the mother and all that she symbolises consciously and unconsciously, a murderous or matricidal rupture of self and object. I explore unconscious drives within the fragile territory of gender identity in instances when femaleness is an unwanted or disputed aspect of psychic or bodily history. For some trans men, their past femaleness can go unacknowledged, and they would not see themselves now, as young women then (see Chapter 5).

This is a bold theoretical leap to make and is not a pronouncement on anyone's specific or individual gender identity. It is an attempt to explore and develop the potential to understand aspects of what might constitute unconscious drives within the complex territory of gender identity and identification, specifically that of some trans men, for whom femaleness is usually an unwanted and often disputed aspect of their psychic or bodily history. The reference to femaleness and womanhood can be perceived as offensive to their identity as trans, which has not been my intention in this exploration. I am conceiving of matricidal wishes as more unconscious than conscious.

I explore the psychoanalytic significance of matricide both in terms of my own theorising and the theories of others (Irigaray, 1991; Jacobs, 2010; Wieland, 2000). I reference Orestes' act of matricide and Athena's decision to absolve him of this act of murder as the beginning of a patriarchal trend that leaves matriarchy unacknowledged. I include thinking about the primal scene and early bisexuality. I consider the role of the father through various lenses: enabling the daughter to separate from her mother, his own relationship to masculinity and aggression and the mother's phallic ambition. I bring in two cases (from psychoanalytic literature) of female children in psychotherapy that demonstrate their poignant struggles with developing a gender identity. I include the importance of early bodily experience, both the primitive, sensory and phantasy aspects of this.

Orestes and Matricide

My proposition is that the Oresteian myth is a better fit than the Oedipal myth here. The Greeks were 'peculiarly preoccupied' with the theme of matricide, and the Orestes myth was the most popular subject in Greek drama (Slater, 1968). Aeschylus' (2009) trilogy 'The Oresteia' recounts the murder of Agamemnon by his wife Clytemnestra and the murder of Clytemnestra along with her lover Aegisthus by their son Orestes.

The first play, 'Agamemnon', was about the King of Mycenae returning from the Trojan War. Clytemnestra, his wife, has been planning to kill him. She desires his death in order to avenge the sacrifice of her adolescent daughter Iphigenia (made by Agamemnon before he set off to war), also to clear the way for her commandeering the crown, and to enable her to be public about her lover Aegisthus. Clytemnestra murders both Agamemnon and his mistress Cassandra.

In the second play, 'The Libation Bearers', Orestes, Agamemnon and Clytemnestra's son, who in infancy had been banished from Argos by his mother out of fear that he would avenge the death of his father, returns after some years to indeed avenge his father's murder following an order from the oracle of Apollo, son of Zeus. Orestes reunites with his sister Electra and influenced by the Chorus, they plan to kill both Clytemnestra and Aegisthus. Orestes carries out these killings and is then pursued by the Furies, maternal goddesses who seek revenge for 'the murder of the mother', and he flees the palace in a mad state.

In the third play, 'The Eumenides', justice and social order are instituted. Apollo intercepts the hounding by the Furies of Orestes, who escapes to Athens where he pleads to the goddess Athena who presides over a trial for him. She supervises a trial made up of 12 Athenian citizens in what may be the first trial by jury. Athena determines that Orestes will not be killed. Apollo steps in to tell the truth about pushing Orestes to kill his mother, thus absolving Orestes of moral responsibility. The endless theme of revenge through killing comes to an end. It sets in motion the trumping of matriarchal law by patriarchal law, so that justice by courtroom trial and injustice via the acquittal are both instituted.

An aspect of Athena's role that has subsequently been questioned is her absolving Orestes according to patriarchal laws that she identified with in her own state of 'motherlessness'. Athena's birth came about through Zeus swallowing Athena's pregnant mother, Metis, who was raped by him. Metis then imparted her knowledge and wisdom to Zeus "From inside his belly" (Hesiod, 1973: 52). The head of Zeus split open after excruciating pain and Athena was born. Jacobs (2010) considers the incorporation and disappearance of Metis as highly symbolic and as the hidden matricide in 'The Oresteia' in which Athena defends Orestes' commitment to patriarchal law as she claims it has been her law too.

The Metis story is a matricidal myth that is inextricably related to 'The Oresteia', yet is only visible in the latter through the figure of Athena whose motherless status functions to secure her loyalty to Orestes. In this way, the Oresteian myth conceals within it the story of the incorporation of Metis. Yet, the myth, like the dream, reveals the traces of its censoring process through distortions, blanks and alterations that, if analysed, can lead to the reconstruction of the original concealed element (Jacobs, 2010: 25).

Jacobs links the two matricidal myths and contends that matricide remains un-theorised and therefore cannot bring forth its underlying law, that of a maternal structuring function. Jacobs questions why matricide, unlike patricide, has re-mained an elusive concept within psychoanalysis, and whether a different theoreti-cal constellation might spring from an investigation into what matricide means and what its theoretical omission has meant for psychoanalytic theory (2010, p. 21). Her investigation opens important questions in relation to presumed and inherited theoretical foundations that can become dogma.

There is a risk in some interpretations of myth that the metaphor of the myth can be lost or replaced by something more concrete and real. It has been suggested that metaphor grows out of real and concrete bodily experiences that have relocated from the physical to the psychical (Freeman Sharpe, 1940). The metaphoric aspect of myth is thus important. When Zeus incorporates Metis and steals her natural maternal position, the metaphor within the myth could be read as matriarchy can-nibalistically incorporated by patriarchy.

Acquittal of the Matricidal Son

Irigaray, in her discussion of 'The Oresteia', contends that the matricidal son has to be saved from madness so as to establish the patriarchal order. The Furies who pursue Orestes for killing his mother are described as: "… women in revolt, rising up like revolutionary hysterics against the patriarchal power in the process of being established" (Irigaray, 1991: 37). She sees the mother's murder lead not only to the non-punishment of the son but also to the "burial of the madness of women – and the burial of women in madness – and the advent of the image of the virgin goddess, born of the father and obedient to his law in forsaking the mother" (1991: 37–38).

Irigaray's main (feminist) domain is that of what it means to be a woman as a subject that is not subordinate to the continuation of the patriarchal law of the father (whether this is represented by Zeus or articulated by Freud or Lacan). In 'The Poverty of Psychoanalysis', she writes that the empire of the phallus requires the support of a society rooted in patriarchal power in which:

> … Natural-maternal power to give birth comes to be seen as the phallic attribute of god-men, and establishes a new order that has to appear natural … We can still read of the upheavals this brought about in the organisation of the imagi-nary or the symbolic in the Greek myths and tragedies …
>
> (Irigaray, 1991: 96)

She contends that in a monosexual economy, bisexuality is not really a true possibility. Irigaray is interested in the maternal body anatomically, symbolically, historically and politically. At a conference on 'Women and Madness' in Montreal in 1981, she presented her paper 'The Bodily Encounter with the Mother', where she sees Western culture as founded on matricide and not on patricide as was suggested in 'Totem and Taboo' by Freud (1912–1913). Her reading of 'The Oresteia' is that of the establishment of patriarchy through the sacrifice of the mother (Clytemnestra) and her daughters (Iphigenia and Electra) and the acquittal of the matricidal son (Orestes) who marks the new order of justice through trial. She claims that the emphasis on Oedipus and castration hides the severance or cutting of the tie to mother through the umbilical cord. She sees the cultural taboo or silencing of the relationship with mother as unleashing monstrous phantasies of women threatening madness and death. These primitive and often projected phantasies belong to the male imaginary and can subject women to a form of cultural hatred. It is daughters that Irigaray warns against the hatred of their mothers or against repeating the murder of the mother.

The act of matricide is open to many interpretations but concretely it is the act of killing one's mother. The physical killing, however, does not eradicate the object psychically. Apollo spurred Orestes on and could be viewed as representing Orestes' harsh superego, by encouraging him to right a wrong. If one applies the Oedipus complex to Orestes, then one can view his act as one of correction: his mother denied him the opportunity to 'kill his father' (whether this is a psychic killing or not). When Orestes kills his mother and her lover, one could say that the mother's lover stands for the father, so in that sense it is an act of matricide and of (Oedipal) patricide once removed. Orestes is described as being in a state of guilt and insanity after the act of killing his mother and her lover, so his is not the guiltless conscience of a psychopathic act.

Matricide by Proxy

Electra plays an interesting role in the unfolding narrative. She and Apollo have a vested interest in Clytemnestra's murder. As the Oedipal daughter, she has been deprived of her actual father's presence since he went to war and has had to contend with a substitute father in Clytemnestra's lover Aegisthus. One could question why she wishes her mother dead. The focus on Orestes' act of matricide leaves Electra absolved of conspiring to plot this murder with her brother; it strikes me that Electra commits matricide by proxy. Clytemnestra's death symbolises both matricide and the murder of matriarchy.

I extrapolate that in some instances, aspects of the conscious and unconscious drive to absolve femininity and femaleness in oneself could speculatively be viewed as committing a form of matricide by proxy through killing off the tie to a (maternal) female body, both in relation to the actual mother and to the symbolic and concrete aspect of femaleness within the natal body. The recognition of the difference between the sexes can take many forms but requires a 're-cognition' of difference. This can ignite a protest that can lead to various resolutions: a capacity to mourn that which I am not or a gender identity choice that reconciles feelings of incongruence.

Phantasy

Klein thought the child's relationship to their own body, mind, family and everyday activities was underpinned by phantasy. With the deepening of her analytic experience, she became more confident that the mother's body and its phantasised contents was what formed the initial and basic symbolic relation to the external world. This was a development of her earlier thinking, influenced by Ferenczi who had proposed that the infant perceived the world in identification with parts of their own body (1913). Another significant influence on Klein was Abraham, who associated the oral stage of development with cannibalistic phantasies and the later anal stage with phantasies of retaining, controlling or expelling the object (Abraham, 1916: 258–275). This corroborated the notion Klein was to build on that phantasies existed from earliest infant life. It was symbolisation that imbued the external world with libidinal significance for her.

Kohon (2018) offers a different angle to Klein's phantasies of mutilation by questioning or suggesting that "What there is in the unconscious is *a danger and a threat* for the man, and *a desire and an envy* for the woman, and not – as is assumed – an overvalued penis and an undervalued vagina" (2018: 282). Kohon moves away from phantasies of body parts to emotional states of mind.

Bion developed the notion of our tendency to attack links, when there is resistance to the coming together of two things, particularly when this link generates feelings of rage about the experience of exclusion. Although Britton brought in the idea of the (Oedipal) missing link (1989), Bion wrote about the attack of or on the link, namely a wish to attack the relationship between objects (Bion, 1959). This could manifest in a child's perception of their mother's relationship not only with an actual other sometimes represented by the phallus but also with her depression or narcissism: an experience of mother as preoccupied or taken away. Father can also be perceived as preoccupied with his work, his sexual relationship, his drives, his depression or alcoholism. It is an experience that can render the parental object as dead or absent to the child. This deadness can ignite murderous rage that sometimes manifests in a pervasive underlying aggressive stance in all relationships. Rage at the exclusion can apply to the parental couple, parental state of mind or the sex that one is not born as. The last of these attacks the link to reality. The rage can also manifest as matricidal rage towards the mother for 'making me a girl and not a boy' or vice versa. This attack also infiltrates the primal scene and so attacks the link between parents in intercourse that conceived one sex, not the other.

How the primal scene locates itself psychically involves a complex network of phantasies in which confused or fused allegiances to mother, father, femininity and masculinity all play out. The capacity to hold in mind a benign link between one's parents is considered to be important psychoanalytically, as the attack on this link can be corrosive or murderous. If I feel matricidal, the murderous wish extends from my mother to both parents, who excluded me from the primal scene.

It is difficult to establish at what age or stage of development a child can register the difference between the sexes. This recognition requires a capacity to mentalise difference, beyond the all-inclusive undifferentiated phase that Fast (1984) refers to for both girls and boys. Whereas Freud postulated that boys and girls believed themselves to be initially male and masculine, Fast dissents from this and believes that children initially take in a broad array of characteristics from people in their surrounding environment to the extent that no attribute is left out. Awareness of the difference between the sexes takes place when the limitations of one's natal sex are fully recognised and the prior notion of unlimited possibilities can be relinquished.

Bifurcation and Object Choice

It was Fleiss (1897) who initially communicated to Freud the idea that all humans begin from a bisexual disposition, an idea that grew in resonance for Freud, who moved more towards emotions that derived from sexuality and the significance of sexuality more broadly (Freud, 1950; Masson, 1984: 4). Bisexuality incorporates the sexual aim and object: the attraction to both sexes and the wish to be both sexes. It opens up the question of whether there is an 'overinclusive and undifferentiated' phase early on in life as Fast (1984) has suggested. I would like to raise the possibility that there is a very early, primitive sense of differentiation between the sexes that is repressed or disavowed, which may lead a girl towards an unconscious matricidal phantasy and the wish to be the other sex; an equivalent may take place in a boy. The early awareness of a bifurcation into two sexes might ignite a protest that can be resolved by gender identity choice, when there are difficulties with mourning the sex that one is not. If the loss of the other sex cannot be acknowledged, a manic solution can be sought.

Writing in 2010, Rapoport points out that bisexuality often gets side-lined but not rejected in theories or debates about gender and sexuality, so that it is neither fully present nor fully absent. She refers to a footnote of Freud's (1905) where he wrote about the "Freedom to range equally over male and female objects – as it is found in childhood, in primitive states of society and early periods of history ..." (1905: 145–146). Rapoport correlates Freud's placing of bisexuality as "the place of origin and the prehistoric past of the individual and the species" (Rapoport, 2010: 71) with Darwin's (1871) assertion that "some remote progenitor of the whole vertebrate kingdom appears to have been hermaphrodite or androgenous" (1871: 525). Nineteenth-century biological scientists were very influenced by the notion of primordial hermaphroditism or bisexuality (Angelides, 2001, in Rapoport, 2010). Although Freud made the shift into the psychical sphere, via psychic bisexuality, it remained tied to biology and physical development.

Rapoport (2010) discusses an intriguing idea, argued by Angelides (2001), that there is 'an erasure of bisexuality in the present tense' by Freud, as an instance of a pervasive cultural phenomenon. The suggestion of bisexuality as praxis would have been too radical at the time, following its assignation as central in the formation of all sexualities (2010: 72). Angelides is implying that Freud relegated bisexuality to the past defensively, as if it was too much to posit it as active and alive in the present. I concur with Rapoport's observation that bisexuality since Freud is often associated with immaturity, an inborn biologically based instinct that is easily associated with primitive organisation whether in animals, infants or psychotic patients, which steers it towards pathology.

In her discussion of bisexuality and 'drive theory', Juliet Mitchell (2018) argues that we are always all bisexual subjects, who seek an object (whether perverse or not) as a way of satisfying our conflicted and coinciding drives for life and death. She sees bisexuality as a condition of our sexuality within our drives (2018: xvii). For Mitchell, as we are always bisexual subjects from birth and throughout our lives, sexual preference (object choice) is a more malleable individual choice. She sees bisexuality as a 'subjecthood position', the choice of object is secondary.

Mitchell returns to bisexuality in her book on 'Fratriarchy' (2023). She places psychic bisexuality in a social and familial context and asks the poignant question: "…does the girl – a *daughter* – exist in the patriarchy, while the boy, with his *brothers* creates the fratriarchy?" (2023: 169).

It is the achievement of bisexuality that interests Mitchell, and how it necessitates an acceptance of sexual difference. She is impressed by and discusses a chapter by Chaplin (2018) in which the transition from psychic to 'genital bisexuality' is beautifully described via a psychoanalytic session. The patient struggles with phases of fusion with mother, phallic bisexuality "in which sexual difference and castration are known but refused" until "there is a form of genital bisexuality in which difference predicated on castration is both known and used" (2018: 212).

Genital bisexuality is understood by Chaplin and Mitchell to necessitate some kind of mother and father union in mind and seen as that which the therapy/analysis must help to achieve. It encompasses knowledge of the fear of castrated/castration as well as a notion of the union of fatherhood and motherhood (Mitchell, 2023: 181). This in turn can provide a capacity for metaphorisation and symbolisation.

In my interviews, bisexuality was nearly always a precursor to identifying as gay, non-binary or trans. The interviewees mostly retained their bisexuality, after identifying as trans, which surprised some of them. This appears to support Mitchell's proposition above that bisexuality is a subjecthood position. It might also suggest that sexuality precedes gender identity or that it moves with it. If say a change has taken place in gender identity from a gay woman who is bisexual to a trans man who is still bisexual; the object of desire has not changed but the orienting of sexual attraction now emanates from a differently defined or felt gender identity.

In a follow-up interview with Joe (2024), four years after the initial interview, he explained that: "I'm a lot more comfortable if people were to know that I'm bisexual than transgender because it's so much harder to understand". He went on to say that "some people are fine with women being lesbian or men being gay, but bisexuality is too complicated for them. So, you really just need to learn how to navigate your current environment".

I think that learning to navigate one's current environment applies to me too as I write about the trans environment, I need to look at myself and the environment of clinical work with trans individuals in order to tread carefully.

Daughter/Father

Britton introduced the idea of the Athene-Antigone[1] complex in women that can arise when there are difficulties with the girl's infantile maternal relationship that is compensated for by idealisation of the relationship with father, either through phallic identification (Athene) or through becoming father's seer (Antigone). In Anna Freud's language, the former denoting 'identification with the aggressor' and the latter 'altruistic surrender' (Anna Freud, 1936, 1968). Apollo, Athene's brother, hailed her suitability for her role "... by virtue of being her father's clone unsullied by intrauterine residence. He also regarded all mankind as essentially the progeny of the father: the mother's role being simply that of incubator" (Britton, 2002: 107–109).

In Athene's position, Britton describes the phallic identification that leads to a triumphant denial of being ordinary as a woman, and in Antigone (the daughter of Oedipus and Jocasta), there is a more general belittling of femaleness through self-disparagement. Both Athene and Antigone hold characteristics that fit Freud's theory of 'female castration' and 'masculinity complex' (2002: 107–117).

The Daughter 'as a Boy in Relation to a Man'

By looking at both Young-Bruehl's biography of Anna Freud (1988) and the paper by Blass (1993) on Anna Freud's first analytic paper (1922, 1923) 'Beating Fantasies and Daydreams', Britton (2002) clarifies that Freud's paper 'A Child Is Being Beaten' (1919) must in part have been influenced by his analysis of his daughter. The beating fantasies in Anna Freud's paper are the fantasies of a girl in which a boy is being beaten by a man. She (Anna Freud) discusses these early infantile masochistic fantasies and the later development of the girl's 'nice story' daydreams. Whereas she saw these daydreams as sublimations of the earlier masochistic fantasies and the masturbation itself as a source of guilt or shame; significantly, Freud viewed the guilt as emanating from the actual content of the masturbatory fantasies. From both these beating fantasies and nice stories, Anna appears to have seen herself as a boy in relation to a man (I refer to this in my discussion of Romi in Chapter 2). There is no mention of the girl's mother at all in her paper. Britton extrapolates further that "Freud makes Anna his son and puts her in the position she occupied as the young man of her daydreams, imprisoned by a knight fearing torture and condemnation only to be triumphantly reconciled" (2002: 111).

It is the influence of his analysis of his daughter Anna on Freud's analytic theories of female sexuality that Britton particularly focuses on:

> I suggest this led to Freud making phallic monism the basis of a revised account of normal female sexual development. His theory rapidly became controversial within psychoanalysis and it remained so ever since. It also made psychoanalysis unacceptable to feminists of both sexes as Freud predicted it would. It seemed not only counterintuitive, but counter to the thrust of his previous thinking about the Oedipus complex in the normal development of both sexes. My belief is that he espoused his new theory of female sexuality as a reaction to his analysis of his own daughter's psychopathology.
>
> (Britton, 2002: 111)

A daughter's relationship to her femaleness cannot be de-linked from her identification with her actual or internalised mother and father. Britton shows how Anna Freud excluded her mother and suggests that Freud's perception of Anna as 'a boy in relation to a man' shaped his theories of female sexuality by making her a boy. Femaleness is thus subsumed, substituted, killed off and masculinised. In this instance, it could be said that Freud colonises Anna's femaleness, which has an impact on his theoretical developments. I make the leap backwards in time to Zeus, who incorporated Metis, and Athena who allied herself with her father and thus to the ascendance of patriarchy. These are singular examples of an analytic case and examples from Greek mythology rather than a body of evidence to support the dominance of patriarchy. My interest lies in the shaping and reshaping of femaleness and femininity in natal females where this is unwanted, refuted and sometimes removed, or where perhaps 'a mother is being beaten'. Matricide concerns the mother/daughter tie, but the father/daughter tie requires consideration too, particularly if a daughter might situate herself as a son to her father rather than a daughter to her mother.

Father/Daughter

The father is a potential and active aid in assisting the girl with separating from her mother. His task is not straightforward, as in time he needs to desexualise his sexually developing daughter who turns to him for her 'freedom pass' from her entangled tie with mother. Simplistically put the father moves into the scene as 'a good object' to counter the 'bad object mother' in the girl's conscious and unconscious mind. But the good object father is not helpful to the daughter if he becomes too good an object or inappropriately seductive, as the daughter needs to move out into the world of other objects away from him. In this way, she too needs to 'desexualise' her tie to her father. This is the location and locus of dissenting views between Jones (1927) and Freud on how a girl manages the move from mother to father and from masculinity to femininity. Mother also plays a crucial role in enabling her daughter to 'flirt' with father and then separate both from her and from him. If the bond between a father and daughter is too threatening for the mother, she can disable this important relationship through her own Oedipal difficulties. Mother's choice of object is significant too in terms of how the child reads the phallic ambition of the mother.

Wieland emphasises the role of the father–daughter relationship in the daughter's negotiation and navigation of her masculinity and femininity; she sees the daughter's unconscious as shaped by the father's masculine unconscious and a collusion with masculine phantasies and anxieties as essential to the formation of femininity (Wieland, 2000: 10).

Benjamin (2004), in response to Freud's (1933) approach to femininity, and influenced by Christiansen (1993), objects to the idea that femininity is a pre-existing 'thing' that the male psyche repudiates but sees it more as constructed by it. She sees the boy's need to defend a passive position, in relation to the Oedipal father, as an active projection into his sister or into the girl. The girl, or daughter, then becomes 'the Oedipal boy' (not unlike Anna Freud was for Freud). This Oedipal girl/boy holds the passivity in relation to father, and also holds excess tension, in the form of the feminine container of excess sexual excitement. Benjamin contends that this containing body is often associated with women or the feminine position, it is what the expulsion of unwanted femininity creates. This differs from my area of exploration which focuses on the expulsion of femininity in and from the daughter. Matricidal wishes can be seen to leave the father out, unless they subsume unconscious patricidal wishes; hostility towards mother might protect a more wished for allegiance or identification with father.

The Sexualised Body

One of my interviewees, Zack, who was aged 27 at the time of the interview, told me about how his past adolescent female body attracted much attention, particularly as he developed a large chest. This led to a promiscuous phase which he thinks of retrospectively as an insecure and self-conscious aspect of his then vulnerable self. Zack later on came out as a lesbian but was not comfortable with this, then identified as non-binary before settling into being a trans man. He was relieved to have found an identity that felt right, after so many years of unhappiness and discomfort, and referred to it as a "final realisation of myself". He thought that part of the unhappiness with his past female body was to do with how he looked and people telling him what to do about that. Zack, as a trans man now, was awaiting top surgery and looked forward to the elimination of that part of his historic female body. The breasts that once received sexual attention that felt positive now felt unwanted and clearly interfered with a sought after masculinised body and appearance. Understandably, his wish now was to pass as male. Zack was thoughtful about his past self and body and did not subscribe to the narrative that he was born in the wrong body. But he was wary of the way in which psychotherapy was prone to label his trans identity as a mental illness or as having "daddy issues" and attempt to talk him out of it (Zack 2020).

My independent curiosity lies with the drive to eliminate his female self and how this shift occurred. I was certainly not a psychotherapist for Zack but an interviewer for the purposes of research. I was struck by the way in which aspects of family disharmony and unhappiness could locate in the sexual body that can then become the battlefield upon which complicated family dynamics are played out. Meltzer describes the sexual drives as fractured at puberty by the eruption that accompanies the maturation of the organs of reproduction (1964–1965: 14).

Boy-Girl

Yanof (2000) wrote about a psychotherapy, over four and a half years, with Jennifer, whose insistent ritual, at the age of 3 years and 9 months, was to roll up a diaper that she labelled her penis and position it in her tights or pants before she would leave her home. The behaviour, said to be driven rather than playful, was explained by this child as her wish to be a boy. This ritual worried her parents who brought her to psychotherapy. Yanof referred to this wish for a penis as a "multilayered compromise formation", a response to the fears of loss and anger about separation (Yanof, 2000: 1445). The oscillations in Jennifer's struggles with femininity and masculinity, separations from her mother, her mother and father's relationship and how these emerged in the transference are described through the nature of the play in sessions.

In one of the sessions in which a paper tree could not be erected to stand on its own, Jennifer is devastated and angry. Yanof shows how she got pulled into the impossible task and was left feeling inadequate. She also shows a development in Jennifer's capacity to reflect on the need to push her therapist into the role of the 'inadequate one'. Over time, this splitting off could begin to be more synthesised within herself particularly in relation to triumph and failure.

This psychotherapy showed a small girl's use of gender as a means to play out difficulties with attachment, sexuality and aggression. The wish to be a boy via the diaper showed a more concretely acted defence against painful feelings. The body limitation (no penis) had become a strong metaphor for a psychological conflict. Yanof showed how the nature of the phantasy moved from the penis to Jennifer's own female body with phallic elements. To my mind, this showed a relinquishment in the need to enact the loss of the other sex and a development over time to accommodate the reality of gender in the body one has. I concur with Yanof's acknowledgement of the importance of individual context and the multi-layered and multi-determined aspects of gender (2000: 1460–1461).

In a paper by Grossman (2001) on contemporary views of bisexuality, Herzog (2002) presented the case of six-year-old Jane who early on in her two-year analysis experienced herself as a 'boy-girl'. Herzog described Jane as knowing she was a girl but entertaining fantasies and beliefs about mixed genders. She had an imaginary pet cockatiel, Matilda, described by Jane thus: "Matilda's a very odd boy, he isn't just a boy, he is a boy-girl. That's why he's called Matilda, although you could also call the bird either Mall or Tilda" (Grossman, 2001: 1372). As Matilda misbehaved, Jane became confused about her role as both the father who could spank and the mother who could groom. She claimed to be both. In reality, she felt her father's lack of presence and involvement and could become very angry about her wish to keep her mother close. When Matilda would not go to bed, Jane displayed an angry movement whilst stamping her leg, killed the bird and then cried. Herzog thought of this as a communication of Jane's tie with her father's conflicts with aggression, as manifested in her girl-boyness. Thereafter, a new character appeared named Lou Shoe, a girl who could express aggression, but described by Jane as being both a girl and a boy. Herzog understood that Jane's "girlness and boyness did not fit together well, and her inherent bisexuality had incorporated her parents' conflicts with aggression". He concluded that "Jane's inherent bisexuality had served as the scaffolding upon which developmental conflicts particular to her family and her endowment were elaborated and then emerged within the analytic encounter" (Grossman, 2001: 1373).

Jane appeared to have difficulties with her father's incoherent relationship to his aggression, as if she wished her parents to fit into more coherent gender roles, so that she could then work out her own identity in relation to them and to herself. Herzog felt that Jane already had the concept of bisexuality, it was not that he had to hold this in mind on her behalf (2001: 1374). Herzog's capacity to contain (and interpret) her conflicts enabled her to both inhabit and enact bisexuality, and through this become less distraught.

The Missing Mother

In the interviews with trans men, I noticed that their mothers were at times missing or vaguely referred to in the material. Fathers were not necessarily positively portrayed, but a male social function was preferred to the more ambivalent daughter/mother, maternal identification. Femaleness and femininity were felt to be incongruent, and a male or masculine embodiment was both felt and sought using the body as a symbol for the realisation of this wish, which brought relief.

For one of the interviewees Milo, who was in his early 20s, the surgery that was desired initially was a hysterectomy. He did not wish to have female reproductive organs in his body or ever risk pregnancy. He felt relief after the operation, as I think it removed the threat of an internal female system that understandably betrayed his male identity. This shows how a physical excision can potentially equate with a psychic belief in that the hysterectomy relieved him of (the threat of) femaleness. His identity as male necessitated concrete action in order to align his body with how he felt himself to be. This left me with curiosity about why female organs were so threatening.

In a follow-up interview, I asked Milo about the place that his pre-transition experience that includes his body has for him. He explained:

> I'm not living in stealth. So, I'm not running around … hiding my transness, or pretending to be cis[2] … that's not how I've chosen to live. … I feel like my

transness and my history being AFB, being assigned female at birth informs my idea of gender and masculinity, and I feel like, I don't feel like I've "killed the female parts of me".

(Milo, 2024)

I asked further about not killing off female parts of himself and yet very much not wanting to have a womb. Milo explained that for him, womanhood and femaleness were "so much more than a womb". And that he wasn't trying to kill off femaleness but that he couldn't bear having a womb and he didn't feel that the body could be "boiled down into a single part".

For Milo, having a hysterectomy was not any kind of (conscious) attack on or flight from femaleness; for him, it was a necessity driven by a certainty about not wishing to have children and perhaps an inconceivability of pregnancy. It was harder to think about the more unconscious aspects of this although Milo did see "the rejection of one symbol of femininity. But I don't feel that that's the entirety of how I viewed my femaleness" (Milo, 2024).

Interestingly, this exchange left me feeling that I had been very concrete in relation to the womb, trying to single it out as that which epitomised femaleness or essentially reproduction. For Milo, this is not what having a womb or wishing to remove it meant. What was very symbolic for me was not as symbolic for him. Perhaps an example of an unreasonable wish for my psychoanalytic ideas to have meaning for him when they did not. Was this my 'psychoanalytic transphobia'? My insight was not corroborated by Milo's experience, making it hard for both of us to see each other's position through this impasse.

Trans identity can offer a symbolic solution, via the body, for a wish to revoke femaleness. In spite of my description of the solution as symbolic, it has an actuality that overrides symbolism. This actuality whether bodily, social or psychic should not be underestimated or undermined. Although I am viewing the past female history as significant, for the trans men that I interviewed, their current trans male identity perhaps inevitably took precedence; this made an exploration of pastness more challenging. The need for linear time to fit into an explanatory framework was much more in me than in them. This has been referred to as 'chrono-normativity' (Freeman, 2010), if I understand this term correctly. It is the antithesis of queering time in which the boundaries of chronology are loosened to allow for more freedom in oneself in the world in time.

The Athene complex that Britton (2002) introduced is relevant to my writing about matricidal wishes or unresolved hostility from the daughter towards her mother. For Klein, it is the mother who has the satisfaction of father's penis as well as breasts and babies that the pre-pubertal daughter does not yet have. The daughter's wish to undo this state of affairs, driven by envy, is to rob the mother of this penis and hence to castrate the mother, but that leaves the mother both damaged and robbed by her wishes which leads on to depressive anxiety and guilt. At its peak, the masculinity complex is one in which the daughter triumphs over mother, manically denies her significance or indeed the significance of mothers more generally as inferior.

It is not unfeasible, therefore, to deduce that in some cases what can be described as 'the masculinity complex' is likely to be influenced by early (conscious and unconscious) difficulties in the maternal relationship. The ways that this can manifest analytically are by the missing mother in the transference, idealisation of the male analyst, denial of sexuality in the patient, a servile attitude in the female patient towards her father (Antigone) or a difficulty with forming a mutually satisfying sexual relationship albeit by no means necessarily a heterosexual one.

I am aware that by looking at unconscious elements of the relationship between a then daughter/now trans man and mother, I subject myself to an old-fashioned tendency to lean on the maternal relationship to locate underlying aspects of identity formation. Stoller's (1975) proposition that transsexuality was influenced by the mother's need and use of her son as a feminised phallus reads as a somewhat stale hypothesis now and in relation to homosexuality is a cliché.

However, a disturbance in the primitive maternal object relationship can render femaleness and femininity as hostile pursuits and a threat to identity. Unconscious matricidal wishes can then become sublimated, and *sometimes* manifest in a drive towards maleness and masculinity as a safer domain.

The Unmourned

In Chapter 1, I refer to Freud and Klein on mourning and the psychoanalytic significance of a capacity to mourn loss. Mourning necessarily requires an acknowledgement of something once had and no longer there. It links to aggression and guilt, can be reactive and remorseful. For Klein, mourning is linked with depression and a capacity to repent for hostile feelings that she saw as especially resonant in infants towards their mothers.

I make the link to matricidal wishes that can be provoked by recognition or disavowal of natal sex that for a daughter is connected to the female and maternal body. Matricidal wishes that might be enacted in the daughter's own body bypass actual damage to the mother. The matricidal hostility could be understood to stem from an oral-sadistic stage of development that can resurface throughout life. During puberty, when the sexual body becomes central, earlier hostilities can be re-activated and locate themselves in the sexual and gender arena.

For some trans men, there can be difficulties for the historical female body to have meaning in relation to loss, if the present overrides the past in the form of 'I am therefore I was', which reverses après-coup into 'now is then', perhaps overriding a meaningful (or overly normative) chronology where the past is antecedent to the present.

Regret about aspects of surgery involved in transitioning can sometimes only be felt and hence mourned later on, after the changes have taken place. Some de-transitioners[3] speak about femaleness as that which was blamed, attacked and irreversibly altered in the body, so that 'gender' became the victim or site of abuse, I expand on this in Chapter 6. My own interviewees did not regret transitioning and varied in their wish or capacity to think about their historical body.

This chapter has focused on daughters and how they might manage awareness of the difference and similarity between the sexes. Femaleness aligns a daughter to her mother's body through symmetrical identification. Mourning or surrendering that which I am not in both sex and gender requires a sophisticated range of psychic manoeuvres that do not have a coherent pathway, and are highly individual in how and when they take shape. I have made links to Klein's Depressive Position which made a significant contribution to psychoanalytic theory. I have tried to show that matricide for a daughter has potency, not unlike Oedipal patricide for a son. I look at matricidal phantasies and wishes as one way to manage unwanted femininity and femaleness. These phantasies necessarily emerge from a complex unconscious dynamic network that is at work from early life and can manifest with force during puberty. The wishes are on a continuum, from ordinary daughter/mother friction to the removal of unwanted parts of the body to enhance gender identity congruence. I have drawn on Greek mythology to illuminate my investigation: Orestes as the acquitted matricidal son, Electra as committing matricide by proxy, Zeus who incorporates Metis the mother and appropriates the womb by giving 'psychic' birth to Athena. He gives birth to the idea that his male head can appropriate a female womb. Through her loyalty to fathers, Athena encourages patriarchy to annex matriarchy with no expiation for the fate of her mother Metis or Orestes' mother Clytemnestra. My interest lies in the myriad conscious and unconscious threads that shape the forming of identity; these threads emerge through identifications, phantasies and phases of development. The route is not linear and does not preclude overlaps, regressions and recurrences.

Matricide for a daughter has potency, not unlike Oedipal patricide for a son. If the Oedipus complex cannot be lived, an alternative complex might manifest in daughters: that of killing femininity or femaleness in which 'a mother is being beaten'. I propose that when the tie between mother and daughter is markedly ambivalent, early forms of aggression can resurface onto and into the female body which can then become the site for enacted matricidal wishes that bypass the actual mother. The female body becomes the enemy that is vulnerable to attack rather than the mother, whether in phantasy or reality. An identification with femaleness in relation to one's mother is rejected and unwanted, and her symbolic structuring power is thus denuded. I include incidents of matricide in Greek mythology such as Orestes' murder of Clytemnestra and Athena's so called motherless state as symbolic in its erasure of Metis.

A constellation of internal objects (maternal and paternal) can shape the ego and superego. If these objects are at war, this can propel universal conflicts of identity and identifications. In some instances of gender identity, a disturbance in the primitive maternal object relationship can render femaleness and femininity as hostile pursuits and a threat to identity. Unconscious matricidal wishes can then become sublimated and sometimes manifest in a drive towards maleness and masculinity as a safer domain.

The capacity to separate and mourn is central, whether a daughter/mother, daughter/father separation or the psychic separation from the sex that I am or am not. I see murderous impulses as universal to us all and part of the aggression of everyday life. If matricidal wishes find an outlet through gender choice, that might be one of many ways of managing the complex nature of identity and the drive to seek a resolution. These themes might illuminate some contemporary clinical challenges and stimulate further investigation into obstacles to mourning unconscious matricidal drives in which 'a mother is being beaten'.

Notes

1 I have used the spelling of Athene here as it is used by Britton (2002).
2 This term is used to describe someone who identifies with their natal sex as assigned at birth. The prefix cis is Latin and means 'on this side of'. It was coined as an antonym to transgender; in 2015, the word 'cisgender' was added to the Oxford English Dictionary.
3 www.4thwavenow.com and Detransition Advocacy Network.

Bibliography

Abraham, K. (1916). The first pregenital stage of the libido. In D. Bryan & A. Strachey (Eds.), *Selected papers of Karl Abraham* (Trans.) (1927, 1979) (Chapter XII). London: Maresfield Reprints.

Aeschylus. (2009). *The Oresteia: Agamemnon, Libation-Bearers, Eumenides* (A. H. Sommerstein, Ed. & Trans.). Harvard College: Loeb Classical Library.

Angelides, S. (2001). *A history of bisexuality*. Chicago: University of Chicago Press.

Benjamin, J. (2004). Deconstructing femininity: Understanding "passivity" and the daughter position. *Annual of Psychoanalysis, 32*, 45–57.

Bion, W. R. (1959, 1984). Attacks on linking. In *Second thoughts* (Chapter 8, pp. 93–109). London, New York: Karnac Books.

Blass, R. (1993). Insights into the struggle of creativity – A rereading of Anna Freud's "Beating Fantasies and Daydreams". *Psychoanalytic Study of the Child, 48*, 67–97.

Britton, R. (1989). The missing link: Parental sexuality in the Oedipus complex. In J. Steiner (Ed.), *The Oedipus complex today* (Chapter 2, pp. 83–101). London: Karnac Books.

Britton, R. (2002). Forever father's daughter: The Athene-Antigone complex. In J. Trowell & A. Etchegoyen (Eds.), *The importance of fathers* (Chapter 6, pp. 107–118). Hove and New York: Brunner Routledge.

Chaplin, R. (2018). How to be both, by not being both: The articulation of psychic bisexuality within the analytic session. In R. J. Perelberg (Ed.), *Psychic bisexuality. A British French dialogue* (Chapter 10, pp. 207–226). London & New York: Routledge.

Christiansen, A. (1993). *Masculinity and its vicissitudes*. Presented at Seminar on Psychoanalysis and Sexual Difference. New York Institute for Humanities, New York University.

Darwin, C. (1871, 1936). *The origin of species by means of natural selection; or, the preservation of favored [sic] races in the struggle for life and the descent of man and selection in relation to sex*. New York: Modern Library; as cited in Rapoport (2010).

Fast, I. (1984). *Gender identity a differentiation model*. University of Michigan, Hillsdale, NJ: The Analytic Press.

Ferenczi, S. (1913, 1952). Stages in the development of the sense of reality. In *First contributions to psychoanalysis*. London: Hogarth.

Fleiss, W. (1897). *The complete letters of Sigmund Freud to Willhelm Fliess 1887–1904* (J. F. Masson, Ed. & Trans.) (1986). Cambridge, Massachusetts: Harvard University Press.

Freeman, E. (2010). *Time binds: Queer temporalities, queer histories*. Durham: Duke University Press.

Freeman Sharpe, E. (1940, 1978). Mechanisms of dream formation. In *Dream analysis* (Chapter 2, pp. 40–65). London: The Hogarth Press and The Institute of Psychoanalysis (Original work published 1940).

Freud, A. (1936, 1968). *The ego and the mechanisms of defence*. London: Hogarth Press Ltd.

Freud, S. (1905). Three essays on sexuality. In *Standard Edition* (Vol. 12, pp. 125–243). London: Hogarth Press.

Freud, S. (1912–1913). Totem and taboo. In *Standard Edition* (Vol. 13, pp. 1–161). London: Hogarth Press.

Freud, S. (1919). A child is being beaten. In *Standard Edition* (Vol. 17, pp. 177–204). London: Hogarth Press.

Freud, A. (1922). Beating fantasies and daydreams. *Writings*, *1*, 137–157.

Freud, A. (1923). The relation of beating fantasies to a day dream. *International Journal of Psychoanalysis*, *4*, 89–102.

Freud, S. (1933). Femininity. In *New introductory lectures on psychoanalysis* (Pelican edition, Vol. 2, Lecture 33). London: Penguin Books.

Freud, S. (1950 [1892–1899]). Extracts from the Fleiss papers. In *Standard Edition* (Vol. 1, pp. 173–280). London: Hogarth Press.

Grossman, G. (2001). Contemporary views of bisexuality in clinical work. *Journal of the American Psychoanalytic Association*, *49*(4), 1361–1377.

Heller, S. (2023). Matriarchy, matricide & mourning. *British Journal of Psychotherapy*, *39*(1), 50–68; February 2023, John Wiley & Sons Ltd. and The British Psychotherapy Foundation.

Herzog, J. M. (2002). Lou Shoe's lament. *Psychoanalytic Quarterly*, *71*, 559–576; as cited in Grossman (2001).

Hesiod. (1973). *Hesiod and Theognis: Theogony, works and days, and elegies* (D. Wender, Ed.). London: Penguin Books.

Irigaray, L. (1991). *The Irigaray reader* (M. Whitford, Ed.). Blackwell: Oxford.

Jacobs, A. (2010). *On matricide: Myth, psychoanalysis, and the law of the mother*, 2007. New York: Columbia University Press.

Joe. (2024). Interview (anonymised).

Jones, E. (1927). The early development of female sexuality. *International Journal of Psychoanalysis*, *8*, 459–472.

Kohon, G. (2018). Reflections on Dora: The case of hysteria. In G. Kohon (Ed.), *British psychoanalysis, new perspectives in the independent tradition* (Chapter 21, pp. 274–289). London & New York: Routledge.

Masson, J. M. (1984). *The assault on truth: Freud's suppression of the seduction theory*. New York: Farrar, Strauss, and Giroux.

Meltzer, D. (1973). The theory of psychosexual development (adapted from lectures at the Institute of Education, University of London, 1964–1965). In *Sexual states of mind* (pp. 5–34). Perthshire: Clunie Press.

Milo. (2024). Interview (anonymised).

Mitchell, J. (2018). Foreword. In R. J. Perelberg (Ed.), *Psychic bisexuality, a British-French dialogue*. London & New York: Routledge.

Mitchell, J. (2023). Part 3, Fratriarchy: Tomorrow, today and yesterday (pp. 169–171) & Oedipal sexual difference (Chapter 8, pp. 173–186). In *Fratriarchy: The sibling trauma and the law of the mother*. London & New York: Routledge.

Rapoport, E. (2010). Bisexuality: The undead m(other) of psychoanalysis. *Psychoanalysis, Culture & Society*, *15*(1), 70–83.

Slater, P. E. (1968). Matricide: Orestes. In *The glory of Hera, Greek mythology and the Greek family* (Chapter V, pp. 161–192). Princeton, NJ: Princeton University Press.

Stoller, R. J. (1975). The transsexual boy: Mother's feminized phallus. In M. Masud & R. Khan (Eds.), *The transsexual experiment*, Volume two of *Sex and gender*, The International

Psycho-Analytic Library (Chapter 3, pp. 38–55). London: The Hogarth Press & The Institute of Psychoanalysis.

Whitford, M. (Ed.). (1991). *The Irigaray reader*. Oxford: Blackwell.

Wieland, C. (2000). *The undead mother: Psychoanalytic explorations of masculinity, femininity and matricide*. London: Rebus Press.

Yanof, J. A. (2000). Barbie and the tree of life: The multiple functions of gender in development. *Journal of the American Psychoanalytic Association, 48*(4), 1439–1465.

Young-Bruehl, E. (1988). *Anna Freud: A biography*. New York: Summit Books.

Zack. (2020). Interview (anonymised).

Chapter 4

Bespoke Masculinity

Non-genital masculinity is not based on being born male. It differs from 'female masculinity' or 'masculine femininity'. It is a gender identity I wish to consider specifically in relation to trans men. The body may or may not be altered hormonally or surgically to corroborate the gender *as felt and seen in the mind's eye*. Lacan dislodged the anatomical penis from the biological to the symbolic which brought to light a momentous shift from body to symbol, a severance from 'anatomy is destiny'. I discuss the trans man's symbolic use of the body that does not undermine the felt or embodied experience of maleness, although aspects of the natal body somewhat like a palimpsest cannot be entirely erased.

We are somatic beings from the beginning. Bodily sensations precede a thinking mind. The movement from soma to psyche connects to both Freud's bodily ego and what Ferrari (1992), an Italian psychoanalyst, called 'The Concrete Original Object' (see Chapter 2). By this, he meant the initial location and source from which mental phenomena are generated.

If unconscious matricidal wishes are enacted on the body in the form of removing femaleness, the identification with father might be enacted via a wish to acquire masculine attributes. This can occur through making alterations in the actual physical body or in phantasy via a phallic identification. Phallic identification can be borne or felt in mind and does not necessitate a physical penis. The lack of an actual penis curiously returns to Freud's applications of this lack to girls and women.

I discuss the tensions between phantasy and reality, the reality of the body-in-phantasy and the phantasy of the body-in-reality, and consider conflation, overlap and confusion between sexuality and gender and the difference between a male social and sexual function for trans men.

Am I a Man or Am I Masculine?

In her discussion about the dislocation and uncertain underpinnings of masculinity, and the reaching out in some instances towards an idealised masculine embodiment, the phrase "penis as the measure of man" is used (Saketopoulou, 2015: 282). If a man is only 'truly' a man if he has testicles and a penis and can procreate with a female, where does that place the gender identity of trans men without invalidating

DOI: 10.4324/9781032718613-5

their masculinity? Unlike the anatomical penis, the concept of the phallus can be thought of as inherently bisexual and ungendered as it denotes a phantasy of possessing magical power, even though it has been argued that it is irrevocably tied to the (permanently erect) male penis (Gallop, Moi). The object (in the psychoanalytic sense) might have this power; in the Lacanian sense, it is what mother has (from father) that the child cannot give her. Although it is derived from and linked to the masculine penis, it is not the actual penis. It is hard to 'de-link' the phallus from the penis, not least as the word phallus is almost automatically associated with the image, symbol of or actual penis. When I refer to the phallus, I am distinguishing it from the penis as part of the anatomy of natal males; it is more antinomy than anatomy. If the penis, that the phallus represents, is not required for masculinity to be authentic, then non-phallic masculinity or trans-phallic masculinity is open to both sexes in all sexualities. The difference being that whereas the phallus is a phantasy, non-phallic, or perhaps more accurately non-genital or trans-phallic masculinity is a lived experience. This tension between phantasy and lived experience is central to my exploration of trans identity. One can live with phantasies and phantasise about lived experience; they are not mutually exclusive.

In psychoanalytic writing, there is a lack of clarity about what is meant by the phallus, not least as it has garnered multiple meanings across different psychoanalytic schools of thought. Lacan addresses some of these difficulties in his paper 'The Signification of the Phallus' (1958, 1982), which was a significant text within feminist thinking and brought psychoanalysis to feminism. I expand on Lacan's paper in the section on 'The Lacanian Phallus' in this chapter.

Seminal Masculinity

Figlio (2010) makes an original contribution in his paper on phallic and seminal masculinity by pointing out that the word 'seminal' has lost its original meaning and is often used without reference to its source. He explores the omission in psychoanalytic theory of the creative and essential part that seminal masculinity offers. He points to the omission of the notion and experience of a male interior space, as this concept is so often attributed to women's bodies and psyches. He states that: "The male seems simply to lack an internal procreative space with structures and processes uniquely male and equal in importance to those in the female. The anxieties associated with them remain marginalized, misrepresented or unrecognized in clinical work" (Figlio, 2010: 120).

He highlights the fact that testicles are not often written or thought about psychoanalytically, even though they are the source of castration anxiety, as well as anxieties and phantasies of their disappearance into the body. Testicles are also a particularly vulnerable part of the body, which may require phallic compensation. Figlio cites Anita Bell who, in the 1960s, made the prescient observation that castration anxiety has been interpreted only in relation to the phallus, thereby encouraging a taboo about the testicle and scrotal sac (Bell, 1965: 189, as cited in Figlio, 2010: 121).

Figlio highlights the trend of moving away from phallic monism that serves further to conceal the non-phallic and seminal aspect that may lie beneath more overt phallic phantasies and dreams. He cites Boehm (1931) who makes the salient observation whilst reviewing the cultural evidence for the Oedipus complex: "I am almost inclined to believe that the child's jealousy of the parent of its own sex is due less to the idea of pleasurable sexual union than to the envy of the capacity to beget and give birth to children" (Boehm 1931: 449, as cited in Figlio, 2010: 123).

Laufer (1976) refers to reality for the adolescent boy who now has the actual capacity to impregnate, thus lending a whole new context to his genitality (Laufer, 1976: 301). I would add to this that incestuous phantasies can become fused or confused with reality, as there is a real physical possibility of incest with mother. For the adolescent girl too, there is the real possibility of incest with her father (Diamond, 1989). Adolescence can also ignite phantasies and accompanying anxieties of sibling incest.

In revisiting Freud's analysis of Little Hans (1909), Figlio noticed that both Freud and Hans' father do not directly address Hans's curiosity about what father did to produce babies. Freud thought that Hans might have reached his own conclusions had he attended to his own "premonitory sensations" of excitement in his penis whilst thinking about it (Freud 1909: 134 as cited by Figlio, 2010, 2024). Figlio infers that Freud roots *the threat of extinction in sensation* making the penis the nexus of narcissistic cathexes, thus promoting a phallic definition of masculine function and castration anxiety that left out both the contribution of the father to having babies and sensations emanating from the male's internal genital space. Semen remained absent from the analysis of Little Hans.

Instead, his theory of castration anxiety refers to the phallic stage, before testicular function, but at a time when sensations in the penis established it as an erotized organ, which could be lost and could serve as a fixation point in regression. And if it corresponded – now, as then – to a cultural stereotype of masculinity, as well as to a fixation point, then alternative representations would not be apparent, because neither analyst nor patient had the language for pursuing an investigation outside these bounds. The male would seem simply to lack an internal procreative space and processes uniquely complementary to those in the female; and therefore, also to lack internal objects of either envy or admiration. By default, analyst and patient would represent internal resources with female imagery, and represent invasion, occupation, usurpation and intrusion with male imagery.

(Figlio, 2010: 124)

In spite of a survey and discussion of theoretical literature on aspects of seminal masculinity, Figlio finds the fields disparate with no clear theory for the observation of non-phallic masculinity, even though depressive anxiety is central to it. Phallic masculinity and its concurrent anxieties take the lead, although seminal phantasies and anxieties exist and are there to be seen. This, he observes, is in spite of much theory and theorising on phallic narcissism, castration anxiety, its defensiveness against femininity, male internal genital structures (Kestenberg, 1968) and male destructive and reparative aims towards the female body (Figlio, 2010: 135).

The defence against (the catastrophe of) seminal failure, for Figlio (2024), finds its way into the erection of masculinity as grandiose in the form of a phantasy of bigness, physically and economically, and culminating in the phallic man as a stereotype: "The magic companion to the phallic narcissist is the penis: An anatomical structure confused with a phantasy of self-enthralment and the enthralment of others" (2024: 134). Figlio reads men's dread of seminal failure and seminal aggressiveness as converted into anxiety over sexual performance. He sees the bedrock male castration anxiety as loss of fertility, and hence related to the original meaning of castration as removal of the testicles (114–115).

Medicalised Masculinity

In her discussion of male impotence, Tiefer states that masculine confidence can never be purchased, as there can never be perfect potency (Tiefer, 1986). If penile/erectile function epitomises 'true masculinity', the loss of it can feel deeply emasculating. Impotence can be injuring to a sense of virility and masculinity, if one's sense of these attributes are located mainly in the penis and its performance. She examines the significance of the use of the impotence label in the social construction of male sexuality. I focus on two aspects of this: firstly, speciality medicine, its expansionist needs and new medical technology and secondly, the male sexual script that is highly demanding. Her paper shows how these factors amongst others combine to bring about a medicalisation of male sexuality and sexual impotence that mainly limits many men although it offers hopeful options to others.

In 'Sexuality as the Mainstay of Identity', Person wrote:

> What so stokes male sexuality that clinicians are impressed by the force of it? Not libido, but rather the curious phenomenon by which sexuality consolidates and confirms gender ... An impotent man always feels that his masculinity, and not just his sexuality, is threatened. In men, gender appears to "lean" on sexuality ... the need for sexual performance is so great. ... In women, gender identity and self-worth can be consolidated by other means.
>
> (Person, 1980: 619, 626, as cited in Tiefer, 1986: 580)

Although this reads as dated in 2024, Tiefer is attempting to trace the social origins of the drivers of masculinity that can make impotence catastrophic, not least as *masculinity is genitally focussed* (Nelson, 1985, as cited in Tiefer, 1986). It is the medicalisation of male sexuality that Tiefer questions, especially the surgical implantation of a device into the penis, the penile prosthesis.

It struck me when reading about this that the procedure for the 'inflatable' prosthesis that was used for impotence in 1978 appeared to be very like an optional part of the phalloplasty surgery for trans men today, 30 years later. It raises the question of whether the penile prosthesis holds more legitimacy when it is 'resolving' impotence in a natal man than when it is bestowing the capacity for erectile function in a trans man? In both instances, *there is a quest for masculine sexual function, or masculinity as sexual function*, albeit the natal man is born with a penis and the trans man is not. For the trans men that I spoke to, their masculinity or maleness was not 'penis focussed'; they mostly felt relief from the impact of testosterone on their physicality and the greater ease with which they were perceived as male in the world. The effects of testosterone corroborated their already felt male identity.

Tiefer remarks on the impotence industry that promotes the potential solution to male sexual dysfunction in the form of the penile implant. She describes the booklet 'Overcoming Impotence' as having a tone that is 'relentlessly upbeat'. I wondered about the purpose or metaphor of this tone as a wish to subliminally convey the promise of a phallus that will not disappoint, perhaps an allusion to a never-ending erection. She points out the message to the reader that the problem will be solved through a mechanical solution that renders the person irrelevant (Tiefer, 1986: 586). It is the absence of focus on the psychogenic aspect of potency difficulties that Tiefer is curious about, as she cynically comments:

> Thus the search for *the* etiology that characterizes so much of the biomedical approach to male sexual problems seems to have less to do with the nature of sexuality than the nature of the medical enterprise.
>
> (Tiefer, 1986: 586)

The medical enterprise in more recent decades has been held to account for its readiness to alter bodies for the purposes of gender identity alignment, sometimes without a thorough assessment of the patient's psychological well-being. This does not negate the reality of surgical procedures bringing much relief to many trans individuals, but in the case of detransitioners, there can be regret and anger about the over-readiness of surgeons, and prior to that the administering of puberty blockers or hormones, setting them too rapidly on a trajectory of transitioning.

Generative Identity and Trans Masculinity

In her discussion of psychoanalytic gender theorising, Raphael-Leff (2008) introduced the concept of 'generative identity': "… defined as a psychic construction of the self as creative, rooted in recognition of procreative difference" (2008: 246). The concept accommodates psychosocial and reproductive developments. She argues that generative identity is progressively consolidated in a child after the age of 18 months, when their notion that they can be 'everything' becomes restricted. The markers she puts forward for it are Sex (I am either female or male, not the other sex, neither or both); Genesis (I am not self-made, two people made me); Generativity (females gestate, give birth and lactate; males impregnate) and Generation (adults make babies; children cannot) (2007: 506). These 'facts of life' echo those of Money-Kyrle. Raphael-Leff explains:

> Sexual difference confronts us with what we are not, instigating further awareness of what we are/have. Generative identity proposes that beyond one's 'core' sense of embodied femaleness or maleness, and, in addition to mental representations of femininity/masculinity and articulation of erotic desires, there is a further psychic construction of oneself as a potential procreator. Freud's primal question 'where do babies come from?' initiates a process of acquiescence to a simple fact of origin: we are not self-made. Formation of generative identity entails recognition of external origins and demarcation of distinct reproductive capacities of the sexes.
>
> (Raphael-Leff, 2007: 506)

She suggests that the less contemporary headings of 'core gender', 'gender role' and 'sexual orientation' that subsume gender identity are recategorised as 'Sexed Embodiment', 'Gender Representations' and 'Erotic Desire'. For her, there is no conscious schismatic division of sex, as multiple cross-sex ambiguities will attach themselves to the basic sense of a gendered self, signifying that corporeality is an ongoing process that is fluctuating and discontinuous (2007: 497–502). Raphael-Leff was writing about the need for more contemporary conceptualisations of gender identity in 2007; in 2024, the need to modernise approaches remains pressing.

Fertility is a complex area for trans men, as both puberty blockers and testosterone change the direction and possibilities of past (female) fertility. The trans men that I interviewed mostly did not want to conceive their own children and were on the whole made aware of this potential loss in the future. However, some trans men do wish to have that option, as was the case with Freddy McConnell, a trans man who stopped taking testosterone in order to conceive, become pregnant and give birth. This opened up complications as he wished to be registered as his child's father and not mother on the birth certificate. In 2019, McConnell recorded the experience of receiving artificial insemination and of his subsequent pregnancy in the documentary *Seahorse*.[1] English Common Law requires those who give birth to be described as mother on the child's birth certificate, even though McConnell had a gender recognition certificate under the Gender Recognition Act in 2004. He was denied a declaration of parentage by the president of the Family Division of the Administrative Court, who stated that McConnell was legally the child's mother and had parental responsibility for the child accordingly. This decision was upheld at the Court of Appeal in April 2020. McConnell gave birth to a second child in the United Kingdom in 2021.

The wish for a trans man to conceive opens up whole new vistas in relation to gender identity, as it is to some degree, a wish to be both female (become pregnant and give birth) and male (retain the right to be registered as the child's father) simultaneously, and has many sides not unlike an apeirogon. It certainly challenges the more traditional psychoanalytic 'facts of life' as proposed by Money-Kyrle

(1971), as it makes way for a new reality in relation to 'the wish to be both sexes', or as Chaplin puts it in her chapter on the recognition or denial of sexual difference, "How to be both, by not being both ..." (Chaplin, 2018).

The situation can be very different for trans men who detransition to their former female gender identity, as they can experience regret from loss of breasts, fertility and voice changes, whether from puberty blockers, testosterone or if they have had top surgery and or hysterectomies (Littman, 2021). I discuss detransitioning in Chapter 6.

Pharmacological Masculinity

Preciado (2013) coined the term 'pharmacopornographic' in his book about the relationship and influence of technocapitalism, global media and biotechnologies on a new bodily experience, one that is exposed to surgery, endocrinology, and biotechnology. This is a body that *wears its psyche externally* as it is subjected to these new technologies that also include technologies of representation such as photography, cinema, television, cybernetics, video games, etc.

> After World War II, the somato-political context of the body's technopolitical production seems dominated by a series of new technologies of the body ... and representation ... that infiltrate and penetrate daily life like never before. These are biomolecular, digital and broadband data-transmission technologies. This is the age of soft, featherweight, viscous, gelatinous technologies that can be injected, inhaled – "incorporated".
>
> (Preciado, 2013: 77)

The (prescient) name that Preciado gives to this new era is 'pharmacopornographic capitalism'. Preciado is looking at the body from the outside in, which creates an interesting new angle to the usual psychoanalytic stance. I associate the external psyche with an exoskeleton. He is also not separating the body (its form, gender and sexuality) from the political context that the body is subject to: freely available pornography online and the pharmaceutical industry that makes substantial profit from the sales of hormone replacement therapy. His thesis implies that capitalism thrives from and feeds the 'requirements' of the mind and body. Preciado states:

> The success of contemporary technoscientific industry consists in transforming our depression into Prozac, our masculinity into testosterone, our erection into Viagra, our fertility/sterility into the Pill, our AIDS into tritherapy without knowing which comes first: our depression or Prozac, Viagra or an erection, testosterone or masculinity, the Pill or maternity, tritherapy or AIDS. This performance feedback is one of the mechanisms of the pharmacopornographic regime.
>
> (2013: 34–35)

I think that not knowing which comes first is highly significant and relevant to the cultural explosion of multigender identities, gender always being rooted in a cultural climate both internally and externally. Preciado sees the death or dearth of an *inside* to be discovered in sex or sexual identity. He sees the pharmacoporno-graphic industry as the *invention of a subject* followed by its global reproduction (2013: 35–36).

In my view, the death of an inside and the externally worn psyche relate to aspects of gender identity that I am exploring in the context of how outer and inner reality coincide, particularly with psychic registration of the difference between the sexes as that which can in time organise aspects of identity. The desire for or feeling of maleness in the mind can drive the motivation for outer reality to match the conviction of inner reality. A trans man's perception of himself will seek cor-roboration not only by his mind's eye but also by the gaze of the other. External real-ity, via the external gaze that looks and perceives a body *might have to alter* in order to correspond and equate with the inner reality of how a trans man feels himself to be. Segal (1957, 1986) gave the term 'symbolic equation' to *extreme* experiences of conflation of outer reality and inner phantasy, in which the symbol substitute is felt to actually be the original object. The substitute is recruited so as to deny the absence of the ideal object or to control a persecuting object. In this sense, the object cannot be represented by a symbol (Segal, H. 1957, 1986). Sechehay (1951) wrote about 'symbolic realisation' in relation to psychotic patients. Fonagy and Target (2000) write about the phenomenon of a dual psychic reality and hence a kind of playing with reality. They describe borderline patients' failure to mentalise adequately as:

> ... the persistence of an undifferentiated mode of representing external and internal experience. This is rooted in a childlike understanding of mental states in which feelings and ideas are construed as direct (or equivalent) representa-tions of reality with consequent exaggeration of their importance and extension of their implication.

> (2000: 853)

Physical reality becomes the same as unconscious as well as conscious feelings or experiences, and this equivalence restricts the capacity to suspend the imme-diacy of their experience, or play with reality. It can be thought of as a defensive attack on or disavowal of difference, or feelings that threaten through their intensity, that cannot be accommodated and lead to concreteness. The concrete state of mind cannot, will not, or does not want to see that 'this means that' which is central for the comprehension of interpretation, metaphor and symbolisation, and hence the reality of difference is eradicated. There appears to be a defensive protest against difference in concreteness, an attempt to make the 'outside' (external reality) con-verge with the 'inside' (internal psychic reality) which creates the illusion of undif-ferentiated symmetry. The writing of Matte Blanco (1975) expands on the structure of symmetry and asymmetry in the unconscious. An attack on or disavowal of difference flattens out the existence of two sexes, the sexual couple and primal scene, and the difference between the generations. These correspond to Money-Kyrle's facts of life, as necessary albeit challenging to metabolise for optimal cognitive development (1971). In the previous chapter, my encounter with Milo about the significance of having or not having a womb evoked concreteness in both of us, so that thinking about it reached an impasse. Milo did not wish to see his womb as a symbol of femaleness, and I struggled to see it as anything other than that.

The Freudian Phallus

In the same way that Freud might have benefitted from Melanie Klein's ideas, he might have also been intrigued by Lacan's ideas about the phallus. According to Laplanche and Pontalis (1973: 312–314), Freud does not make a particular distinction between the penis and the phallus, and the term phallus appears in his writing infrequently. He refers to 'the phallic stage' (1923) as a stage of libidinal development following on from the oral and anal stages of development for both sexes, a stage which is highly significant as it includes the castration complex as well as the establishment and resolution of the Oedipus complex. The 'having or not having' the phallus is not quite the same for Freud as the Lacanian meaning of this presence or absence as a signifier of desire, although Freud does encompass in his use of the term both the anatomical part of the body and the virility that it symbolises in the child's mind in relation to objects.

Although Freud cited the phallus in his theory of symbolism as a universal object of symbolisation, its blueprint as the male penis has subsequently been controversial. There is some ambiguity in the use of penis or phallus for Freud, its unconscious or conscious meaning, how it fits into a symbolic equation or is used interchangeably: the daughter substitutes her wish for father's phallus with her wish for a baby.

This ambiguity extends into penis envy:

> The term '*Penisneid*' crystalises an ambiguity which may be a fruitful one, and which cannot be disposed of by making a schematic distinction between, say, the wish to derive pleasure from the real man's penis in coitus and the desire to possess the phallus *qua* virility symbol.
>
> (Laplanche & Pontalis, 1973: 314)

The Lacanian Phallus

The phallus as devised and defined by Lacan represents potency but is not the penis. As Bailly puts it:

> The whole point of the word *phallus* is that it refers to an entirely imaginary object invested with an *entirely imaginary and undefined power*: it is the imaginary-ness that is important ... Lacan appropriated the word to denote the

imaginary object-of-power that the infant hypothesises *draws mother away,* or that *perhaps I have, which brings her back:* it is an imagined perfect object.

(Bailly, 2009: 76)

That which takes mother away more often than not is the father or something that the father has and can give the mother. The father enters the scene of both reality and the unconscious and sets in motion the notion of a third. Lacan calls this new metaphoric structure the Name-of-the-Father. It does not have to denote a live and present father but can be abstracted as the 'Other' person who brought the child into existence (2009: 79). The Other also has the function of liberating the child from a frightening form of (more primitive) omnipotence; it also reformulates mother's omnipotence in the child's mind as she has needs and is not entirely self-sufficient and all powerful. This Other for the child is both a loss of being all powerful and also an aid to reducing mother as all powerful and hence frightening (2009: 80).

The child's submission to the paternal metaphor also paves the way towards Symbolic functioning. Mother has to enable this metaphor to take shape in the child's mind, through sufficient forms of communicating it. If these do not happen, a failure for the child of these structuring developmental moves can occur. The absence of the communication to the child of the Other in her (mother's) mind can lock the child into something trapped, dyadic and frightening with mother, or the belief that (s)he is the mother's phallus: a law unto himself. Both these scenarios can lead to extreme forms of social instability and the potential absence of the symbolic realm.

Early awareness of the phallus and moves towards acknowledging it can assist the child towards acceptance of the symbolic castration that is set in motion by this metaphoric structure of the Name-of-the-Father/phallus hypothesis. It functions as protection from anxiety and in time, the child can come to realise that no one has the phallus. This stage can be reached through the acceptance of castration, the phallus eventually becomes relegated to the field of lost objects, objects that were once lost but can be regained.

Inequity in the Distribution of the Phallus

Gallop (1981) points out that Lacan pursues work on sexual difference that refers to Jones in the very year that Jones died in 1958. Phallocentrism appeared 'wrong' or disproportionate to Jones, as he states in his article on symbolism: "There are probably more symbols of the male organ itself than all other symbols put together" (Jones 1916: 103). However, in spite of this finding and Jones' dissent from Freud on female sexuality, Gallop sees Jones as sidestepping this 'disproportion' and moving away from it into a more general discussion of sexual symbols that are equally applicable to males and females. So, although Jones gets credit as it were, for advocating an equal place for female sexuality in psychoanalytic theory, Gallop reads this missed opportunity as a denial or disavowal (*Verleugnung*), the very word that Freud applied to the traumatic experience of the perception of castration, especially the absence of the woman's penis. She states:

> ... it is striking that Jones's response to the discovery of a sexual inequity first in symbolism and then in psychoanalytic theory coincides with Freud's description of a certain response to the discovery of an inequity in the distribution of the phallus.
>
> (Gallop, 1981: 255)

When Jones proposes *aphanisis* (1927), the total loss of sexual libido, as an alternative to castration anxiety (the fear of phallic loss) in the comprehension of female sexuality, Gallop sees this move of Jones in 1916 from the phallic to sexual symbols as one that he repeats in 1927 when he moves from phallic symbols to sexual symbols. She sees this as Jones acting out the very mechanism (*Verleugnung*) that Freud advocated *when a disturbing perception is disavowed.*

Lacan takes an altogether more blatant approach to the phallus by stating that "The phallus is the privileged signifier" (1966: 692). Lacan moves *from symbols to signifiers*: it is through the function of the phallus as a (privileged) signifier that its symbolism can be conceived. Gallop, perhaps somewhat ironically, sees that what Jones looked was access to both modern linguistic theory and the rule or 'domination' of the signifier over the speaking subject. She sees Lacan's insistence on returning to Freud's concept or experience of castration as a conceit, as it revisits and relocates the centrality of the phallus or "retains a term that unveils the obscene privilege of the phallus". Gallop states that "... it is glaringly disproportionate for one particular signifier to "designate" all the effects of signification" (1981: 257).

The Feminist Phallus

Jane Gallop and Judith Butler, American feminist academics, attempt to decode the phallus and its meaning. They are both well versed in the psychoanalytic writing of Freud and Lacan and are both highly skilled in their capacities to excavate meaning from these texts. My focus here is the penis/phallus distinction, Butler's concept of the 'Lesbian Phallus' and my own ideas on the 'Trans Phallus'.

What emerges from my reading of their understanding is the difficulty for the phallus as a concept to dissociate itself from the penis, although it is not the same as the penis. This appears to happen even if we think of the phallus as ungendered and equally applicable as a concept to male and female experience. It is *robustly masculinised* which could be attributed to how it was held in Freud's mind originally in relation to infantile sexuality and the phallic stage. As Gallop put it:

> The phallic phase is organized by the opposition phallic/castrated (one either has a phallus or one has nothing); adult sexuality, according to Freud, is organised by the distinction masculine/feminine. The phallus thus belongs to a monosexual logic, one that admits to no difference, of no other sex; whereas the

penis can be inserted into the realm of adult sexuality, where it can encounter the feminine. ... To distinguish penis from phallus would be to locate some masculinity that does not necessarily obliterate the feminine. Yet it remains an open question whether there truly exists any adult sexuality, whether there is any masculinity that is beyond the phallic phase, that does not need to equate femininity with castration.

(1988: 125)

Gallop recognises the need to think of a masculine that is not phallic and to think of sexuality that is not caught up in the phallic phase. This both necessary and impossible task throws the penis/phallus distinction into a double-bind that can remain endlessly circular (1988: 127). My understanding of Gallop's grievance with the Lacanian position on the phallus is that although phallocentrism is not the same as androcentrism for Lacanians (because the phallus is not a penis) and although the signifier phallus is distinct from the signifier penis, it does at the same time always refer to the penis. In this way, Lacanians want to have their cake and eat it: they wish to polarise synonyms and locate meaning in language but perhaps also control meaning through language (1988: 126). Lack of this capacity to control the meaning of the phallus leads to what Lacan called symbolic castration.

The phallus as that which is robustly masculinised brings to mind the painful struggle for some trans men to embody masculinity, almost as if it can be equated with a phallus as always out of reach and never quite fully possessed. In a moving description of a trans man's struggle with his experience (Hertzmann & Newbigin, 2020), there is a masculinity that can never be achieved in spite of so many attempts. I quote from *A Person Beyond Gender*:

The fear is of rejection. The fear is of not belonging and the reminder of alien status. The fear is of the shame and humiliation I feel because I am not a biological man [...] The fear is that the men say, "You're not a man – get out of this changing room!" because then what? Then where do I go? Where do I belong? The fear is of how painful it can feel to be transgender in a binary world ... Where do I go when I am not a woman and cannot possibly go into the female changing room? There is nowhere else to go.

(2020: 274)

Parker (1986) attempts to understand how reference to the body regulates and limits the discipline of psychoanalysis. He explores the Freudian and Lacanian stances on the place of the body and how it fits between the unconscious and the anatomical. Given that Freud saw hysteria as a "malady through representation" (Laplanche & Pontalis, 1973, as cited in Parker, 1986), Parker asks whether representation can be viewed as the "... malady of psychoanalysis ..." (1986: 98), because it relegates hysteria to an unconscious realm prior to and other than the body. He juxtaposes Lacan's sentence "There is nothing in the unconscious which accords with the body" (Lacan, 1958, 1982) with Freud's 'instruction' to keep psychoanalysis separate from biology. The 'swerving' from the body is seen in Freud's *Three Essays* and the deviation is seen in Lacan's semiotic order that does not refer to the body but to internal relations between signifiers. It is in relation to the phallus that the distinction between signifier and referent can collapse, as Gallop pointed out. Parker argues that "... the phallus cannot not be confused with the penis" (1986: 101) and that the body never ceases to haunt the presumed autonomy of the unconscious. The conundrum appears to lie at the frontier between the mental and the physical, where Freud placed the drive, and between psychoanalysis and biology that cannot remain permanently divorced.

The Lesbian Phallus

In Butler's paper on the lesbian phallus, she writes that "... any reference to a lesbian phallus appears to be a spectral representation of a masculine original ..." (2011: 33). She discusses the difficulty of the accessibility of anatomy through an imaginary schema that denotes the indissolubility of the psychic and the corporeal (2011: 35–36). She questions where and what the body is, if it can only be psychically and phantasmatically invested albeit through projection: "Bodily contours and morphology are not merely implicated in an irreducible tension between the psychic and the material but *are* that tension" (2011: 36). Butler elaborates that although the process of signification is always material, that which allows for a signifier to signify is never only its materiality, it necessitates an expansion of linguistic relations. There is constant ongoing negotiation between *referent* and *signified*, the materialities of language and the world it attempts to signify (Butler, 2011: 38).

The place of the maternal body as a palimpsest for all other emotional, psychological, physical, gender and sexual development is significant. Lacan's 'Mirror Stage' (1949, 1977) and concept of 'The Real' (1953) are relevant here as are the foundations of Object Relations in (classical) psychoanalytic theory. There is no escape from the reality of the maternal body as the *original* body. I discuss the lesbian phallus as being tied to and yet freed up from an original. Nguyen writes about the lesbian phallus:

> For the phallus to maintain its power, it needs to remain veiled as, according to Lacan, its exposure would also be a revelation of its lack (Jagodzinski, 2003). As such, the lesbian phallus might be the ultimate phallus, for it exists only in an endlessly deferred chain of signification (Rosenberg, 2003). The lesbian phallus *can* not be the dildo/strap-on in ways that the male phallus can never *not* be the penis, and the removal of the lesbian strap-on does not produce the same sense of de-phallicization as the removal of the penis. The lesbian phallus does not experience the threat of being severed as it is already severed and is instead located elsewhere, but exactly where cannot be determined. Thus the lesbian phallus is "radically unbegotten" and "the more we want to see it, the more the lesbian phallus becomes a joke at the expense of the visual field altogether".
>
> (Nguyen, 2008: 678–679)

This next section that I quote is highly applicable to the trans phallus. Nguyen quotes Hart:

> ... the lesbian dick *is* the phallus as floating signifier that has no ground on which to rest. It neither returns to the male-body, originates from it, nor refers to it. Lesbian-dicks are the ultimate simulacra. They occupy the ontological status of the model, appropriate the privilege, and refuse to acknowledge an origin outside their own self-reflexivity.
>
> (Hart, 1996, as cited in Nguyen, 2008: 678–679)

Hsieh (2012) proposes that feminists and psychoanalysts turn away from the metaphysical language of the phallus. She admires Butler's analysis of the lesbian phallus but feels that it is still founded on the realm of the phallus, thereby reproducing the master's system. Hsieh appears to be both apprehensive towards and advocating psychoanalysis in current thinking about femininity and sexuality. She elaborates that:

> In the 'post phallic' scene of poststructuralist feminism, Power is sexing rather than sexed, and sexual oppressions can only be tackled when the encompassing Power/Discourse is deconstructed. With the turn to Power it seems that feminisms are done with the Phallus.
>
> (2012: 101)

Hsieh cites Moi (1999) who in turn cites Wittgenstein's (1953) notion: "A *picture* held us captive. And we could not get outside it, for it lay in our language and language seemed to repeat it to us inexorably" (Wittgenstein, 1953: 1. 115). Moi puts forward the idea that the opposition of sex and gender, the language of phallus and penis and the endless discussion of the outside and the inside fall into this concept of the picture that holds us captive (Moi, 1999, as cited in Hsieh, 2012: 102).

Lacan takes issue with Abraham for introducing the notion of part objects, disliking both Melanie Klein's notion of introjected body parts and Ernest Jones' adoption and acceptance of these ideas. Lacan does not think that the phallic phase should be understood as a repression. In the light of these 'rejections', Butler asks:

> If the position for the phallus erected by Lacan symptomizes the specular and idealizing mirroring of a decentred body in pieces before the mirror, then we can read here the phantasmatic rewriting of an organ or body part, the penis, as the phallus, a move effected by a *transvaluative denial* (my italics) of its substitutability, dependency, diminutive size, limited control, partiality. The phallus would then emerge as a symptom, and its authority could be established only through a metaleptic reversal of cause and effect. Rather than the postulated origin of signification or the signifiable, the phallus would be the effect of a signifying chain summarily suppressed.
>
> (Butler, 2011: 49)

Further questioning emerges for Butler about whether the body (in pieces or parts) before the mirror is (initially) without the phallus, symbolically castrated, but comes to have or assume the phallus through specularised control (through the ego that is constituted in the mirror). She sees the phallus already there, however, in the described body that is in pieces before the mirror hence "… the phallus governs the description of its own genesis and, accordingly, wards off a genealogy that might confer on it a derivative or projected character" (2011: 49).

Rose explains the Lacanian phallus thus:

> … the phallus is not a fantasy, if what is understood by that is an imaginary effect. Nor is it an object (part, internal, good, bad, etc…) in so far as this term tends to accentuate the reality involved in a relationship. It is even less the organ, penis or clitoris, which it symbolizes. And it is not by accident that Freud took his reference for it from the simulacrum which it represents for the Ancients.
>
> For the phallus is a signifier …
>
> (Rose, 1982: 79, as cited in Butler, 2011)

Butler is sceptical about Lacan's claim that the phallus 'is not an imaginary effect' (2011: 50), as she sees it elevated to the status of a privileged signifier by his own convergence of meaning onto it. Butler takes up the way that the phallus is dependent on the penis, seeing a relation of identity holding between them. But this dependence is complicated as the phallus is bound to the penis through 'determinate negation'. By this she means that the phallus both needs and negates the penis but also that "… the phallus would be nothing without the penis" (Butler, 2011: 51). The question that follows is why the phallus requires this particular body part, and why it could not symbolise other body parts, which paves the way to the lesbian phallus. This (other) phallus incorporates both *having* and *being*, the threat of castration and castration anxiety (2011: 51). Butler cleverly shows how the lesbian phallus is no different to the 'non lesbian phallus' and from this she concludes that the phallus takes up an ambivalent site of identification and desire that differs in a significant way from normative heterosexuality. The (Lacanian) 'veiled' phallus has a place within lesbian sexual exchange just as it does in other manifestations of sexual exchange because it is an idealisation not a reality that a body can approximate, and hence the phallus is a 'transferable phantasm' (2011: 50–53).

I have cited much of Butler's discussion as I think it has relevance to an understanding of the trans body and the resignification of feminine to masculine. She points out that her introduction of a lesbian resignification of the phallus pulls into question the stability of masculine and feminine morphologies, as does trans identity qua "the crossings of phantasmatic identification" that Butler cites. It might be controversial to posit the idea that maleness for a natal female is 'phantasmatic' and more equitable to think that there are phantasmatic aspects to the adoption, adaptation and inhabiting of the other sex.

The Phallus in a New Temporality

> The phallus is what one had in the past but lost or what one has in the present but fears losing in the future. This is the normative temporality of the phallus; that the phallus has been or will be lost, that the phallus is imbued with pastness whether in the present or in the future. This overwhelming pastness of the phallus, its insisting connection to loss even when it is present is what we call psychoanalytically castration anxiety.
>
> (Gallop, 2019: 16–17)

Gallop (2019) introduces the idea of thinking about the phallus in a different temporality to the one in which it is held in (Freudian/Lacanian) psychoanalytic theory. She is interested in transposing the phallus into a new temporality, where it might appear not only in the past but as something promising in the future. She sees the (normative) temporality of castration anxiety as that of losing it once and for all. With a different kind of queer temporality, there is the scope to move from castration to phallus as well as in the other direction (2019: 20). What can return in this new temporality is different to the normative phallus, that which belongs to a man and not a child, that which can impregnate a woman. It is a perverse phallus, albeit no less exalting.

Gallop advocates a departure from 'the normative hold of reproductive sexuality' to enable entry into other phallic temporalities and sees the limitations of a temporality that only goes in one direction, namely that of progressive decline. She applies the notion of castration to experiences such as aging or the onset of disability where something once had, is lost, but can be regained in a different form. She thinks of castration anxiety as combining a loss of sexuality with a loss of gender identity.

In some respects, the trans man's phallus shares in this perverse temporality that is unbound by normative physicality. The notion of the phallus 'in the mind's eye' that Gallop discusses seems relevant to the experience of non-phallic, or non-genital masculinity in the trans man. In her demarcation between femme and butch lesbians, she describes femmes as phallic because of how they look and butches as phallic because of what they do. The issue of *being the doer* is significant in relation to whom in the primal scene the infant boy or girl identifies with, and later on what role or identification in phantasy one wishes to have sexually when with another. A trans man may not be comfortable in his pre-transition identity as a girl with a boy, or a girl with a girl, but might be more comfortable as a trans boy with a boy or a trans boy with a girl. This strikes me as being connected to an identification with the (phantasy of) the person who 'does' to the other rather than the person who 'receives' from the other. Clearly, there can be multiple identifications between two people within the sexual act, as Freud pointed out in a letter to Fleiss in 1899 (Masson, 1985: 364). My interest lies in a specifically masculine identification, which may denote (in phantasy or reality) more control or power, the control or power of possessing the phallus. This might denote the illusion of masculinised sexual control in relation to the desired other; in this context, the identification in the primal scene is more with the father than mother.

Female Masculinity

> ... I do have a few proposals about why masculinity must not and cannot and should not reduce down to the male body and its effects.
>
> (Halberstam, 1998: 1)

Although I am differentiating non-phallic masculinity from female masculinity, they have some things in common. The term 'female masculinity' as described and elaborated by Halberstam has sought to define a form of masculinity that is *not rooted* in the (natally) male body and can be enjoyed and experienced *in and of itself*. It dissents in its meaning from male and masculine forms of masculinity. My attempt to distinguish female masculinity from the non-genital masculinity of some trans men throws up the distinction between *what it means to be masculine as a female who wishes to retain a female identity* and *as a trans man who wishes not to*. There has been conflict between these identities and identifications, not least as trans men can at times be perceived as turning away from femaleness and hence turning away from feminist ideologies. This differentiation is central to the identity of trans men: the drive to identify *as male* and *be identified as male* and not remain a masculine female (lesbian) or retain aspects of female identity. The wish not to be identified as a lesbian appears, for some trans men, to be a central aspect of trans male identity.

In the book 'Female Masculinity', Halberstam attempts to prise masculinity away from the white male middle class body and hence away from structures of privilege, power and patriarchy at large. A case is made for the recognition of another form of masculinity rooted in the female body that is not new and has been in existence (albeit covertly) since the 19th century. Reference is made to 'epic masculinity' as characterised or stereotyped in Bond films in which the white male hero's masculinity is supported by a massive sub-structure of government groups, the army, well-funded scientists, beautiful good and bad women and (always) a bad guy (1998: 4).

My understanding of Halberstam's approach and analysis is that, writing in the late 20th century, there is frustration of a lack of space for female masculinity that does not hinge on male masculinity. The adolescent tomboy girl is seen as struggling with the onset of puberty as this goes against her masculine identity. I would add here that the onset of puberty ushers in a reality that affirms femaleness for the tomboy girl in a way that can be especially difficult if this (visceral) femaleness is unwanted or disavowed. It is a particularly difficult aspect of development as femaleness and female sexuality in the form of growing breasts and menstruation make themselves known corporeally. The disavowal or rejection of femaleness becomes impossibly challenging.

Whereas pre-pubescent tomboyishness is acceptable to parents, Halberstam points out that it is not so easily accepted post puberty, when pressures can come in (for the daughter) to become and look more feminine and hence to conform to and comply with her birth gender. Portrayals of female tomboys in popular cinema, as surveyed by Halberstam, show this more as a resistance to grow into adulthood rather than the more specific resistance to adult femininity. I am not convinced that these are distinct entities, as growing into adulthood as a female might well include an acceptance of femaleness and femininity and all that this might entail whether it is desired or not.

The mission that Halberstam sets out to achieve in this book is to make female masculinity "plausible, credible and real":

> For a large part of my life, I have been stigmatized by a masculinity that marked me as ambiguous and illegible. Like many other tomboys, I was mistaken for a boy throughout my childhood, and like many other tomboy adolescents, I was forced into some semblance of femininity for my teenage years. When gender-ambiguous children are constantly challenged about their gender identity, the chain of misrecognitions can actually produce a new recognition: in other words, *to be constantly mistaken for a boy, for many tomboys, can contribute to the production of a masculine identity* (my italics). It was not until my midtwenties that I finally found a word for my particular gender configuration: butch.
>
> (1998: 19)

Initially Judith, now Jack Halberstam saw the adoption of 'butch' as a viable term for her own masculinity. This precedes a subsequent trans identification as Jack Halberstam with the preferred term: trans* as it advocates that the asterisk better captures the provisional nature of sex or gender reassignment. It endorses the non-specificity of the term 'trans' and expands it beyond "the life narratives of a specific group of people" (Halberstam, 2018: 53).

The description above could also apply itself to the identity of some trans men, who feel masculine albeit not necessarily butch. There is a significant distinction between the female masculinity of a lesbian woman who may or may not wish to identify as butch and some trans men who do not want their masculinity to have female associations or necessarily wish to be 'stereotypically' masculine. There have been tensions if not wars, between feminists, lesbian women and trans men, in which trans men can be seen to have turned away from femaleness and signed up to masculine maleness and feminists can be seen to have rejected trans men or trans women. The derogatory term 'Trans Exclusionary Radical Feminists', known as 'Terfs', has gained currency in the last ten years. This clash of allegiances reflects the tensions that can and do emerge in the fragile yet highly differentiated territories of sexuality and gender.

Self-Tailored Masculinity

When I interviewed Zack, he was 27 years old. He had initially come out as a gay woman and then on feeling more freedom to experiment with his gender identity came out as non-binary before identifying as a trans man. This particular trajectory was common to a number of my interviewees. Zack explained that he was not especially masculine when younger and that his masculinity had roots in 'femmeness' and gay culture.

> I was never like super tomboy or like that masculine like when I was younger so when I did come out people were like: "but you were never like that masc, you were always kind of feminine". I was like: "Yeah, I still am kind of femme but I'm just a man". So, for me my gender is very rooted in a base of femme-ness still, so I don't see myself as a super masculine dude and I think that's because partially for me, I came to my gender like through gay culture ... so for me my gender was always like: "Oh, like this is what a man is to me" and that was never hyper-masculine or anything like that. My gender is very much based on that almost parodying of masculinity, and that to me has been the basis for who I am basically.
>
> (Zack, 2020)

Zack was comfortable with a form of masculinity that was not too masculine, a masculinity that incorporated femininity, but not as a female. The 'parodying of masculinity' implies a detachment from masculinity and sexuality, and perhaps Zack's adolescent sexual presentation implied a parodying or parading of femininity as a way to manage emotional struggles. There are aspects of Zack's behaviour that relate to Riviere's (1929) notion of womanliness as a masquerade and Butler's notion of gender as performative. In Zack's case, manliness becomes performative or the masquerade for a self-tailored or bespoke gender, one that includes some femme and some 'masc' but not too much of either.

The notion of wishing to embody parodic masculinity suggests that masculinity is being invoked and provoked simultaneously: a mockery of the real thing (masculinity) that nonetheless becomes the real thing: "I'm a man", but not the kind of man who merits parody, and yet parodic masculinity is enticing. If the kind of extreme masculinity in and of itself is parodic, then the parody of that masculinity becomes *a parody of a parody*. The 'parody of a parody' is reminiscent of what Britton (1995) referred to as: "phantasy used as a defence against phantasy", in the case of Klein's child patient Dick who created a refuge in a phantasy in order to protect himself from the symbolic representation of this phantasy being met with in the external world. I'm curious about the draw for Zack to a group that excludes women sexually and parades male to male masculinity and sexuality. Perhaps this group formed a symbolic representation of Zack's own ejection of female sexuality. Within this particular niche of gay culture, there is an idolisation and idealisation of leathered and tattooed maleness, perhaps an external carapace of toughness that Zack was drawn to and wished to inhabit.

Zack was much more at ease with gay male culture than with lesbian culture. He can see that there has been an effeminate take on his masculinity and eventually realised he was "like a gay trans dude, I was like: Oh, I'm gender queer and sexually queer, cool" (Zack, 2020). The object of attraction has remained or returned to being male but following much change in Zack's gender identity from a straight woman to a gay trans man. Bisexuality is maintained throughout the gender identity changes. This raises interesting questions about whether gender identity moves in parallel with innate bisexuality. The object of desire is still male for Zack, but he is now a gay trans man and that feels right for him.

After I brought up the distinction between being male and being masculine, Zack responded:

> … I think like masculinity in the like concrete definition (laughed) whatever that is like, it just didn't fit … it wasn't right. Whereas now like I'm just doing whatever I want basically and yeah sort of fitting it to myself instead of me trying to like fit into whatever I thought I was.
>
> (Zack, 2020)

Zack acknowledges that he never liked his body and never felt at home in it for most of his life:

> … I was just trying to pinpoint a reason why I didn't feel at home in my own skin umm. Whereas now I realise it's because I was a man and so yeah weight doesn't matter at all.
>
> (Zack, 2020)

At the time of the interview, Zack was excited to have booked in for top surgery, he had been taking testosterone for under a year and was happy with the effects. He has let go of his prior wish for a very specific male look.

I put it to him that his past relationship to his body is somewhere in his history in spite of his moves through different identities and that complicates his relationship to aspects of his body. When I asked more about him referring to his past self as always having been a boy, Zack explained that although he did not really subscribe to *that* narrative which is a common trans narrative and was not true for him in the sense of being "trapped inside a woman's body", he saw himself more as trying to find himself and evolving at the same time as being the same person then as now: "… yeah I was a dude, so yeah, I do refer to myself as a man". There is an understandable wish to have always been 'the gender that I am now', which can subsume past depression (Zack, 2020).

The Masculine Vaginal, Female Phallus and Trans Phallus

If the phallus can be de-linked from the penis and is ungendered, the vagina can be thought about as a female phallus. Even if it were to be called 'Phallussa', it would still have a male origin: it is difficult to de-gender associations to the phallus. Griffin Hansbury (2017), a psychoanalyst who identifies openly as trans, has written about a female symbolic counterpart to the Phallic in his paper: 'The Masculine Vaginal: Working with Queer Men's Embodiment at the Transgender Edge'. In this paper, Hansbury clarifies his concept as the embodied experience of many trans men, he also thinks this concept is applicable to natal gay or heterosexual males. He discusses a clinical case of a gay man who treated his anus as a vagina, physically and symbolically. Hansbury describes the versatile relationship of the body to its various representations as the 'transgender edge'. This is a space in which men who are cisgender[2] or not can develop the freedom to explore 'other gender' aspects of their sexual fantasies and experience: what Kubie referred to as the "drive to be both sexes" (1974: 352). This "is a border that, when unpoliced, becomes porous, allowing outlaws to penetrate, sliding into a zone not easily defined" (Hansbury, 2017: 1010).

Hansbury describes the Vaginal:

> I hope here to delink the Vaginal from the strictly female so that, like the Phallic, it can be more acceptably accessed by the analyst working with people of all genders and all sexes. This concept goes beyond the conceptual to the real, embodied experience of many transgender men, who live in whole, partial, and/or temporary "female" bodies.

(2017: 1010)

He goes on to ask 'a transmodern' question:

> … can we conceive of the vagina and the symbolic Vaginal as multivalent, by turns feminine and masculine, depending on who is using it, in what style, and to what aim?

(2017: 1015)

The anatomical penis is dislodged from the biological to the symbolic for Lacan, in 'The Signification of the Phallus' (1958, 1982). He saw it as central to the whole symbolic order inhabited by the human subject. This brought about a momentous shift from body to symbol, a severance from 'anatomy is destiny', rendering all human subjects as symbolically castrated with their own individual relation to the phallic signifier. As Wilson, who introduces Hansbury's paper, describes:

> Anatomical form and function – a classically normative pairing – are increasingly *queered*, as the simple binaries of male/female, heterosexual/homosexual, vagina/anus are questioned, problematized, and deconstructed.

(Wilson, 2017: 1006)

Moss (2017), in his paper 'Pussy Riot: Commentary on Hansbury', argues that the 'psychoanalytic edge' subsumes the 'transgender edge'. He asserts that the Masculine Vaginal for Freud would be "… a product of psychic polymorphous fantasy …" and that "… Hansbury is granting extraordinary, transmutative power to psychic reality" (Moss, 2017: 1053–1054). This power eradicates the difference or edge between psychic and material realities as seen in psychosis or hallucinations in which the object that is perceived is not there. Saketopoulou (2017), another respondent to Hansbury's paper, is more embracing of the emergent possibilities of his new ideas calling for the need for "new translational forms" and a new discourse in order for diverse and non-normative gender identities to be understood clinically (2017: 1040).

Non Genital Masculinity and the Trans Phallus

The masculine Vaginal as invoked by Hansbury introduces the concept as a helpful psychic and symbolic space to be acknowledged, explored and opened up for interpretation. It undoes the shame sometimes associated with female or feminine identification or desire. My interest is in thinking about this more specifically in relation to trans men who identify as male and masculine and who are usually more concerned with having top surgery (an excision of the more visible female anatomical part of the body). This brings into focus the notion of trans-genitality as well as the complex awareness of having a vagina.

Phantomisation is a not an unusual aspect of transgender embodiment (Ramachandran & McGeoch, 2008). Trans men can experience the feeling of having a penis without any genital reconstructive surgery (Hansbury, 2017: 1011). I have referred earlier in this chapter to the Lesbian Phallus and to Female Masculinity. Hansbury introduces the 'empowered male vagina', not as emasculated or castrated but as a counterpart to the Phallic accessible to all genders and sexes. For Moss (as mentioned earlier), and undoubtedly others, this lends extraordinary transmutative power to psychic reality (2017). There are clearly very differing stances to sexuality and genitality within trans identity.

I introduce the trans phallus as an aspect of non-genital masculinity; it is transient, transplantable, transportable and transgressive, not least as it is psychically and imaginatively created. It is not unlike Winnicott's notion of transitional space (1951, 1987) although in this instance, it can bridge the transition between gender identifications. The trans phallus is also akin to a conception that is met by a realisation not unlike Bion's theoretical proposition that thoughts precede thinking. An infant can have an innate pre-disposition to expect a breast (the pre-conception), the realisation occurs when it meets the breast, but the thought only arises from the frustration brought about by the absence of the breast which provides the apparatus for the thinking of thoughts (1967, 1984). I have brought in Bion as the phallus is linked to an absence that creates a desire. It is that which is in the mind of the infant's mother that he/she cannot fulfil. Similarly, the trans phallus is elusive, powerful and desired. The trans phallus like the Lacanian or Lesbian phallus is linked to a lost object that splits the subject.

The term 'phallic' is metaphoric and symbolic, it denotes a particular kind of masculine functioning, personality trait or aspect of identity initially derived from a stage of genital psychosexual development as described by Freud (1923). If one joins this word up with masculinity, it expands the metaphor and locates it more specifically in relation to a masculine and non-feminine way of being. If one negates the term 'phallic' through the description and term 'non-phallic masculinity', it both negates and enhances the metaphor into something more transient and less categorisable as I suggest might befit the desire and bespoke masculine identity of some trans men.

Some trans men choose to undergo phalloplasty surgery. This involves the creation of a penis, which can take place by using a flap of skin from the body, usually taken from the arm (radial forearm free-flap, RFF) or from the thigh (anterior lateral thigh pedicled flap phalloplasty, ALT). In the RFF surgery, tissue is removed from the donor site as well as the blood supply. The blood supply is then anastomosed to a recipient blood supply at the site of transfer. With either of these procedures, the donor skin is rolled into a tube shape and grafted to the inguinal area. Usually this is done after a hysterectomy and vaginectomy or vaginal mucosal ablation in order to reduce the risk of fistula. A scrotoplasty may also be done that includes or excludes testicular implants. A urethral connection might also be made using cheek or vaginal mucosa as well as the placing of an erectile implant. The whole phalloplasty procedure involves many surgeries across different stages, and depending on these choices, the penis might have erotic sensation and might not. Metoidioplasty is an alternative to phalloplasty, it comes from the Greek word 'towards male genitalia'. As testosterone causes the clitoris to grow, metoidioplasty uses local tissue to enhance the clitoris further (to 1 3 inches, with the girth of a thumb), and there is no skin grafting involved (Transgender Care, UCSF, Crane, 2016).

Transmasculinity

A couple of interviewees whom I saw for a follow-up interview told me how their past experience before they identified as trans was helpful to them and to other cis men, in relation to masculinity. They felt that they had empathy and kindness towards women that came from their own lived experience. They knew what it was like to be on the receiving end of particular forms of masculinity that included misogyny. Cis men were interested in talking to them and learning from them. In effect, they were saying that trans men could really understand women from the inside, and cis men could learn from their experience and approach. This would only be possible if the cis men were trans-friendly.

In a follow-up interview, after a question from me about what place their pre-transition experience holds for them, Joe explained:

> I think honestly it just teaches you to be kind to people. When you experience so much prejudice yourself, it makes you more open minded. Actually, I definitely think that trans men have a big responsibility of, umm, of you know, teaching other men how women should be treated … because women are trying to do this almost 24/7, but they don't feel like they're being listened to by the man that they are trying to reach. And trans men have a privilege of being listened to by men. I hear a lot that trans men get interrupted a lot less in the workplace than pre-transition because of how they were perceived.

(Joe, 2024)

When I put the same question to Milo in a follow-up interview, he explained:

It's not like … I'm not living in stealth. So, I'm not running around umm, hiding my transness or pretending to be cis. That's not how I've chosen to live … I feel like my transness and my history of being AFB, being assigned female at birth like informs my idea of gender and masculinity, and I don't feel like I've killed the female parts of me. … I think a lot of people view gender as like either you're male or you're female and like these traits are either masculine or feminine and that there's not like it's, it's not just a big mushy spectrum of human experience … being assigned female at birth, that means that I was socialised for certain things, like talking about how I'm feeling, or sharing my emotions or like actively listening. … Which is not to say that men can't do that. And I think that, that is in a way the role that trans people can play in the world is, kind of highlighting that there's so much human experience that we share that it feels a little ridiculous to just put people in boxes.

(Milo, 2024)

Milo went on to explain that his pre-transition self helps to inform his ideas about masculinity and how he feels as a man. That he was not wanting to sever anything but that his was a different kind of masculine experience.

In earlier interviews, there was something experienced as potentially threatening from cis men in social situations where it was unclear how they might react to transness. Some interviewees tended to socialise in groups that were more queer and hence trans-friendly; in these groups, transmasculinity was more likely to blend in and not stand out. The effects of testosterone and top surgery for most of the interviewees helped significantly to reduce social self-consciousness, which brought much relief. However, the ongoing fear of being 'outed' was often still experienced, although this inevitably depended on the environment.

Testosterone

In a follow-up interview with Joe, he had begun to take testosterone and was mainly very happy with the effects of it on his appearance and voice. One thing that he was struggling with was the change of now being perceived as a black young man, which exposed him to racist presumptions that he was not subjected to as a young black woman prior to his transition. This required a new kind of identity adaptation from him that exposes the complicated linkage of race and gender in relation to external forms of prejudice.

Joe was relieved to not be misgendered as often as he was pre-testosterone. He noticed that he'd become more resilient and less prone to emotional states. The way Joe understood this was that a lot of his most emotional moments were caused by things that don't happen anymore. He thought that there was "a new chemical balance that testosterone gives the brain" (Joe, 2024). This experience of changes brought about by testosterone is not new but is interesting to consider in relation to trans men.

'This American Life' (2002), an American radio series, broadcast four episodes on differing experiences of testosterone. In 'Act Two, Infinite Gent', Alex Blumberg spoke to Griffin Hansbury about the extreme changes that he experienced after taking testosterone, not least as he'd been started on a very high dose, following his transition to being a trans man. He felt a pronounced increase in libido and the way in which he perceived women, a pervasive sexualisation, in a way that was hard to contain; he became interested in understanding science which he had not been interested in previously; he found it hard to cry. He described the quality of the crying as 'very dry' with 'very little tears'. His transition was from being a butch dyke to learning how to be a man in the world. He noticed how aggressively other cis men could be whilst walking on the street, which required him to 'puff himself up'. He spoke about the joy of being called 'Sir' which interviewees had mentioned too. Hansbury said he had a love/hate relationship to 'passing' as many aspects of his past history had to be concealed in certain environments: "that my whole deeper self becomes invisible and my history becomes invisible". When asked about the biggest thing that he missed, he said it was having new close relationships with females. In this interview, Hansbury mentions setting up an online advice column called: 'Ask a Guy Who Used to be a Girl', but that it hadn't yet come to be (This American Life, 2002).

In my discussion of masculinity, I suggest ideas and am not offering any kind of definitive pronouncements. I explore the term 'masculinity' broadly, concretely and symbolically not only in relation to natally assigned men but also in relation to many manifestations of gender identity. The more usual bodily interventions for trans men, as far as I'm aware, are testosterone and mastectomies, perhaps the more externally or socially perceived tropes of maleness. Phalloplasty surgery is less likely to be pursued; this may be because it is more complex and invasive. Amongst my interviewees, phalloplasty was not sought, perhaps corroborating the idea that the lived experience of bespoke masculinity does not necessitate a penis. What was wanted was to be visually and aurally perceived as male, achieved hormonally via testosterone, with the aim of reducing or removing femaleness facially, vocally and in the case of mastectomies, bodily.

Physical intervention and psychological intervention are different ways of getting help with gender identity struggles that are not mutually exclusive, although there might well be more resistance to psychological help if trans men suspect that the therapist is at worst prejudiced and at best ambivalent. If one understands non phallic as non-penile, although biologically valid, the complex psychological terrain of transmasculine identity can be missed, one that embodies the tension not only between masculine and feminine but between sex and gender. It is bespoke, as the maleness and masculinity are worn like a made to measure tailored suit, or second skin (Bick) that is idiosyncratic, personally inhabited, and removed from the concreteness of biology.

Notes

1 Documentary Seahorse: The Dad Who Gave Birth (2019), directed by Jeanie Finlay. https://seahorsefilm.com. The first British transgender man to carry and give birth to his own child in 2018 was detailed in the documentary Seahorse in 2019.
2 This term is used to describe someone who identifies with their natal sex as assigned at birth.

Bibliography

Bailly, L. (2009). The paternal metaphor, the role of the father in the unconscious. In *Lacan* (Chapter 5, pp. 74–87). London: Oneworld Publications.

Bick, E. (1968). The experience of the skin in early object relations. *International Journal of Psychoanalysis*, *49*, 484–486.

Bion, W. R. (1967, 1984). A theory of thinking. In *Second Thoughts* (Chapter 9, pp. 110–119). London: H. Karnac (Books).

Britton, R. (1995). Reality and unreality in phantasy and fiction. In E. Spector Person, P. Fonagy, & S. A. Figueira (Eds.), *On Freud's "Creative writers and day-dreaming"* (pp. 82–106). New Haven and London: Yale University Press.

Butler, J. (1993, 2011). The lesbian phallus and the morphological imaginary. In *Bodies that matter* (Chapter 2, pp. 28–57). New York & Oxon: Routledge.

Chaplin, R. (2018). How to be both, by not being both: The articulation of psychic bisexuality within the analytic session. In R. J. Perelberg (Ed.), *Psychic bisexuality: A British French dialogue* (Chapter 10, pp. 207–226). London & New York: Routledge.

Diamond, D. (1989). Father-daughter incest: Unconscious fantasy and social fact. *Psychoanalytic Psychology*, *6*(4), 421–437.

Ferrari, A. B. (1992). *L'ecclissi del corpo* [The eclipse of the body]. Rome: Boria.

Figlio, K. (2010). Phallic and seminal masculinity: A theoretical and clinical confusion. *International Journal of Psychoanalysis*, *91*(1), 119–139.

Figlio, K. (2024). Seminal masculinity (Chapter 7, pp. 113–133); Incapacity and ambivalence in seminal masculinity (Chapter 8, pp. 134–151). In *Rethinking the psychoanalysis of masculinity, from toxic to seminal*. London & New York: Routledge.

Fonagy, P., & Target, M. (2000). Playing with reality: III. The persistence of dual psychic reality in borderline patients. *International Journal of Psychoanalysis*, *81*, 853–873.

Freud, S. (1909). Analysis of a phobia in a five-year-old boy, (Little Hans). In *Standard Edition* (Vol. 10, pp. 1–149). London: Hogarth Press.

Freud, S. (1923). The Infantile Genital Organisation: An interpolation into the theory of sexuality. In *Standard Edition* (Vol. 19, pp. 139–145). London: Hogarth Press.

Gallop, J. (1981). Of phallic proportions: Lacanian conceit. *Psychoanalysis and Contemporary Thought*, *4*(2), 251–273.

Gallop, J. (1988). Phallus/penis: Same difference; beyond the phallus. In *Thinking through the body* (Chapter 6, pp. 124–133). New York: Columbia University Press.

Gallop, J. (2019). *Sexuality, disability and ageing: Queer temporalities of the phallus.* Durham and London: Duke University Press.

Halberstam, J. (1998). *Female masculinity*. Durham and London: Duke University Press.

Halberstam, J. (2018). *Trans* a quick and quirky account of gender variability*. Oakland, California: University of California Press.

Hansbury, G. (2017). The masculine vaginal: Working with queer men's embodiment at the transgender edge. *Journal of the American Psychoanalytic Association*, *65*(6), 1009–1031.

Hart, L. (1996). Doing it anyway: Lesbian sado-masochism and performance. In E. Diamond (Ed.), *Performance and cultural politics* (pp. 69–77). New York: Routledge.

Hertzmann, L., & Newbigin, J. (2020). A person beyond gender: A first-hand account. In L. Hertzmann & J. Newbigin (Eds.), *Sexuality and gender now* (Chapter 11, pp. 256–287). London: Routledge.

Hsieh, L. (2012). A queer sex, or, can feminism and psychoanalysis have sex without the phallus. *Feminist Review, 102*, 97–115.

Joe. (2024). Interview (anonymised).

Jones, E. (1927). The early development of female sexuality. *International Journal of Psychoanalysis, 8*, 459–472.

Jones, E. (1916). The theory of symbolism. *British Journal of Psychology, 9*, 181–229.

Kestenberg, J. (1968). Outside and inside: Male and female. *Journal of the American Psychoanalytic Association, 16*, 457–520.

Kubie, L. S. (1974). The drive to be become both sexes. *Psychoanalytic Quarterly, 43*, 349–426.

Lacan, J. (1949, 1977). The Mirror Stage as Formative of The Function of the I as Revealed in the Psychoanalytic Experience. In J. Lacan, *Écrits: A Selection*, London: Tavistock, 1977.

Lacan, J. (1953). The Symbolic, the Imaginary, and the Real: Inaugural meeting of the SFP, 8th July 1953, Paris.

Lacan, J. (1958, 1982). The meaning of the phallus. In J. Mitchell & J. Rose (Eds.), *Feminine sexuality, Jacques Lacan and the école freudienne* (J. Rose, Trans.) (1982) (Chapter 2). New York, London: W.W. Norton and Panthean Books.

Lacan, J. (1966). *Ecrits*. Paris: Seuil.

Laplanche, J., & Pontalis, J. B. (1973, 1967). Phallus. In *The language of psychoanalysis* (1973) (pp. 312–314). London: Karnac Books.

Laufer, M. (1976). The central masturbation fantasy, the final sexual organisation and adolescence. *Psychoanalytic Study of the Child, 31*, 297–316.

Littman, L. (2021). Individuals treated for gender dysphoria with medical and/or surgical transition who subsequently detransitioned: A survey of 100 detransitioners. *Archives of Sexual Behavior, 50*, 3353–3369.

Masson, J. M. (1985). *The complete letters of Sigmund Freud to Willhelm Fleiss 1887–1904* (J. M. Masson, Trans. & Ed.) (August 1, 1899) (pp. 363–364). Cambridge, Massachusetts & London, England: The Belknap Press of Harvard University Press.

Matte Blanco, I. (1975). *The unconscious as infinite sets: An essay in bi-logic* (pp. 35–47). London: Duckworth.

McConnell, F. (2020). The guardian.com/society/2020/nov/16/trans-man-loses-uk-legal-battle-to-register-as-his-childs-father. Documentary Seahorse: The Dad Who Gave Birth (2019), directed by Jeanie Finlay. https://seahorsefilm.com

Milo. (2024). Interview (anonymised).

Moi, T. (1999). What is a woman? Sex, gender, and the body in feminist theory. In *What is a woman? And other essays* (Chapter 1, pp. 3–120). New York and London: Oxford University Press.

Money-Kyrle, R. E. (1971). The aim of psychoanalysis. *International Journal of Psycho-Analysis, 52*, 103–106.

Moss, D. (2017). Pussy riot: Commentary on Hansbury. *Journal of the American Psychoanalytic Association, 65*(6), 1049–1059.

Nguyen, A. (2008). Patriarchy, power and female masculinity. *Journal of Homosexuality, 55*(4), 665–683.

Parker, A. (1986). Mom, *Oxford Literary Review*, Vol. 8, No. 1/2, Sexual Difference (1986), pp. 96–104, Edinburgh University Press. http://www.jstor.org/stable/43964592. Accessed 15.12.2017.

Person, E. S. (1980). Sexuality as the mainstay of identity: Psychoanalytic perspectives. *Signs, 5*, 605–630.

Preciado, P. B. (2013). *Testo junkie: Sex, drugs and biopolitics in the pharmacoporno-graphic era.* New York, NY: Feminist Press.

Ramachandran, V. S., & McGeoch, P. D. (2008). Phantom penises in transsexuals: Evidence of an innate gender-specific body image in the brain. *Journal of Consciousness Studies, 15*, 5–16.

Raphael-Leff, J. (2007). Femininity and its unconscious 'shadows': Gender and generative identity in the age of biotechnology. *British Journal of Psychotherapy, 23*(4), 497–515.

Raphael-Leff, J. (2008). 'The casket and the key': Thoughts on creativity, gender and generative identity. In *Female experience* (2nd ed., Chapter 13). London: Anna Freud Centre.

Riviere, J. (1929). Womanliness as a masquerade. *International Journal of Psychoanalysis, 10*, 303–313.

Rose, J. (1982). The meaning of the phallus. In J. Mitchell & J. Rose (Eds.), *Feminine sexuality, Jacques Lacan and the école freudienne* (Chapter 2, pp. 74–85). New York & London: W.W. Norton & Company.

Rosenberg, J. (2003). Butler's 'Lesbian phallus', or what can deconstruction feel? *Gay and Lesbian Quarterly, Journal of Lesbian and Gay Studies, 9*, 393–414.

Saketopoulou, A. (2015). Diaspora, exile, colonization: Masculinity dislocated. *Studies in Gender and Sexuality, 16*(4), 278–284.

Saketopoulou, A. (2017). Between Freud's second and third essays on sexuality: Commentary on Hansbury. *Journal of the American Psychoanalytic Association, 65*(6), 1033–1048.

Sechehay, M. A. (1951). *Symbolic realization: A new method of psychotherapy applied to a case of schizophrenia.* New York: International Universities Press.

Segal, H. (1957, 1986). Notes on symbol formation. In *The work of Hanna Segal* (Chapter 4, pp. 49–65). New York: Aronson.

This American Life. (2002). Infinite Gent, 220: Testosterone, Act Two. [Radio Broadcast] https://www.thisamericanlife.org/220/testosterone/act-two-1. Retrieved 20th April, 2024.

Tiefer, L. (1986, May 1). In pursuit of the perfect penis: The medicalization of male sexuality. *The American Behavioural Scientist, 29*(5), 579–599; Periodicals Archive Online.

Transgender Care, UCSF. (2016). Curtis Crane, June 17th, 2016. https://transcare.ucsf.edu/guidelines/phalloplasty. Retrieved 19th May, 2024.

Wilson, M. (2017). Body and symbol: Introduction to Hansbury and commentators. *Journal of the American Psychoanalytic Association, 65*(6), 1005–1008.

Winnicott, D. W. (1951, 1987). Transitional objects and transitional phenomena. In *Through paediatrics to psycho-analysis* (Chapter XVIII, pp. 229–242). London: The Hogarth Press.

Wittgenstein, L. (1953, 1974). *Philosophical investigations* (G. E. M. Anscombe, Trans.) (1974) (1. 115, p. 48e). Oxford: Blackwell.

Zack. (2020). Interview (anonymised).

Chapter 5

Bespoke Temporality

Although past things are related as true, they are drawn out from the memory, – not the things themselves, which have already gone, but the words conceived from the images of the things that have formed in the mind as footprints in their passage through the senses.

(Saint Augustine 1943: 289)

St Augustine in his *Confessions* tries to make sense of the relationships between the past, present and future and how these resonate in the mind given the labile nature of time. The notion that identity is not rooted in chronology is pertinent to some experiences of trans individuals who might not welcome the historicising of their experience as defining or contributing to their identity, whether this is their own historicising or one that comes from someone else. In some instances, the experience of transgender identity can be conceptualised as existing somewhere outside linear time, in a more unconscious than conscious domain, which both cancels and questions developmental time. Past time can be set up against present time in what can become a negation of origin that includes conception: 'I am not the baby girl I was born as, and never really have been'. The degree of accommodation and interpretation of past history is of course hugely variable and individual, and I am not advocating any general overview.

I will refer to the distinction that Scarfone makes between the sequential developmental line of maturational infantile sexuality and the infantile sexual that remains as the unconscious centre of adult sexuality and precludes evolution and maturity (2014: 335). An understanding of trans identity might require the therapist to develop what the Botellas (2005) describe as a particular capacity for retrogressive movement in order to enter into the patient's non-representability so that a perception of the void can be grasped and then become representable. This can manifest as countertransference that necessitates deep empathic identification. The retrogressive movement would also require an entry into what could be termed *trans-temporality*, a temporality that can challenge the axis of vertical, horizontal or generational coordinates. Trans-temporality can reconfigure historical and familial coordinates.

DOI: 10.4324/9781032718613-6

Après-Coup Revisited

Freud's Nachträglichkeit (noun) or nachträglich (adjective) has had various translations, one of which is après-coup, a well-recognised psychoanalytic term that denotes the past as re-enlivened in the present. Freud mentioned it in a letter to Fleiss in 1896, in which he mentions psychical material being subjected at times to a *re-arrangement* or *re-transcription* (Masson, 1985: 207). Stratchey translated it as 'deferred action', and Kernberg translated it as 'retrospective modification' (House, 2017; Kernberg, 1993). Stratchey was attempting to convey the idea of a link between two moments but this also implies linear movement, unlike the concept of après-coup which is retroactive. Faimberg[1] (2005) points out that the translation choice highlights a specific way of conceiving temporalisation and psychic causality (Faimberg, 2005: 109). House (2017), in his lucid and helpful article, explains the difference between these terms. He likens the temporality of deferred action to fireworks or landmines. "The results ... have been determined in the past by what was desired when the device was constructed. Retrospective modification has the opposite temporal structure. Its results are determined in the present on the basis of current needs" (House, 2017: 776).

It was Lacan (1953) who homed in on this term or concept in relation to Freud's Wolf Man case (1917–1919), and, as House puts it "... gave *nachträglich* retroactivity" (2017: 777). Lacan (1955) states:

> It's not what happens afterwards which is modified, but everything that went before. We have a retroactive effect – nachträglich, as Freud calls it – specific to the structure of symbolic memory, in other words to the structure of memory.
>
> (Lacan, 1955: 185)

In 2002 (de Mijolla in Faimberg, 2005: 121) Laplanche gave this definition of après-coup:

> It establishes a complex and reciprocal relationship between a significant event and its resignification in afterwardness, whereby the event acquires new psychic efficiency.[2]

In a recorded conversation between Jean Laplanche and Martin Stanton (1991), revised for a published chapter 'Notes on Afterwardness' (1998), (Laplanche, 1999), Laplanche argues for or perhaps enriches the bi-directional aspect of Freud's concept of afterwardness. He acknowledges that Freud's concept combines a retrogressive and progressive direction, and adds his own account of this:

> ... right at the start, there is something that goes in the direction of the past to the future, from the other to the individual in question, that is in the direction

from the adult to the baby, which I call the implantation of the enigmatic message. This message is then retranslated, following a temporal direction that is, in an alternating fashion, by turns retrogressive and progressive (according to my general model of translation-detranslation-retranslation).

(Laplanche, 1999: 265)

I wish to focus on après-coup as applied to aspects of temporality in gender identity. We all live or exist in time, and usually have a birth date, and narrative of origin. The memory of this personal history is partly conscious and partly unconscious; it continuously unfolds into neither a tidy nor a clear division. It relies in its unfolding on the personal and individual form that the structure of memory and the memory of structure takes. The conscious part of the mind has the freedom to direct and redirect the narrative, not least because memories are not facts (see Widlöcher, 1994). Psychoanalytic approaches facilitate a revisiting of memories that might have become ossified as facts, with the opportunity to unleash and consider unconscious processes, which can aid restructuring or revision.

Toby, a 29-year-old interviewee, explained in relation to his trans identity that:

I've got reason to feel that it's genetic, I've got reason to feel that it's caused and I've got reason to feel that it's chosen. But what I now feel coming to the end of it ... is ... whatever I did is, I anchored this decision around the age of about five years old. ... I am now exactly how I imagined myself to be when I was that age, who I wanted to grow into, what I considered to be iconic, I now embody all of that.

(Toby 2020)

Toby's approach to his trans identity fits with Kierkegaard's phrase that "Life can only be understood backwards; but it must be lived forwards" (Kierkegaard 1843).

The Infantile Sexual, Gender and Temporality

When the word 'infantile' is used psychoanalytically it usually refers to something childlike or regressive that in turn refers to a period in time prior to the next phase of development. The explanation can be limited to a temporal phase. Scarfone (2014) deploys Laplanche in excavating a deeper understanding of the 'Infantile Sexual', which can be understood as a-temporal, not just a sequential part of growing up that eventually matures. Scarfone distinguishes between the sequential developmental line of maturational infantile sexuality and the infantile sexual that remains as the unconscious centre of adult sexuality and precludes evolution and maturity (Scarfone, 2014: 335).

Scarfone (2002) differentiates between 'infantile sexuality' and the 'infantile aspect of the sexual', as he feels the meanings of these terms can become blurred.

He connects Freud's tendency to use myths when the question of origin arises, with the timelessness of the unconscious. Myths are connected to periods that are outside time, outside origin and outside chronology. Whereas Freud used 'actual' initially (as in actual neuroses rather than psychoneuroses) he then moved to a psychic timelessness in his conceptual system. Scarfone sees an extratemporal dimension connecting infantile sexuality with the infantile aspect of the sexual. He sees the sexual as a remainder, surplus or excess that is specific to psychoanalytic space and time as conceived after Freud, and does not see a clear differentiation between infantile sexuality and adult sexuality. As I understand Scarfone, he is not in favour of a reversion or reduction to a historical beginning, and is more in favour of 'the actual' as a temporal category specific to the unconscious:

> The actual is what is not inscribed in a chronology but lies beneath the chronological level and functions as the generator of history that is itself not able to be historicized. It seems to me that this is what the infantile aspect of the sexual represents, in that it transcends the particular event, the vicissitude, and thus, by necessity, can only be transferred, that is, transmitted as an excess part, never entirely admitted into a process that could be completed, come to an end.
> (Scarfone, 2002: 106)

One could replace the word 'actual' with the word 'gender' in this quote, as also being to some degree outside of chronology and resistant to being historicised. Gender can be conceptualised as that which is transferred or transmitted as a remainder, surplus or excess and hence not unlike Scarfone's description of the sexual.

According to Scarfone's discourse, psychoanalysis does not deal with the past, but more the actual and active present as it infiltrates the transference from an unconscious reservoir of hitherto unspeakable experience. He refers to the *Unpast* (Scarfone, 2015) as the haunted present that neither becomes past or future history, but repeats. A patient can move from narrating and remembering to repeating in the transference the unrepresentable aspects of experience that require representing so as to enter the psychic domain where they can be expanded and worked through.

The aliveness of the present and its poignancy fits well with some experiences of gender identity. The notion of time that is not rooted in past chronology is pertinent to the experiences of my interviewees, who largely did not welcome the historicising of their experience in the context of the past informing the present. A preferred lens through which to view earlier life struggles to include puberty, was a 'gender framework lens'. Gender was seen as 'the root of the struggle' leading to states of depression, suicidality, anorexia and self-harm. In this way gender or perhaps more accurately the embodiment of a gender can become an all-encompassing umbrella term that subsumes multiple psychological difficulties, which can reduce the precipitating complexity of these difficulties. This does not devalue the notion of gender as that which was the cause of difficulties, but points to the comorbidity of other psychic struggles.

When I asked Seth, an interviewee aged twenty-four, about the possible notion of self-hatred in connection with the drive to transition, he replied that:

> … if I were to be retrospectively tracked down, I would say that self-hatred or discomfort was just gender dysphoria, which was part of being trans for me at least.
>
> (Seth, 2020)

I asked Seth about how psychoanalytic practitioners could become more sought by people who might have gender-identity struggles. He replied:

> … I would worry that there would be a kind of thinking in that Freudian model: a kind of "Are you gay because X?" "Are you trans because X in your childhood and your relationship to your parents?" … something like that.
>
> (Seth, 2020)

In my interview with Zack, who was 27, I asked about his approach to psychotherapy:

> I never really wanted to talk about gender with a therapist   there was also this fear that someone would try to talk me out of it … that someone would you know 'oh this is just because of daddy issues or it's related to something here' you know like 'have you really thought about this'… and I know that for a lot of trans people the way you have to defend it is to be like 'look I know myself, I know my body better than anyone else does, therefore I am the one who can make this decision for myself'.
>
> (Zack, 2020)

Zack went on to say:

> I think that talking to a therapist … could have probably helped me a lot sooner and helped my come to terms with my life.
>
> (Zack, 2020)

And in relation to the age at which he started transitioning, which was 26:

> I know eighteen-year-olds who've been on T[3] for longer than me, so sometimes I wish that I had done this a lot sooner so that I could have been happier quicker.
>
> (Zack, 2020)

Zack expresses many feelings about the notion of therapy and therapists, spanning the fear that his wishes would have been looked at through a somewhat clichéd

Oedipal constellation, to the idea that a therapist might have speeded things up and relieved his unhappiness sooner. The wish for attunement into his specific struggle and the anxiety of misattunement are both present.

Coming out of or into Time

It is ambitious to try and tie gender to time and time to gender as these concepts are to some extent amorphous. In a developmental context a sense of one's gender develops physically and emotionally in a sequence of linear and chronological time, that of infancy, childhood, latency, adolescence and adulthood, namely the life cycle. The physicality of gender shows itself through secondary sex characteristics that disrupt the body and sexualise it: into (usually) either male or female, and more unusually intersex. Growth and development work within the ordinary sequential flow or movement of lifetime. When gender develops, emerges or is felt to exist psychically in a different form and register to the gender assigned at birth or manifesting in the body, the sequence of developmental and generational time is altered, arrested, negated, renavigated and reformed. The relational axis of the sex I was born as or into turns and twists chronological foundations so that past, present and future are no longer sequential. The temporality of gender sets its own pace, undoes the (more linear) movement of sequential development in the body over lifetime.

The interpretation of temporality as experienced when gender identity has altered, can be thought of as a reversal of après-coup that disrupts the causal chains of life history, or "Where the Past Begins" to borrow Tan's book title (2018). This new vertex can disturb the vertical generational links between mothers and daughters or fathers and daughters and the horizontal links between brothers and sisters, between sisters and between brothers.

The relationships between parents and their hitherto sons or daughters are also altered. A mother/daughter relationship converts to a mother/son relationship and a father/daughter relationship converts to a father/son relationship. The dynamic of female to female in the case of mother and daughter or female to male in the case of daughter to father are dissolved and disoriented. The alteration of gender cuts across what might be referred to as 'Oedipal time' or Oedipality as it locates in time.

Holmes (2000) points out the Oedipal nature of the patient/therapist couple in his discussion about use of metaphor as a narrative device that is fundamental in dynamic therapy. He describes that:

> It lies transitionally between patient and therapist and is not wholly the property of either. It is thus 'oedipal', in the sense that it both pulls patient and therapist together and separates them from the lure of narcissistic fusion or collusion.
>
> (Holmes, 2000: 138)

In writing about time, the German novelist Erpenbeck (2020) asserts that:

> Time has the power to separate us, not only from others, but also from ourselves –
> a fact that's hard to grasp. We know that time also separates us from circum-
> stances that might have turned us into very different people. We know it, but we
> don't understand it.
>
> (Erpenbeck, 2020: 42–43)

In her expansive writing about time, Baraitser (2017) explores the nature, history, culture and political implications of temporal experiences in multiple contexts.
Events that resist or frustrate the regular flow of time interest her, particularly in
relation to practices of care. She writes about discipline or transdisciplinary formation, not as a linear development but (following Michel Serres 1991) as *temporally
folded*: this involves a process whereby old and new events can be placed side-by-
side, the new can reanimate the old or imbue it with fresh meaning (Baraitser,
2017: 32–34, 180). I found aspects of these ideas pertinent to experiences of
gender-time or time in gender in which the present gender identity revises the past gender experience so that gender identity can be thought of as temporally folded. Although
I cannot do justice to the wide-ranging writing about time in her book, this particular
concept resonated for me in relation to what I have termed 'après-coup masculinity'.

One generalising and potentially reductive way of thinking about the wish to
undo one's female gender is as a defence against father/daughter incest. As the
feminine and female sexuality are excised from the body, so is the risk of incest,
sexual abuse or pregnancy. Freud's trajectory, often considered to be a both reduc-
tionist and heteronormative description of the Oedipal constellation is the daughter's wish to marry her father and have his baby albeit in phantasy, and her 'goal' is
to manage to find another man or partner with whom she can achieve this. At issue
here is the distinction between phantasy and reality, as my proposition of a defence
against incest implies that in the daughter's mind this idea has become a feared or
wished for reality, albeit located unconsciously, given that the 'solution' can be
seen in the form of bodily- and gender-identity alterations. This defence against
incest, which is more unconscious than conscious, might manifest in situations
where a daughter is strongly identified with her father and or in which her father
might collude in an Oedipal coupling with his daughter that excludes the mother.
In instances of sexual abuse, a more conscious defence is likely to manifest. This
description is generalised and schematic.

In her analysis and interpretation of Laplanche, Butler joins Fletcher (2014) in
asking the poignant question: "…how do we account for gender if Oedipus is no
longer the exclusive framework in which we consider the formation of gender?"
(Fletcher and Ray 2014: 127). I'd like to add to this question: how do we find new
psychoanalytic ways of working with non-normative gender identities if Oedipus
is no longer the exclusive framework?

Laplanche (1999) makes a pronounced distinction between instinct and drive.
The infant's development is necessarily subject to impingements from the other,

usually the primary caretaker. These impingements are transmitted enigmatically, from the unconscious of the caretaker/parent/other to the unconscious of the infant. In her reading of Laplanche, Butler suggests that given the varied forms of these transmissions, they do not presuppose the Oedipal structure. Seduction is the generalised term that is given to the adult's intervention which separates the drive from the instinct:

> The instinct makes the drive possible, but the drive institutes a life of fantasy that is qualitatively new, and which is not constrained by the teleologies of biological life.
>
> (Butler, 2014: 123)

In conceptualising the impact of the rupture that the drive institutes, Butler concurs with Laplanche in the 'transgression' of an Oedipal structure that presumes a mother and father as the archetypal template for parenting. She sees gender as embedded in the enigmatic adult messages that transmit adult desire. For Laplanche gender assignment is considered as an unconsciously transmitted desire that emanates from the sexual unconscious of the parents (2007).

Traumatic Time

Seligman (2016) has written about how central disorders of temporality are to traumatised subjectivity. In a discussion of Seligman's paper on the experience of time, Vermeule states:

> It isn't just that the future, like the present, cannot be different from the awful past, but that the future as a category of experience has hardly any dimensionality at all: *Temporality itself is collapsed, obscured or absent, not only by the persistence of a terrible past, but by the mangling or deprivation of the possibility of an orderly flow of events in the meaningful emotional and interpersonal area.* This is of course not a matter of the clock, but rather a disorder of temporal sequentiality as a basic principle of the subjective sense of self.
>
> (Vermeule, 2016: 143)

Vermeule goes on to locate the "orderly flow of events" (2016: 143) within the parent–infant bond, following a quoted section of Seligman's paper in which he describes a benign and intuitive sequence of relating between a mother and a two-month-old baby. The mother's capacity to match the baby's initial gesture "vitalizes" the forward flow of time (Seligman, 2016: 115). It gives time and the sense of oneself in time meaning, through a capacity to feel vital, effective and linked to an object. Vermeule refers to this image as more one of constellation than causation (2016: 144).

Given that time cannot be arrested, and it is within the movement of time that we live, grow, develop and become sexual, what can be altered is the gender identity I feel and have, albeit not necessarily aligned with my birth sex. Although *this cannot alter time* or the primary objects that have looked after me *in time*, it can alter the *constellation of who I am in relation to others and who they are in relation to me*. In this sense time *can be negated* and perhaps also the original primary object, at least in phantasy. I can now identify as a son instead of a daughter in relation to my mother and father, and this 'born again' identity cuts through the Oedipal constellation and the generational constellation. This identity is *self-generated*, and bypasses the 'laws' of nature, biology, physiology, chromosomes and endocrinology. It disorders and reorders the status quo of prior relationships, it moulds and shapes a new landscape, one that dissents fundamentally from that which was there before. In this context gender identity alters temporality, and retranslates reality.

Returning to one of my interviewees, Zack, although he did not subscribe to the idea or narrative that he was "always a boy trapped inside a woman's body", he found it meaningful to apply his current gender identity as a trans man to his historic female self in his attempt to understand his past behaviour and unhappiness. He explained his promiscuous phase in his female teens as a result of a deep sense of self-consciousness that emanated from being trans and hence dissociated from his (female) body. Zack spoke about never really feeling at home in his body "… because I was a man …" (Zack, 2020).

I Am Therefore I Was

A change in gender identity can bring forth a unique temporality that can appraise the past through the lens of the present into 'I am therefore I was'. This temporality moves from the present back in time which is different to the past becoming re-enlivened in the present in the form of après-coup. Rather than a resignification in 'afterwardness', it is a resignification of 'beforeness'.

Although Zack did not feel that he was born in the wrong body, he did apply a retrospective temporality to his current maleness in the form of 'I am therefore I was', or 'What is now, was then'. This explained his past unhappiness in a female body. It also alters linear developmental temporality into bespoke temporality, which is tailor-made, and designed to fit the body well.

Zack expressed his relationship to his body:

> … all bodies are constantly containing within them the trauma of your life … and you know you don't just forget about things … especially people who are told that their bodies are wrong. When you look at your body, yeah, it constantly carries within itself your past life and you see it quite vividly on your own skin. So, for me when I see my chest or whatever, I still see like this little boy that was struggling to find acceptance and love wherever he could, and not knowing why like no matter what he felt like shit and didn't feel like himself.

(Zack, 2020)

In an article 'Time and the *après-coup*' (2003), Birksted-Breen opens up for exploration the different temporalities of developmental time, *après-coup* and what she refers to as 'reverberation time'. She discusses the psychoanalytic concept of 'here and now' as it is used clinically, and how "the past is always a past as reinterpreted in the present" through current internal object relations and how these get played out in the analytic scenario. She describes the present as having a complex relationship to the actual past, and the analytic dyad as that which reshapes the past (2003: 1503). She speaks of the past at the end of an analysis, and specifically the childhood parents as a past which has been retrospectively resignified, and hence one that has been shaped *après-coup*. It is this meaning of retrospective resignification that I am adopting in relation to gender identity and the modus operandi of 'I am therefore I was', in my discussion of Zack earlier.

The term *après-coup* has garnered various psychoanalytic meanings. Whereas Lacan (1953, 2004) initially drew attention to Freud's concept *Nachträglichkeit* in his discussion of the Wolfman, Laplanche and Pontalis (1973: 111–114) highlighted its importance in Freudian theory where it links to a reconfiguration in the mind subsequent to sexual maturation: "Human sexuality, with the peculiar unevenness of its temporal development, provides an eminently suitable field for the phenomenon of deferred action" (1973: 112). Within psychoanalytic practice interpreting in the 'here and now' subsumes the existence of après-coup, as the session material in the present is often seen to be a relived or re-experienced version of past object relationships. I wish to focus on the aspect of this concept when something in the present is perceived with a retrospective meaning and the application of this phenomenon to gender identity.

Birksted-Breen (2003) discusses the workings of a complex temporality in the 'here and now' that incorporates the ambiguity of the two directions of temporality: the past in the present and the present in (or perhaps as) the past. The past in the present is generally presumed to be a reinterpreted past as seen in the present unfolding through the prism of internal object relations within, into and onto the setting of the analysis and the specific analytic dyad. Birksted-Breen refers to this as "... *a new creation of the past*" (2003: 1503). This phrase has particular poignancy in relation to gender identity when the past identity is at times *revisioned through the present lens of who I am now*, that can convert into *who I have always been: I am therefore I was*. This 're-vision' can revise unwanted history and tamper with temporality that includes natal sex, childhood and sexual development; but can also offer opportunities for transforming the self as a-temporal or has having control of one's own relationship to temporality.

The Sexual Unconscious

For Laplanche the unconscious is the enabling condition for language and in this way of thinking he dissented from Lacan's view that the unconscious is structured like language. Laplanche (1987) understood the infant as being on the receiving end of not only care but also 'enigmatic signifiers' through the attachment relationship to its caretaker. These signifiers are transmitted through the sexual unconscious of the parent. The infant is thus subjected to or perturbed by not only the asymmetry of the parent/infant dyad but also to messages that cannot be translated or decoded by the infant. This was described by Laplanche as "… a thorn in the flesh of the ego …" (1987: 129), denoting an irritation that impels the child's attempt to try and make sense of the enigmatic message by trying to translate it. As it cannot be translated it sediments and forms the subject's sexual unconscious through primary repression. The enigma, which is unconscious for the parent, is translated through the borrowing of existing cultural forms of the family and from the mytho-historical, and through what is already intelligible both socially and culturally. Laplanche discussed gender as "… a product of culture nominated in the effort to cull the untameability of the infantile sexual" (Laplanche, 1987 as cited in Saketopoulou, 2017a: 51).

Saketopoulou (2023) introduces the concept of traumatophilia with a specific focus on what subjects do *with* their trauma as different to what can be done *about* it, which she terms 'traumatophobic'. She is interested in the creative and constructive side of trauma as opposed to the 'recovery from injury that has happened' approach. She does not advocate a psychoanalytic narrative that cures trauma, or restores and repairs mental health. For her, the work of trauma is in how to manage to inhabit its afterlife. She is more concerned about the promise of healing and overcoming pain that can move away from a way of relating to trauma that embraces its psychic imprint, lives through it rather than purging it. She adopts Laplanche in her thinking on the retranslation of the enigma (trauma), and its potential for psychic transformation (2023: 131–135).

Psychic Equivalence

This is a mode in which inner and outer reality are equated, so that one's thoughts become reality, and other viewpoints or interpretations are not feasible. It is usually applied to patients who have poor mentalising capacities, and was initially introduced by Fonagy and Target, in a series of papers about psychic reality and its failure in borderline patients (1996). They proposed the term 'psychic equivalence' to specify "… domination by psychic reality in Freud's sense …" (Fonagy & Target, 1996: 218). Two forms are used: 'psychic equivalent' and 'pretend mode', which differ in the assumed relationship between internal and external realities, in a small child. They maintained that the subjective sense of oneness between what is internal and external in the development of children is a universal phase. For the small child, inner experience is equivalent to and hence mirrors external reality, and this extends to feeling that others have the same experience that he does, and that the very young child does not yet have the capacity for the *merely representational* nature of ideas and feelings (1996: 217–219). Psychological and physical pain are equated in instances of psychic equivalence, so that psychological pain is experienced as bodily pain.

In an article about a mentalisation based approach specifically to aid functional somatic disorders, (Lutyen, Van Houdenhove, Lemma, Target, & Fonagy, 2012: 129–130), patients are described as expressing that one's body can feel like an 'alien self-part' or 'a machine that is out of control and that doesn't function properly'. The term 'psychic equivalence' might apply to aspects of gender identity struggles, in which there is often a desired equivalence or alignment of the gender in mind with gender in the body. At times there can also be an equating of emotional struggles (in the mind) and gender struggles (in the body), that can be hard to disentangle.

Ray, 28 at the time of the interview, described never fitting in to his assigned gender identity:

I had no kind of connection to any kind of womanhood, to like feeling of womanhood ... I felt something really ineffable excluding me from womanhood, I couldn't really understand why and it caused a lot of stress, I guess ... I didn't have any negative feelings towards womanhood or women or like the idea of being ... but I knew it wasn't me. ... when I saw myself in the mirror wearing dresses it felt incongruous ... it felt so incongruous and wrong...it was just kind of disorienting I guess, yeah ... there was something that didn't blend.

(Ray, 2020)

The term psychic equivalence connotes symmetry, which has been written about extensively by Matte Blanco (1975). His original ideas attempted to explain the laws that govern the unconscious, in mathematical terms, with the purpose of new possibilities for understanding psychoanalytic work. The aspects of his work that I wish to pluck out are the principle of symmetry, asymmetry, symmetrical identification, succession and temporality as I see their relevance and application to gender identity. Freud's words that "The governing rules of logic carry no weight in the unconscious; it might be called the Realm of the Illogical" (Freud, 1940: 168–169 in Matte Blanco, 1975), are acknowledged by Matte Blanco's principle of symmetry in which the system Unconscious treats *the converse of any relation as identical with the relation*. His example of asymmetry is that 'if John is the father of Peter, the converse is: Peter is the son of John' and here the relation and its converse are not identical; whereas 'If John is the brother of Peter, the converse is: Peter is the brother of John' and here there is symmetry because the converse is identical with the direct relation. From this Matte Blanco extrapolates that "When the principle of symmetry is applied there cannot be succession" (1975: 38–39).

My extrapolation from these ideas and principles is into the realm of gender identity, in which there is asymmetry between male and female, but perhaps not so in the unconscious. And in female to male trans identity there can be no biological succession, unless parts of the female body are retained as was the case with Freddy McConnell, who paused taking testosterone so that he could conceive

(McConnell, 2020). I refer to this in Chapters 3 and 4. This situation cuts into the biological/gender complexity of the trans womb.

In the principle of generalisation Matte Blanco introduced the idea that

> ... the system Unconscious treats an individual thing (person, object, concept) as if it were a member of a set or class which contains other members, it treats this class as a subclass of a more general class, and this more general class as a subclass of a still more general class and so on.
>
> (Matte Blanco, 1975: 38)

Fink (1989) adopts and applies these ideas to elements of time, space and difference between part and whole that all cease to exist when the principles of generalisation and symmetry are applied. These apply to primary thought processes in the main, that occur in the unconscious and are more id based, rather than secondary thought processes that are more conscious and ego based.

Fink (1989) utilises Matte Blanco's ideas to show through case studies that time does not exist in the thought system of symmetry: "An event that occurred yesterday can also occur today or tomorrow or at any other occasion in the past or in the future and therefore by excluding temporality, everything has happened, is happening, or will happen, all at the same time ..." (Fink, 1989: 482). This collapse of sequential time lends itself to my attempt to think about trans temporality in which for some trans men, time becomes elastic: now is then and then is now; which can erase the notion of developmental time, causal chains and historical meaning. Of course, the merging of time present, past and future is also ubiquitous, and something we are all prone to do. It can however acquire specific characteristics in relation to gender identity as located in time or outside of time. The experience of incongruity in relation to one's body must to some extent dismantle aspects of experience in one's lifetime.

Seduction in Time

Laplanche (1999) sees the drive as forming a kind of rupture and is thus qualitatively new and a separate entity to instincts that have aims that are more biological or self-preservative. Butler describes this drive as sexuality in general, that may be pre- or para-genital (Butler, 2014). This sexuality is fantasy based, the fantasy being that which is generated by the impingement of the other. These impingements are transmitted through enigmatic signifiers that can feel overwhelming, and occur at a time when the child is receiving necessary bodily care that is vital to its thriving and survival. Butler views the generalised scene of seduction that Laplanche advocates as the initiation of the sexual life of the child, and as separate and different to (experiences of) sexual abuse (Butler, 2014: 122).

The child cannot make sense of all aspects of the transmission of messages from the adult. It is the parts that are enigmatic, the remainders or source-objects of the drives, that form the child's unconscious. The unconscious for Laplanche is not bound by temporality or time which he understands as the binding of thoughts into something linear that can create a discourse. He firmly dissented from Lacan's view that the unconscious is structured like language, which then makes it temporal (Fletcher, Stanton, & Stanton, 1992: 25). What is striking about Laplanche's stance and theorisations is that he makes a definitive move away from a family structure that is 'informed' by the paternal law, heteronormativity and Oedipal constellations. This is a move away from both Freud and Lacan. It is the chain of enigmatic messages that inscribes itself onto and into the skin (or primitive skin-ego) of the infant, just as their mother or father or caregiver have similarly absorbed enigmatic messages themselves. It is the untranslatable residues of the messages that form the unconscious. There is a foreign dimension to desire that remains foreign, and to some extent unknown: it is the source of the drives and that which forms the self as a desiring subject (Butler, 2014: 126).

Excluding Oedipus: A New Translation

Laplanche relegates the Oedipal structure from its primal position, making it culturally contingent rather than universal. This position dissents from Lacan's central concept of the paternal metaphor (Fletcher 1992: 118). As the enigmatic signifier takes precedence over the paternal law and Oedipal structure, aspects of sexuality are no longer biologically determined or shaped to fit a heterosexual norm. In this respect, Laplanche offers a nuanced psychoanalytic perspective on the formation of desire, sexuality and gender.

Working with gender identity in its multiple manifestations requires clinical fluidity and agility in the mind of the clinician. Clinicians may need to expand and develop new Oedipal configurations in relation to gender variance. This does not mean that issues of exclusion, triangularity, murderousness, cannot be considered and worked with. There is work of translation required in the clinicians' minds, a retranslation of classical theory that would fit better with the current climate of gender variability. If this does not happen there is a risk that psychoanalytic work will not be sought out or benefitted from by patients who present with or may have underlying gender identity struggles.

When Saketopoulou (2017) comments on the paper 'The Masculine Vaginal' (Hansbury: 2017), she speaks of the importance for the analyst to be open to emergent possibilities in the analysis which she recognises in Hansbury's capacity to remain open and enabling of his patient's struggles and at times extreme risk taking. These experiences are thought about by Saketopoulou as a translation of the infantile sexual; an unbinding of translations that were previously bound with the aim of freeing up enigma and opening the possibility for the patient of a new translation. I agree with Saketopoulou's advocating of new translations for both the patient and the analyst. She is referring specifically to work with non-normative subjects. She recognises that subcultural communities facilitate discourses that are alternative within the analytic space, discourses that can retranslate the sexual in a better fit for the patient (2017: 1036). Sometimes this will mean a better fit than their original object, who might not have accommodated the gender identification of their child. This approach of rethinking the analytic working tools blends into my notion of the concrete thinking that at times resides in the mind of the therapist. Scarfone (2014) puts it well: "… what we need to do in analysis is not to discover hidden sexual meanings, but to uncover the personal equation by which the individual analysand deals with his sexual complexion" (Scarfone, 2014: 342).

Extinction of Temporality – As Rebellion?

Green (1927–2012), a French psychoanalyst who practiced in France explores how Freud used the concept of temporality in psychoanalysis. He speaks of repetition compulsion as "the murder of time" (2008: 1037), because in the very act of repeating, time stops short rather than being transformed into thoughts that can be analysed. Green, following Freud, distinguishes repetition compulsion from the timelessness in the unconscious. The repressed does not collaborate, it takes up its own room in the unconscious separate to the experience of reality.

When this is applied to time in the session, Green explains Freud's schema: where a path from a to b (in the patient) is cut off due to repression, it is unavailable. The patient then develops a network (alpha, beta, gamma, delta) that is called the lateral cathexis. Green's proposition is that there must be a connection between the unavailable 'a to b path' and the network as a whole represented by the ego's lateral cathexis (Freud, 1895). Whereas Freud described neurons, Green describes associations and stresses the importance of noticing the (bilateral) movement backwards and forwards, as well as the oppositional aspect of the representative system and the system of motion or movement. This tension and difficulty between construction and destruction, Green terms the extinction of temporality (Green, 2008: 1037–1038).

I think that these ideas are also applicable to a conceptualisation of or struggle with gender identity. A developmental pathway that moves in time is diverted or repressed and takes a lateral move into a new gender. Chronology is interrupted and so is the intergenerational system. A whole new network is set up that defines its own relationship to time and to objects that exist in time; time and being in time are thereby self-generated and self-generational. By self-generational, I mean that gender identity alters the relationship to parents, and hence to the generation they belong to as mother/daughter can become mother/son. The invention of a new temporality stands in antithesis to Freud's advocating 'remembering, repeating and working through' (1914). It brings forth a new form of working through that is less contingent on more conventional approaches to temporality.

Tense Present

In a chapter about the importance of taking time to transition, Israeli-Nevo (2018), who describes her experience living as a transwoman (sic), conveys how much she needed to have time in the present tense to process many aspects of her transition.

She discusses how trans subjects in a transphobic world are forced into a position of not being present, of being dissociated from their bodies, loved ones and general environment. This can throw trans individuals into an imagined future that is safer, but also unreachable and out of time. Taking time to transition can create a pull into the present and into the time cycle. For Israeli-Nevo, there was something comforting about forming her body in the present without trying to fit it in as having been imagined in the past. She wished to have time that was not pressured by others to either forgo her decision to transition or move on with it. She describes how in an encounter with a male acquaintance, he didn't recognise her at first, and this situation brought about a moment described as an excessive affective moment that was temporally delayed for the other person and pulled him into a mindful present, in which their misrecognition was re-cognised (2018: 62–63).

In her chapter she expands on the many meanings of taking one's time in transition, and on the present not having only positive connotations. She cites Muñoz's (2006) critique that points to the privilege of a white queer future, that queers of colour do not have and cannot have this kind of imaginable temporal horizon (Muñoz 2006: 825). She also cites Phillips (2015) in relation to linear time as that which Western, white and capitalist societies are rooted in, particularly in relation to the present moment in which marginalised populations can feel trapped (2015: 12).

Uncanny Temporality

The notion of negation is embedded in Freud's paper 'The Uncanny' (1919). He elaborates on the discomforting and disturbing experience of the familiar becoming unfamiliar: "Thus *heimlich* is a word the meaning of which develops in the direction of ambivalence, until it finally coincides with its opposite, *unheimlich*" (Freud, 1919, 1990: 347). There is an uncanny element to gender reassignment, a juxtaposition of the unfamiliar with the familiar. We have to step outside and beyond the established categorisations that root us in the familiar or homely/heimlich. This perception of the unfamiliar is not unlike a lateral cathexis that requires us to plug into a whole new network, as described earlier.

The analytic setting invites the emergence of uncanny temporality as past, present and future combine and distort. The past can feel alive or dead, familiar or unfamiliar. Chronology loses its linearity as thoughts and feelings can either surface or become repressed through the analytic process that brings forth the 'here and now' as well as the 'there and then' of life experience, mainly in the transference. Analytic time and gender time create an interesting juxtaposition.

Gozlan (2015), a Lacanian psychoanalyst, describes analytic work with a 40-year-old transsexual[4] (male to female) woman, he refers to as 'S'. He felt caught up in a universe in which masculinity and femininity were experienced (both by his patient and himself) as concrete facts, outside time, space and movement. Gozlan understood this experience as a re-enactment of S's childhood experience of enmeshment with her mother until she was 12, and sent to boarding school. Her father was an absent figure. S could not feel masculine or feminine, and so was stuck, persecuted and confined, as was Gozlan's experience. He did not see her difficulty as that of choosing a gender, but rather as a disavowal of internal difference:

> ... between time and timelessness, union and separateness, being and doing – that manifested itself through gender and where femininity and masculinity came to represent polar opposites and already made categories, neither of which she could embody and which she tried to escape through her gender oscillation.
> (Gozlan, 2015: 64)

S was unable to settle into an identification in which there was a possibility of the tolerance of otherness, so that her maleness could not tolerate her femininity and vice versa. Gozlan understands temporal boundaries as crucial in aiding the capacity for differentiation, and sees sexual difference as an area in which temporality and atemporality are held in suspense. If they cannot be, as was the case for S, who could not relate to her body as a signifier for integration that was wished for (but rather a dreaded repetition of past enmeshment with mother), she was unable to return to the past, unable to settle in the present, and the future was not imaginable (2015: 65). Seligman as discussed by Vermeule earlier corroborates the arrest of past, present and future as viable constructs.

For Gozlan, it was important not to get caught up in the decision for S about whether to transition, but his concern was what S did in relation to her reality and desire (2015:70). This impasse of integration within the self, born of complex internal and external family dynamics, highlights the fragile relationships between temporality, the location of sexual identity, and the wish for a concrete solution enacted in or on the body.

In this chapter I have explored the unique temporality of trans identity, and suggest that it can bypass linear and developmental time. As it can inhabit a space that is outside historical time, it meets conceptualisations of the unconscious more than the conscious. It resonates with Scarfone's atemporal category of the Infantile Sexual in that it transcends history as generated and historicised, and with time as *temporally folded* (Baraitser, 2017). I have leaned on the concept of après-coup, and applied it to experiences of resignification in 'afterwardness' and 'beforeness'. This space in time, or time in space can be thought of as an extinction or reinvention of temporality and a potentially creative solution to embodiment.

Notes

1 Faimberg (2005) mentions other authors' proposed translations: retrospective attribution (Thomäs & Cheshire, 1991), afterwardness (Laplanche, 1998) and retranscription of memory (Modell, 1990).
2 This is translated by Faimberg (2005).
3 T is used as shorthand for testosterone.
4 This is the term used by Gozlan (2015).

Bibliography

Augustine of Hippo, Saint. (1876; 1943). *The confessions of Saint Augustine* (J. G. Pilkington, Trans.). New York: Liveright Publishing Corp.

Baraitser, L. (2017). *Enduring time*, pp. 1–188. London: Bloomsbury Academic.

Birksted-Breen, D. (2003). Time and the *après-coup*. *International Journal of Psychoanalysis*, *84*, 1501–1515.

Botella, C., & Botella, S. (2005). *The work of psychic figurability*. London and New York: Routledge.

Butler, J. (2014). Seduction, gender and the drive. In J. Fletcher & N. Ray (Eds.), *Seductions & enigmas, Laplanche, theory, culture* (chapter 5, pp. 118–133). London: Lawrence and Wishart Limited.

Erpenbeck, J. (2020). Time. In *Not a novel* (pp. 42–44). London: Granta Publications.

Faimberg, H. (2005). *The telescoping of generations: Listening to the narcissistic links between generations*. London: Routledge.

Faimberg, H. (2005). Après-coup. *International Journal of Psychoanalysis*, *86*(1), 1–6.

Fink, K. (1989). From symmetry to asymmetry. *International Journal of Psychoanalysis*, *70*, 481 489.

Fletcher, J. (1992). The letter in the unconscious: The enigmatic signifier in the work of Jean Laplanche. In J. Fletcher & M. Stanton (Eds.), *Jean Laplance: Seduction, translation, and the drives* (pp. 93–120). London, ICA.

Fletcher, J., & Ray, N. (Eds.) (2014). *Seductions & enigmas, Laplanche, theory, culture*. London: Lawrence and Wishart Limited.

Fletcher, J., Stanton, M., & Stanton, M. (Eds.) (1992). *Seduction, translation, drives*. London: Institute of Contemporary Arts.

Fonagy, P., & Target, M. (1996). Playing with reality: 1. Theory of mind and the normal development of psychic reality. *International Journal of Psychoanalysis*, *77*, 217–233.

Freud, S. (1895) as cited in Green 2008.

Freud, S. (1914). Remembering, repeating and working through (Further recommendations on the technique of psycho-analysis II). *Standard Edition* (Vol. 12, pp. 145–157). London: Hogarth Press.

Freud, S. (1919). The uncanny. In *Standard Edition* (Vol. 18, pp. 145–172). London: Hogarth Press.

Freud, S. (1940) as cited in Matte Blanco 1975.

Gozlan, O. (2015). The "real" time of gender. In *Transsexuality and the art of transitioning* (chapter 5, pp. 58–72). East Sussex and New York: Routledge.

Green, A. (2008). Freud's concept of temporality: Differences with current ideas. *International Journal of Psychoanalysis*, *89*(5), 1029–1039.

Holmes, J. (2000). Psychotherapy and general practice: Evidence, narrative and the 'New Deal' in mental health. *Psychoanalytic Psychotherapy*, *14*(2), 129–141.

House, J. (2017). The ongoing rediscovery of après-coup as a Central Freudian concept. *Journal of the American Psychoanalytic Association*, *65*, 773–798.

Israeli-Nevo, A. (2018). Taking (my) time: Temporality in transition, queer delays, and being (in the) present. In O. Gozlan (Ed.), *Current critical debates in the field of transsexual studies, in transition* (chapter 4, pp. 59–71). London & New York: Routledge.

Kernberg, O. F. (1993). Convergences and divergences in contemporary psychoanalytic technique. *International Journal of Psychoanalysis*, *74*, 659–673.

Kierkegaard, S. (1843). KJN, 167/SKS 18, 194; JJ 167

Lacan, J. (1953, 2004). The function and field of speech and language in psychoanalysis. In B. Fink, H. Fink, & R. Grid (Eds.), *Écrits: A selection*. New York: Norton.

Lacan, J. (1955). *The seminar book II: The ego in Freud's theory and in the technique of psychoanalysis, 1954-1955*, J. A. Miller (Ed.), (S. Tamaselli, Trans.). New York: Norton, 1988.

Laplanche, J. (1987). *New foundations for psychoanalysis* (J. House, Trans.). New York: The Unconscious in Translation, 2016.

Laplanche, J. (1999). The drive and it's source object. *Essays on otherness* (Chapter 3, pp 117–132. London & New York: Routledge.

Laplanche, J. (2002). Après-coup. In A. de Mijolla (Ed., Trans.), *Dictionnaire International de la psychanalyse* (p. 121). Paris: Calmann-Levy.

Laplanche, J. (1998, 1999). Notes on afterwardness. *Essays on otherness* (pp. 260–265). London and New York: Routledge.

Laplanche, J. (2007). Gender, sex, and the sexual. *Studies in Gender and Sexuality*, 8(2), 201–219.

Laplanche, J., & Pontalis, J. B. (1973, 1967). 'Phallus', in *The language of psychoanalysis*, 1973: 312–314. London: Karnac.

Lutyen, P., Van Houdenhove, B., Lemma, A., Target, M., & Fonagy, P. (2012). A mentalisation-based approach to the understanding and treatment of functional somatic disorders. *Psychoanalytic Psychotherapy*, 26(2), 121–140.

Masson, J. M. (1985). Periodicity and self analysis. In J. M. Masson (Ed., Trans.), *The complete letters of Sigmund Freud to Willhelm Fliess 1887-1904* (pp. 207–263). Cambridge, Massachusetts, and London, England: The Belknap Press of Harvard University Press.

Matte Blanco, I. (1975). *The unconscious as infinite sets: An essay in bi-logic* (pp. 35–47). London: Duckworth.

McConnell, F. (2020). the guardian.com/society/2020/nov/16/trans-man-loses-uk-legal-battle-to-register-as-his-childs-father

Modell, A. (1990). *Other times, other realities*. Cambridge, MA: Harvard University Press.

Muñoz, J. E. (2006). Thinking beyond antirelationality and antiutopianism in queer critique. *PMLA*, *121*(3), 825–826.

Phillips, R. (2015). Constructing a theory and practice of black quantum futurism: Part one. In R. Phillips (Ed.), *Black quantum futurism: Theory & practice* (Vol. 1, pp. 11–30). Philadelphia: AfroFuturist Affair.

Ray (2020) Interview (anonymised).

Saketopoulou, A. (2017). Between Freud's second and third essays on sexuality: Commentary on Hansbury. *Journal of the American Psychoanalytic Association*, *65*(6), 1033–1048.

Saketopoulou, A. (2017a). Structured like culture: Laplanche on the translation of parental enigma. *Division Review*, *17*, 51–52.

Saketopoulou, A. (2023). Toward a theory of traumatophilia (chapter 4, pp. 131–168), *Sexuality beyond consent: Risk, race, traumatophilia*. New York: New York University Press.

Scarfone, D. (2002). Sexual and actual. In D. Widlöcher (Ed.), *Infantile sexuality and attachment* (chapter 5, pp. 97–110). London: Karnac.

Scarfone, D. (2014). The three essays and the meaning of the sexual in psychoanalysis. *The Psychoanalytic Quarterly*, *83*(2), 327–344.

Scarfone, D. (2015). *The unpast: The actual unconscious*. New York: The Unconscious in Translation.

Seligman, S. (2016). Disorders of temporality and the subjective experience of time: Unresponsive objects and the vacuity of the future. *Psychoanalytic Dialogues*, *26*(2), 110–128.

Serres, M. (1991). *Rome: The book of foundations*. Stanford, CA: Stanford University Press.

Seth (2020). Interview (anonymised).

Tan, A. (2018). *Where the past begins: Memory and imagination*. London: 4th Estate.

Thomä, H., & Cheshire, N. (1991). Freud's concept of *Nachträglichkeit* and Strachey's 'deferred action': Trauma, constructions and the direction of causality. *International Review of Psychoanalysis 3*, 401–445.

Vermeule, B. (2016). The writer and the analyst on and in time. *Psychoanalytic Dialogues*, *26*, 142–146.

Widlöcher, D. (1994). A case is not a fact. *International Journal of Psychoanalysis*, *75*, 1233–1244.

Zack (2020). Interview (anonymised).

Chapter 6

No Man's Land

It can be challenging for a psychoanalytic stance and a trans stance towards gender identity to find common ground, without the more obvious oppositional pitfalls around unconscious processes and historical narratives intruding, but it is not or should not be impossible. 'Transpsychoanalytics' (Cavanagh, 2017) is an attempt to bring trans theory insights and experience into dialogue with psychoanalysis, "… without erasing the tensions between the psychoanalytic emphasis on the unconscious and the project for trans liberation" (Osserman, 2024: 1–2). Within the shifting landscape of gender, adults that include parents, teachers and clinicians (medical, psychiatric, psychological and psychoanalytic) are required to keep up with children and adolescents so as not to neglect them (Corbett, 2016). Not neglecting children's (gender variance) needs can have a breadth of possibilities different to a need for action, which is sometimes seen to be the best solution to unhappiness and body incongruence by the child, adolescent, young adult, older adult, parent or clinician. Taking physical action is often more instinctive (and certainly more impulsive) than pausing for reflection that includes consideration of unconscious processes. Acting on a problem can give the delusion of solving it.

Winnicott (1971) highlighted the important distinction between doing and being. He understood *being* as that which occurs in early ego organisation, through object-relating of 'the pure female element' whether this was in males or females. The object-relating of the male element he understood as pre-supposing separateness, which comes later to the basic establishment of being from birth. "The male element *does* while the female element (in males and females) *is*" (1971: 80–81). This division might read as old fashioned now, and much has been written about the attribution of passivity to femaleness. A particularly interesting stance is explored by Benjamin (2004), who states that "femininity cannot be seen as a thing separate from masculinity, for the two are truly constructs created in the same moment, for the same purpose". She sees it as constructed by the male psyche, one that needs to be shored up from the threat of Oedipal loss, exclusion and overstimulation (Benjamin, 2004: 46).

There has been much conflict within the psychological and psychoanalytic field about the ethics of early intervention with puberty blockers in gender development. The rise in adolescent referrals has become an international phenomenon, noticed

DOI: 10.4324/9781032718613-7

across North America, Europe, Scandinavia and elsewhere (Zucker, 2019). The issue of consent came to a head in December 2020, (Bell-v-Tavistock, 2020) when a case was brought against GIDS (the Tavistock's Gender Identity Development Service), which resulted in a High Court ruling deeming that patients under 16 should not be assumed to have the capacity to consent to interventions. There was a subsequent Appeal by the Tavistock that was upheld (Bell-v-Tavistock, 2021); as a result, it was decided that "it was for clinicians to exercise their judgement knowing how important it was for the patient's consent to be properly obtained according to the particular individual's circumstances" (2021: 5). There are ethical tensions around the parameters of care deemed to be affirmative, as I go onto discuss in more detail below.

One school of thought promotes the notion that children and adolescents ought to be given the freedom to *know themselves* in relation to their gender identification. This has been termed 'the gender affirmative model of care'[1], which has become the prevalent course of action in working with teens identifying as trans in different contexts. Ehrensaft is an advocate of this method; she states: "When it comes to knowing a child's gender, it is not for us to tell, but for the children to say" (Ehrensaft, 2017: 63). But as Marchiano (2021), a Jungian analyst based in Philadelphia, points out:

> … it may foreclose thinking about a young person's development by conflating gender dysphoria with trans identification, and it may concretize an adolescent's desire to transition, without extended exploration and assessment.
>
> (Marchiano, 2021: 824)

The exploration that becomes possible post transition, or post detransition can be thought of as requiring more of what Klein termed 'depressive position' functioning. This capacity necessitates both mourning and repentance for more aggressive and disorganised impulsive ways of being. In Klein's writing this is specifically described as the infant's early attacks onto and into the mother's body. This is relevant to my understanding of what can take place in the drive to transition from female to male, in which the mother's body has a place in the unconscious. Ambivalent feelings towards a mother from a daughter are not unique to trans men, and I have discussed this more in Chapters 2 and 3. Whereas once the contention was about the age of consent for sex, it has now become about the age of consent for puberty blockers. In question also is the individual capacity (discussed later in this chapter) for intra-psychic (the internal dialogue between different parts of the psyche) consent, agreeing and endorsing the part of the self that knows one's felt gender. I will discuss detransitioning as a contentious and at times more silenced or hidden aspect of gender identity that merits consideration, empathy, acknowledgement and research.

Sometimes the reality of the transitioned body does not live up to prior wishes or phantasies, and can lead to a wish to detransition. This can bring about a melancholic aspect of gender identity as once desired and not achieved, or can be thought of as a secondary and more delayed melancholic experience; the first one having precipitated the drive to transition. The disappointment of having to live with irreversible changes to the body, via hormones or surgery, that were once actively and determinedly sought or encouraged, is a painful process and requires a capacity to mourn earlier wishes and look back at a younger and driven self; or indeed at how that younger self might have been driven by others, whose focus albeit well-meaning was in the direction of active physical changes. Psychic difficulties that are complex and often comorbid require in-depth exploration, and more opportunity for careful consideration, before embarking on major changes to the body that cannot be entirely reversed. This is easier said than done when a clinician is faced with a (usually but not exclusively) young person, who might well have been experiencing a deep sense of gender incongruence for a protracted length of time.

Disavowed Affects Find Hosts

Silber (2019), a clinical psychologist based in the United States, who works primarily with children, adolescents and families attributed to Harris (2005) the notion that "disavowed affects find hosts: one of them, located in gender". Silber goes onto say: "In a plea for complexity, it is not to suggest all ruptures are expressed through varying gender and not all gender variance (variance by definition) is the same" (2019: 136). Her article (2019) sets out to better comprehend what might be encrypted in gender in the form of ruptures in which there has been an "inability to hold tensions of sameness and difference, both within the self and within the relational matrix" (2019: 136). Silber argues, via her clinical work with children and adolescents, that it is not only race that connects to ancestry but also gender, albeit in a different way (2019: 134). She cites Brubaker's statement:

> The landscape of identities has become more complex, fluid and fragmented. As new categories have proliferated and old categories have come to seem ill fitting, we increasingly face uncertainties and ambiguities in identifying ourselves and categorizing others. ... the very act of categorization itself-have been challenged.
>
> (Brubaker, 2016: 41)

Marchiano (2021) documents the experience of detransition for one of her young patients, that she refers to as Maya, who came for help once she had decided to dis-identify from her trans male identification and re-identify as female. One of the aspects of Maya's early history was the sudden loss of her aunt, which had caused a significant rupture. At the time of her aunt's death, there was no space for grief, and so it remained frozen, unmourned and unformulated. Marchiano wondered if Maya's adolescent gender dysphoria may have been her psyche's way of "giving expression to split-off and unformulated grief related to significant attachment ruptures" (2021: 818). Jung is cited as having been prescient in stating that "the body is often the personification of the shadow of the ego. Sometimes it forms a skeleton in a cupboard and everybody wants to get rid of it" (Jung, 1950, in Marchiano, 2021: 818). Marchiano acknowledges Jung's foresight into the desire in contemporary culture to escape or alter the body "… as a way of avoiding contact with reviled, instinctual parts of ourselves" (2021: 818), which may also have relevance when distress is somatised via eating disorders, self-harm or gender dysphoria. Marciano speculated whether Maya's trans identification was her attempt to relegate intolerable affect to the body, so that the emotional losses became concrete, and her vulnerable feminine side gained more illusion of control through a masculine identification (2021: 818–819). As the psychotherapy progressed, a more defensive aspect of Maya's wish to transition became clearer, especially in connection to her mother and how she perceived her mother's expectations of her (then) daughter. The transition had allowed her to claim some authority and aggression.

The testimonies of detransitioners' experiences (many posted online) offer useful insight into gender dysphoria and varied approaches to clinical practice. Entwistle (2021) asserts that "It seems unlikely that gender clinicians envisage that females would detransition after being prescribed testosterone, mastectomy and hysterectomy but they have" (Entwistle 2021: 15). In recent years case studies of gender detransition in psychoanalytic journals and more data in medical journals is beginning to emerge (Butler & Hutchinson, 2020; Entwistle, 2021; Expósito-Campos, 2021; Marciano, 2020, 2021; Zucker et al., 2018, 2020). This has given insight into what can at one stage of life necessitate action, and at another become more available for reflection; later reflection with retrospective insight can help an understanding of earlier actions and medical interventions. This does not undermine the positive experience of gender transition for non-detransitioners, who can and do experience much relief from hormonal intake and or surgical procedures.

People who have chosen to stop their pathway toward transition are referred to as 'desisters' and those who opt to reverse their transition are referred to as 'detransitioners'. Articles written on this subject suggest that there is a dearth of guidance or support for this cohort, which may in part stem from anxieties that paying attention to the experiences of desisters and detransitioners might compromise the legitimacy of persisters' experiences (Butler & Hutchinson, 2020, Cohn, J. 2023).

Safe Disclosure & Premature Foreclosure

From 2019 in the United Kingdom, services modelled on commissioning guidance from NHS England for adults of 17 years and above allowed for self-referral, precluded psychological formulation or therapeutic intervention as standard practice, and recommended hormonal intervention after two appointments. This led to more hormonal and surgical interventions in young patients who bypassed pubertal development and the necessary mental health treatment in their pathway towards interventions, which could have detrimental effects not foreseen and potentially regretted later on (Griffin et al., 2021).

The substantial growth in gender variance in recent decades has led to more gender-identity clinics in the United States, the United Kingdom, the Netherlands,

Finland and some other European countries. The Gender Identity Service (GIDS), which was based at the Tavistock (1966–2024), was Britain's only specialised gender service for children and adolescents. The Tavistock recorded a 25-fold rise in referrals since 2009, most marked in biological girls ('assigned female at birth'), who made up the majority of referrals at the time of this data (GIDS, 2020). A chequered history of prejudice and denial towards transgender individuals has required a shift in the epistemic understanding of clinical and medical structures of *what it means to be trans*. The exponential growth of individuals wishing to move along the pathway towards transition has necessitated more specialised clinical input, provided by specialised GIDS clinics. There is much variance within and between clinical approaches, ranging from the 'gender affirmative' approach to the more psychoanalytic/exploratory model which takes into account conscious as well as unconscious influences on the mind's capacity to make a choice, takes personal history and family dynamics into account, and requires more time. These differing approaches run the risk of becoming binary, and hence oppositional, which they may not necessarily need to be. Lemma discusses the complex ethics of 'autonomy' when it comes to making life changing decisions to or on the body (Lemma, 2022; Lemma & Savulescu 2023). Premature foreclosure can occur when children and adolescents are at times propelled into medical transitioning too quickly, which can result in the later wish to detransition with its attendant complexities.

Ethical Supply Chains

Wren, who worked for many years at GIDS, discusses (2021) the 'hammering' that this service experienced from both internal and external sources. She speaks plainly about the difficult ethical questions that the work of this clinic faced, a clinic that from the outset took a stance of 'non-judgemental acceptance'. The shift in social attitudes towards sex and gender minorities alongside the right to self-determination by the mid-2000s inevitably had an impact on how the clinic operated. She states:

> If treatment was only to be offered following a period of therapeutic exploration, how much exploration was 'enough'? If puberty blockers were prescribed to hold open future gender options, might they also serve sometimes to narrow down these options? Which children were at risk if we withheld treatment? What features of an autistic presentation and what degree, would hamper an ability to consent? How could we balance possible future suffering (if the person came to see the physical changes made as unwanted or unnecessary) over suffering in the here and now?
>
> (Wren, 2021: 47)

Ironically, in the light of later developments, these kinds of questions gave GIDS a reputation for being cautious or conservative. But, as Wren describes, the overload of referrals after 2015, the removal of any filter for referrals in

2016 and the major increase in online discussions about gender identity all contributed to a changed landscape. Some of these changes came from gender non-conforming young people more able to speak out online, and increased awareness of improved medical interventions and greater social accommodation of modifications to the body. Waiting lists soared, with a noticeably high proportion of assigned female at birth referrals as an internationally recognised pattern. One noticeable challenge for the staff at GIDS was a greater intolerance from families towards the relatively slow-paced model of care that it offered (Wren, 2021: 48).

In her reflections on one of the accusations levelled at GIDS about the insufficient research evidence to enable medical therapies to be offered with confidence, Wren makes the salient point that:

> Put simply, many questions around treatment are not settled by science alone, because scientific knowledge is itself social knowledge. When we devise treatment plans, we inevitably work within what society considers a just response to suffering; our research is based on culturally derived ideals about what constitutes a good and worthwhile life; treatment decisions reflect prevalent notions of self-determination, including of the rights of minors.
>
> (Wren, 2021. 48)

Wren explained that GIDS didn't trade in firm convictions, which meant operating with a degree of uncertainty and at times accompanying moral unease. She cites the 'epistemic injustice' that trans, non-binary and queer people are subjected to as knowledge holders within healthcare systems, because "society as a whole lacks an adequate interpretative framework to understand their experiences" (2021: 48). She goes onto say that for some advocates, this justice based approach stretches itself to the demand "that all gender-diverse people, including the young, should have the unquestionable right to make fully autonomous treatment decisions – the full freedom, we might say, *to make their own mistakes*" (my italics). Although this was never GIDS' stance, it is an argument that is being debated in the courts. Wren asks poignant questions about parental discretion, how children and adolescents' competence is ensured, and last but not least "… if young people, with or without their parents, are deemed competent, where does the responsibility lie if there are subsequent feelings of regret?" (Wren, 2021: 48). Put slightly differently and in relation to adults Lemma asks "… what justifies the epistemic superiority of certain people to determine when others are 'mistaken' about their own interests and self-understanding?" (Lemma, 2023: 48).

Ethical considerations play a vital role in gender identity, whether this is in the wish to transition or the wish to detransition. The four principles of biomedical ethics, as outlined by Beauchamp and Childress (2013), have become the cornerstones of biomedical ethics in healthcare practice. These are autonomy, non-maleficence, beneficence and justice. The role of autonomy in the doctor–patient relationship has changed over time from one that was grounded in paternalism – denoting a deferral to the doctor's view – to a more joint decision-making process involving both participants.

Lemma and Savulescu (2023), in their article: 'To be, or not to be? The role of the unconscious in transgender transitioning: identity, autonomy and well-being', skilfully address ethical complexities that are necessarily part of the decision-making process towards medical transition. Although I cannot include all aspects of the intricate analysis in their article, I will summarise elements from it that I found pertinent. The concept of 'well-being' is dissected in relation to 'acceptance' and 'best interests', which opens up the question of what constitutes an ethical response to transgender individuals' consciously stated claims about how best to promote their well-being. One of the article's central claims is the extent to which *unconscious forces may undermine autonomy*, for both children and adults. They look at how 'acceptance' of an individual's self-diagnosis as transgender can work against best interests where distress, as located in the body, results from another psychological and/or societal problem. Importantly they advocate acceptance that the transgender individual has a unique perspective on what can make a positive difference to their predicament. However, there are tensions and conflicts between the individual's own desires and evaluation of their own interests and right to choose what they consider to be in their best interests, and the authority embedded in medical and psychological 'expertise' in relation to what makes a life go well. Drawing on ethical debates on well-being that include a composite welfarist view, Lemma and Savulescu lean towards a fundamental principle of bioethics, which suggests patients should be offered interventions that are in their best interests. This might include consideration of the benefits of medical transitioning if the psychological benefits exceed the physical harms.

Values inevitably come into consideration, even though they are subjective and idiosyncratic when applied to gender as this quote demonstrates: "… how one feels in one's body relative to one's idiosyncratic experience of gender is a subjective state, such that it would be very difficult to assign an objective value to it" (Lemma & Savulescu, 2023: 67). The ethical component of values also traverses the societal, cultural and political terrain. In recent decades one cannot take politics out of gender-ethics, or gender-ethics out of politics. The binary of us and them has many manifestations, whether it is the trans individual at the mercy of healthcare services; the healthcare services' accountability; children, adolescents, or young adults and their parents; gender and government policy and differing models of care or schools of thought in relation to gender identity. This can leave a zone of danger, a 'no man's land' in which one can be shot at from both sides, blurring the parameters of safety.

Lemma extends her exploration of ethics in her book *First Principles: Applied Ethics for Psychoanalytic Practice* (Lemma: 2023). Within this broad and in-depth examination many foundational elements of ethics are carried over to the dilemmas that clinicians face in their psychoanalytic practice, in order to advocate an 'ethical self-discipline'. My interest lies in the ethical dilemmas that are embedded in complex aspects of gender identity to include questions of autonomy, well-being and self-knowledge.

It can be hard to distinguish distress that might result from other psychological and/or societal problems. In previous research I found that the trans men that I interviewed invariably presented experiences of anorexia, depression, suicidality, self-harm and autistic spectrum disorder, alongside their transition from female to male. The comorbid aspect of trans identity does not undermine the validity of their lived gender identity but nonetheless merits serious consideration as part of the complex choice making process. A counter argument, and indeed one that several interviewees made, was that other psychic struggles *were caused by* gender-identity issues, and hence gender was the *central* difficulty. The comorbidity is posited not with the intention of decentring gender-identity issues, but as an important concurrent consideration.

The Certification of Self

Salient aspects of the research data that Lemma and Savulescu (2023) gather in their article are focussed on whether 'self-certification as transgender' may reflect other psychological and/or societal problems. I will mention three of these (points 1, 3 & 4 in their article) that are relevant to my chapter. The first strand states that cross-sex identity during childhood is "overwhelmingly predictive of homosexual orientation in adulthood" (Lemma & Savulescu, 2023: 67) and the importance of safeguarding against conversion therapy by another name. In my research and interviews with trans men, they all identified as female and gay before embarking on the route towards a trans male identity. Most of the interviewees did not like being identified as lesbians in their past history prior to identifying as trans and expressed discomfort and incongruence with this identity. Remaining female and gay was unwanted and rejected (see Patterson, 2018). Returning to Lemma and Savulescu's research, the third strand mentioned is that as natal girls are twice as likely as natal boys to be referred to GID services, this urges the investigation of the role that social processes may play in the over-representation of girls. The fourth strand as quoted:

> The number of medically transitioned people coming forward now who regret transitioning is rising and has led to the creation in the UK of the Detransition Advocacy Network. These narratives indicate that some people consider that they had not been challenged enough to explore their reasons for wanting to transition. The recent legal case against the GID at the Tavistock Clinic is a case in point.
>
> (Lemma & Savulescu, 2023: 67)

The meaning of autonomy is convoluted when unconscious factors can interfere with a capacity to consent and the ability to gauge one's sense of well-being. The wish to detransition highlights the difficulty of what was once a strongly held belief, subsequently and retrospectively reconsidered après-coup. As Lemma and

Savulescu point out, the possibility of future regret does not provide a strong argument for withholding treatment; however, encouraging the patient to reflect on the possibility of future regret can be very helpful in the decision-making aspect of treatment (Lemma & Savulescu, 2023: 68).

The role of the unconscious has been curiously absent from the more public debates on gender identity, even though it is held in the minds of clinicians who work or write psychoanalytically. This is an example of the kinds of division that I discuss in relation to 'No Man's Land' later in this chapter. The Cass Report (April 2024) is long, detailed and wide-ranging, and makes a concerted effort to understand the unprecedented demand and change in the demographic of young people accessing gender services with reference to the complex interplay of biological, psychological and social factors. However, it was noticeable that there was no mention of psychoanalytic ways of working with gender variance, and the words psychotherapy or psychotherapists occur a total of six times in the entire 388-page document, three of these in the bibliography. Reference to the unconscious only appears twice, once in a reference and once in relation to unconscious bias in questionnaire design. Within the report's section on training and education, recommendations around a consortium to develop a competency framework refer to 'The Association of Psychotherapists' (2024: 212) which, as far as I'm aware, is not an existing organisation. Four of the main (although not only) accrediting organisations in the United Kingdom: The British Psychoanalytic Council, United Kingdom Council for Psychotherapy, The Association of Child Psychotherapists and British Association of Counselling and Psychotherapy are not mentioned. The training suggestions are advocating specific training for gender dysphoria, but appear to overlook a large existent body of psychotherapists, many trained to work specifically with adolescents. As this report is designed to encompass wide ranging studies and research, these absences feel somewhat stark. Another difficulty of the report is the absence of material from GIDS, as GIDS was unwilling to provide it, not least perhaps as it had been under attack in the last few years. Perhaps unsurprisingly, the Cass Report and Dr Hilary Cass have been at the receiving end of polarised views in the form of strong projections and objections. Some of these have been specifically in relation to its approach to puberty blockers, although NHS England are more the 'decision makers' in this context.

This absence of the unconscious might be in part because gender can have connotations of immutability, certainty and conviction, in spite of the more fluid aspects that it also denotes. Although gender is embodied, it is the mind that gives shape to the thoughts and feelings about and towards the body. Gender identity or identification cannot be divorced from desire, object relationships and unconscious phantasy that are conflictual and in flux. As Lemma reminds us, "… the representation we have of our bodies in our minds is profoundly shaped by the projections of others – often early attachment figures – onto our bodies" (Lemma & Savulescu, 2023: 69). Lemma and Savulescu favour the inclusion of the processing of unconscious influences on the mind and brain as part of the period of exploration, optimally through psychoanalytic psychotherapy prior to decision making for transgender individuals.

They argue that this can increase the range of autonomous functioning, as it incorporates the possibility of considering the unconscious meaning of transgender identification. By contrast unqualified acceptance, whether this resides in the transgender individual or in the nature of affirmative care, can lead to premature foreclosure, and this in turn can sometimes lead to the wish to detransition. Conscious choices have blind spots that can only become more visible if they are noticed or highlighted by clinicians with experience of working with unconscious processes. Lemma and Savulescu argue that time for self-reflection is ethically significant as it supports autonomous decision making through the piecemeal elaboration of unconscious meaning that can only emerge over time. In their words: "this is why unqualified acceptance of conscious claims can lead to unintended harms" (Lemma & Savulescu, 2023: 71).

Zucker (2020), a Canadian psychiatrist, points out that the field of gender social transition in prepubertal children suffers from the "vexing problem" of no randomised control trials of different treatment approaches, which leaves the frontline clinician having to rely on lower-order levels of evidence in deciding what the optimal approach to treatment might be. He argues that there are three main approaches for children: firstly, active psychosocial treatment to reduce gender dysphoria so that the child's eventual gender identity is likely to adhere more to their biological sex, secondly, watchful waiting without the clinician recommending a direction one way or the other and thirdly, gender social transition, meaning that the child's social gender is lived as the 'putative desired gender', and shifted away from the gender assigned at birth. He believes that if a social transition model is adopted (the third option) the rate of gender dysphoria persistence will be much higher as the child moves into adolescence and young adulthood. I suggest that the likelihood of a move towards medical transitioning and the potential for detransitioning can also increase, if the social transitioning is enacted prematurely via an affirmative approach that can overlook less visible complexity. This does not suggest or advocate for a negation or denial of gender dysphoria at an early age.

In his article about gender dysphoria in children, Schwartz (2012) a psychologist in the United States who has written prolifically on the subjects of sexuality and gender, points out how the medical sciences push against ambiguity and refrain from emphasising the lack of data from controlled studies. He describes the challenge for clinicians of making the "child/parent symptom matrix" fit a liberal psychiatric treatment model (2012: 461). Schwartz is surprised by the lack of ambivalence in relation to their gender identity in trans children, and the lack of experiential dimensions in both subject and observer. He is struck by the "assumed mutability of gender" of which children propose to avail themselves, and by the differences in approaches with which a clinician can lean into the child's narrative: either literally, or symbolically and metaphorically, via an interpretive process. When clinicians hold essential gender in mind, Schwartz thinks that their approach is likely to be less psychologically minded not least as children speak more symbolically than adults. He cautions against the assumption (Edwards-Leeper & Spack, 2012) that gender is a primary physical rather than psychological condition, especially in children. He is empathic towards parents and clinicians caught up in the turmoil of the child's demands that can lead to the belief that gender is biologically real, rather than a subjectivity (2012: 473–476).

Marchiano and Silber, echoing Schwartz, Zucker as well as Lemma and Savulescu demonstrate how useful and essential a space for reflection is. This is usually a space that was not necessarily available for representation in the past, so that grief or trauma had the potential to become arrested or somatised. What I have taken from these authors is that the absence of metaphor, symbolisation or representation can leave a lacuna that can attach itself to gender.

The metaphor of 'the affect finding a host' is poignant, not least as the body becomes the host of the affect when the psyche is unable to bear the pressure of hosting affect that cannot be represented. Unrepresentable states of mind have been written about widely in psychoanalytic literature, Bion (1962) refers to Beta elements and 'nameless dread', the Botellas refer to psychic figurability (2005), Levine refers to not-yet-emerged elements in the mind (2012: 44). Lombardi (2002, 2008, 2017) has written about the importance of the body in the consulting room, not only the mind, and how helpful it is for the analyst to attune themselves to the way in which a patient brings in their body and all that it is attempting to communicate through its unrepresentable struggles. Lombardi is unusual in his capacity for the sensitive use of his own bodily countertransference, which can sometimes be overlooked in psychoanalytic work, in which the mind, psyche and mental apparatus can often take precedence.

Castration, Metaphor & Reality

In her examination of metaphor, Freeman Sharpe (1940: 201) maintains that the use of metaphor in language is psycho–physical, and she cites Grindon (1879) who claimed that "No word … is metaphysical without its having first been physical" (Grindon, 1879, as cited in Freeman Sharpe, 1940). Freeman Sharpe's theory is that it is only after the control of bodily orifices (in my understanding this denotes an inside, outside, retention and emission) that metaphor can evolve in language or the arts. Early experiences of infant life are expressed through metaphor, thus converting the material to the immaterial (1940: 202).

Three decades later, Fonagy and Target, express things similarly:

> Because abstract thought evolves from a bodily state it should not surprise us that cognition inevitably retains a link to the physical (bodily) acts from which it originates at the level of unconscious meaning and metaphor.
>
> (Fonagy & Target, 2007: 440)

Chaplin (2018), in 'How to be both by not being both: The articulation of psychic bisexuality within the analytic session' writes about the necessary psychic moves in (early) psychic bisexuality, that are requisites for the move from psychic (being both) to genital bisexuality (not being both). Through a clinical description Chaplin shows how she became caught up in her patient's protest about sexual difference, partly due to her patient's struggle to move into a capacity for metaphor or to metaphorise in her thinking. This relates to a capacity for representation (the primal scene) and symbolising. Her patient's reluctance to acknowledge sexual difference (she was excluded from being like the boys or men) made it harder for her to hold a parental couple in mind and hence relinquish a pre-oedipal state of being, in which she could be both (sexes). When Chaplin disrupted this delusion, her patient reacted strongly.

Chaplin states:

> We are born bisexual and yet we have to acquire bisexuality … [this involves] the renunciation of phallic bisexuality to genital bisexuality in which sexual difference is accepted and interiorized. This is the transition from bisexuality as defence to bisexuality as resource.
>
> (Chaplin, 2018: 224)

The subjective bisexual position for Chaplin via Freud, forms the basis for symbolisation and the capacity to think. In Mitchell's (2023) reading of this, patient and analyst between them acquire a newly achieved bisexuality as the basis for 'sexual difference', having overcome phallic bisexuality (2023: 181). The overcoming of phallic bisexuality as the 'being both' has to be relinquished as 'not being both' which necessitates an acceptance of castration (Chaplin is discussing her work with a female patient).

Marciano quotes Alderman who states: "when metaphors are made literal, the literal body becomes a vehicle for metaphoric expressions" (Brett Alderman in Marchiano, 2021). In some instances of transgender identity, a wish can be realised through using the body as a symbol which seems to echo Alderman's words. It is when this symbolic use of the body does not resolve or realise the wish, that the literal use of the metaphor requires translation.

Marchiano's paper includes material from a transcript of Livia, a 23-year-old detransitioned woman who had a mastectomy and hysterectomy when she was 20 and 21, respectively. Livia spoke at the Detransition Advocacy Network event in Manchester, United Kingdom in 2019. She put emphasis on the role of reality in her transition and detransition:

> It's really hard to focus on one thing but the word that's stuck in my mind the most is 'reality.' I feel like for me transition was a way to get out of my reality as a homosexual woman …. When we started this conversation the word that was important to me was 'reality'. And reality to me is that … a hysterectomy and removal of your ovaries doesn't make you any less female. So, it doesn't make any sense to me why this is called transition or a sex change because it's not it's castration. And now that I am trying to care for my health as much as possible, I spend a lot of time on hysterectomy support sites and message boards for women – for women because only women get hysterectomies, and only women deal with the consequences of a hysterectomy.
>
> (Livia, Marchiano, 2021: 826)

Livia is articulate about the unwished-for reality as a homosexual woman, and the drive towards transition as a way of side-stepping or even denying this reality. I found that my interviewees expressed similar feelings about their past female homosexual identity. This throws up the potential for internalised homophobia that then becomes externalised. In an article co-written for the *British Journal of Psychiatry Bulletin* (2021) re-evaluating the evidence for sex, gender and gender identity, the authors (Griffin et al.) discuss research papers about comorbidity amongst referrals to child and adolescent gender clinics in The Netherlands, Finland and the United Kingdom (de Vries et al., 2011; Holt et al., 2016; Kaltiala-Heino et al., 2015). In the UK-based research paper (Holt et al., 2016), it was amongst natal females that same sex attraction was especially prevalent, with only 8.5% of those referred to GIDS describing themselves as mainly attracted to boys. The authors of the *British Journal of Psychiatry Bulletin* paper are perturbed by this, and wonder about current societal acceptance of young lesbians even within youth LGBTQ+ culture. They state:

> It is possible that at least some gender-non-conforming girls come to believe themselves boys or 'trans masculine non binary' as more acceptable or comfortable explanations for same-sex sexual attraction, a kind of 'internalised homophobia'.
>
> (Griffin et al., 2021: 294)

Returning to Livia whom I mentioned earlier in this chapter, I am interested in her use of the term *castration* instead of *transition*. Castration and more usually castration anxiety are known terms in psychoanalytic literature, most obviously the small boy's anxiety of (phallic) castration in Freud's writing. It is more unusual to hear it used outside of psychoanalysis in the way that Livia is using it with more brutal connotations of having had a body part cut off or cut out. The literal and historical meaning of castration is the mutilation of testicles that render the body sterile. It also has a symbolic meaning that links to prohibition and law; this could be the law of the father or the law of the mother when the gratification of the child's desire is forbidden. Castration and its concomitant anxiety, although originally testicular have shifted to the penis as the threatened organ. I discuss this in Chapter 4.

Figlio points out the narrowing of an understanding of castration to phallic loss as located in the lost penis. He sees "castration proper" more as a loss of seminal function, a loss of being, not of an object. Figlio argues that "the phallic defence defends, not just against feminine vulnerability, but against seminality" (Figlio, 2024: 115, 130).

Mann introduces the idea of 'Castration Desire' (1994) as the small boy's desire to lose the penis so as to strengthen his identification with his mother, as a denial of difference and phantasy of fusion. He sees castration anxiety as a later development that enhances separation from the mother. His discussion left me wondering about the small girl's relationship to 'castration desire', particularly when linked to top surgery and hysterectomy which could be considered psychoanalytically as a return to a pre-pubescent body, one that was less differentiated into female and male. I am not suggesting that all trans related surgeries necessarily have unconscious regressive elements to them, but wondered about the drive to remove parts of the body that are quintessentially female (and reproductive), that can, in some cases, later on be perceived as a castration. Mann goes onto say that "The girl cannot wish to lose what she has not got" (Mann, 1994: 519), which is true in some respects, although the wish to 'lose' it necessitates an acknowledgement of what is there as well as the phantasy of *what is not there*, the phantasy of castration that Horney refers to. I think that she can very much want to lose what she has got and gain *what she has not got* in the form of innate maleness, or that which mother desires whether this is the father, the boy brother or the penis/phallus. This might drive her to 'castrate' aspects of her femaleness, in order to lose femaleness and achieve maleness as *that which was lost to her*. Horney (1926) expressed this poignantly in relation to castration phantasies in feminine development:

> I picture their origin as follows: when the woman takes refuge in the fictitious male role her feminine genital anxiety is to some extent translated into male terms – the fear of vaginal injury becomes *a phantasy of castration*. The girl gains by this conversion, for she exchanges the uncertainty of her expectation of punishment (an uncertainty conditioned by her anatomical formation) for a concrete idea.
>
> (Horney, 1926: 336) (my italics)

Dolto (1908–1988) was a French psychoanalyst who had a special interest in working with children. She wrote about 'Castrations' as a way to understand the losses incurred during developmental phases, when infantile desire is thwarted as a necessary move towards socialisation. This is a different take to that of Freud's on the dissolution of the Oedipus conflict, in which the (literal) fear of castration is that which limits the small boy's wish to marry his mother. Although Freud's ideas have been challenged, parental and clinical observation of children often affirms an early wish to assert ownership and partnership with the parent of the opposite sex and rejection of their same sex parent, optimally followed by acceptance of who belongs to who in the home environment. As an aside to this, a daughter who wishes to 'marry her father', or has a strong identification with her father and struggles to dissent from this in the direction of an identification with her mother has relevance in relation to the drive to pursue a masculine identity.

By treating the phallus and castration as imaginary and symbolic, Lacan attempted to translate Freud's ideas. For Lacan a symbolic castration is part of the route for the child towards accepting the Law-of-the-Father, within which the mother is not the sole 'property' of the child. Dolto uses the term 'symboligenic' (2023: 55) in relation to the castrations for the child, and these symboligenic castrations can either promote forwards development or be experienced as painful and pathogenic. She thought that castration was part of every stage of development: umbilical, oral, anal, pre-Oedipal and Oedipal (Dolto, 2023: 51–59). Bailly in Dolto (2023) stresses that Dolto's term 'symbologenic' is unlike the Kleinian understanding of symbol formation, and needs to be comprehended more in relation to Lacan's Borromean knot of real, symbolic and imaginary that form the structure of the psyche; in this sense it enhances the development of the Symbolic realm for the child (Dolto, 2023: 5–6).

As I understand Dolto, she sees castrations as pathways to managing necessary developmental separations or in her words 'tests of symbolic partitioning', initially from the mother and then from the father – required both for socialisation, and law within the family. Weaning separates a mother/infant dyad and moves the dynamic from an unseparated state to one in which the maternal presence takes on symbolic value as different. If the memory as a link is cut off, say if the mother disappeared or died, the child is left with the impossibility of symbolising a disappeared link. When this occurs, these drives that have become unbound abruptly from the relationship that validated the child's existence, return to the body of the child.

This notion of the trauma of loss becoming embodied is very relevant to how the psyche manages an overflow of affect that it cannot register or contain. This links to Marciano's patient Maya's experience of the sudden loss of her aunt as mentioned earlier in this chapter.

Detransitioner Experiences & Self Diagnosis in the Online Era

In the following section I include testimonies from detransitioners online, who speak openly about their experiences.

I quote a woman in the States who transitioned to a trans man and has retransitioned to being a woman. She now identifies as a biological woman and finds it distressing when she is identified as a trans woman. She hates her voice (impacted by testosterone) and would like to have voice feminisation surgery, but it is prohibitively expensive. She developed dysphoria after starting to take testosterone and missing being a woman. She expressed her misgivings online. I quote from what she said on YouTube:

> "Growing up, I couldn't pinpoint what my issues were and then I realised that it might be a gender issue"; "Before I went on hormone therapy, I wasn't required to see any therapist or any sort of doctor at all"; "The biggest mistake that I made was that I did not get the right therapy or medical advice needed"
>
> ('I Detransitioned. Here's what they will NEVER TELL YOU', YouTube)

> "Don't just see a therapist who will affirm what you think. Their job is not to tell you what they think you want to hear". She described the Trans Industry as a multi-billion dollar industry which is 'there to make money". She felt that detransitioners were being "shoved under the rug and hidden".
>
> ('I Detransitioned. Here's what they will NEVER TELL YOU', YouTube)

Below is a selection of reasons given for detransitioning in a female detransition and re-identification survey that took place between 16 and 30 August 2016, and was shared through online social networking sites:

> "No effort was made to explore if there were other mental health issues", "I feel I was duped into believing I was something I'm not", "Concern about loss of fertility", "Wanted to be a lesbian girl again", "Became more comfortable with my gender non-conformity, grew more into my femalehood", "Realised the dysphoria was the result of abuse", "My trauma was not examined at all".
>
> (Griffin et al., 2021: 296)

In a documentary called 'DETRANS', the first person to speak describes with her suffering from depression and use of the internet to self-diagnose. She became interested in having a male persona, and spent a lot of time online; the online experience felt real. She says: "Transitioning was the closest I could become to killing myself, without actually doing it". She recognises now her wish then "to alleviate pain, not to be who I was, and escape my identity as female" (DETRANS Documentary PragerU, 2023).

This has some resonance with my proposition in Chapter 3, in the context of matricide as an unconscious killing off of femininity associated with motherhood in the self.

Data provided in this documentary (Leor Sapir, PhD, Fellow at Manhattan Institute) asserted that double mastectomy on teenage girls increased 13-fold between 2013 and 2020; and between 2016 and 2019 alone, these procedures went up by 500% (DETRANS Documentary PragerU, 2023).

The documentary 'No Way Back' was made in the United States in 2023 (Deplorable Films). It charts the experiences of detransitioners, and how they look back at their younger selves and current bodies, usually with a sense of painful regret. They acknowledge the influence of the internet on their decisions to transition, and how they can now see that there were other underlying emotional struggles that located in gender dysphoria. There are also grievances about the speed with which they were able to start the process of transition, with insufficient exploration (from clinicians) at the early stages. The film includes material from a wide range of clinicians and researchers who speak about the huge phenomenon of gender dysphoria, the prevalence of the 'Informed Consent' model in the United States, and aspects of the industries that underlie and profit from gender transition. Dr Julia Masson, a paediatrician, speaks about how there is resistance from the American Academy of Paediatricians to address the ease with which hormones can be accessed by young trans individuals. Dr William Malone, an endocrinologist, likened the ease of access to medical/hormonal aspects of transition to the opioid epidemic of Oxycontin. The journalist Jennifer Bilek's articles (2018) which question the institutionalisation of transgender ideology are referred to in the documentary. She voices her view that the transgender phenomenon is not connected to identity but part of corporate marketing selling a product very successfully. In the documentary, there is mention of research that questions the transgender trajectory for young people from Sweden, Finland and England; but a resistance to questioning this in the States. The author and journalist Lisa Selin Davis makes a plea for more to be done to re-think many aspects of the current climate of gender transition, while remaining open to gender variance. She acknowledges the dangers of speaking out about these kinds of reservations.

In a study in the United States of 100 individuals initially treated for gender dysphoria with medical and/or surgical transition who then detransitioned, Littman (2021), a physician scientist, set out to describe this population in order to understand better some of the underlying factors of the motivation both to transition and detransition. The study was not initiated to assess the prevalence of detransition as an outcome of transition, but rather to identify reasons for and narratives of detransition, so as to inform clinical care and future research. It is one of the largest samples of detransitioners to date, and included more natal females (69.0%) than natal males (31.0%), with 55.1% of natal female participants reporting that their gender dysphoria started at puberty or later. The online survey was active between 2016 and 2017, and participation was voluntary. A majority of participants (56.7%) felt that the evaluation by a doctor or mental health professional preceding transition was not adequate, with 65.3% reporting that the clinicians did no evaluation of whether their desire to transition was secondary to trauma or a mental health condition. Almost half of the participants (46.0%) reported their pre-transition counselling as overly positive, and not sufficiently negative about the risks (26.0%) (2021: 3360). The reasons for detransitioning from the survey's participants are outlined:

> The most frequently endorsed reason for detransitioning was that the respondent's personal definition of male and female changed and they became comfortable identifying with their natal sex (60.0%) ... other commonly endorsed reasons were concerns about potential medical complications (49.0%); transition did not improve their mental health (42.0%); dissatisfaction with the physical results of transition (40.0%); and discovering that something specific like trauma or a mental health condition caused their gender dysphoria (38.0%).
>
> (Littman, 2021: 3361)

Over half of the participants (51.2%) thought that transitioning had delayed or prevented them from either dealing with, or being treated for, trauma or a mental health condition. Participants' answers refer to themes including the dawning of a severe disconnect between self and body, becoming critical of transition as emanating from self-hatred and deep discomfort with secondary sex characteristics associated with childhood trauma. Although there were no specific questions in the survey about homophobia, almost a quarter of participants described internalised homophobia and difficulty with accepting oneself as lesbian, gay or bisexual. This included the notion that transitioning to male would normalise an attraction to girls; that being a gay trans man was preferable to being a lesbian and that being the opposite gender would diminish the fear of repressed same-sex attraction. Elements of misogyny (named as such) from natal female participants were evident, in the form of internalised misogyny and homophobia as an attempt to distance oneself from womanhood and femaleness, due to internalised lesbophobia and misogyny as well as a history of sexual trauma (2021: 3363).

An important finding within this survey, was that only 24.0% of participants informed the doctor or clinic that had initially facilitated their transitions that they had detransitioned.

Littman acknowledges that although her study documents the existence of de-transitioners, the prevalence of detransition as an outcome of transition is unknown, as clinic rates are likely to be underestimated (2021: 3364). The findings of her study show the complexity of gender dysphoria and that the failure to explore co-morbidities can lead to "misdiagnosis, missed diagnoses, and inappropriate gender transition" (2021: 3364). Littman suggests that an inclusion of a non-judgmental question about detransition and desistance into nationally representative surveys that assemble health data, clinical practice and electronic medical records could help with difficulties with obtaining accurate rates of detransition (2021: 3366). Important within the findings of this study is that although some detransitioners regret transitioning, some do not and remain detransitioned and some retransition. Another finding of significance is that of the differences in baseline characteristics between natal female and natal male detransitioners.

In the chapter 'A Person Beyond Gender' (Hortzmann & Newbigin, 2020), the narrator describes his physical experience:

> I have never tried to be male either pre- or post-transition. I have always been me, and "me" is male. So, on the contrary, I have spent the vast majority of my life *trying to be female*, trying to be something I am not, never was, and could not be, trying to fit into and adapt to the uncomfortable limitations of my female body and society's predetermined roles, behaviours, and expectations that are dictated by anatomy.
>
> (2020: 274)

Here the narrator describes their experience of top surgery:

> Top surgery was the stuff of miracles for me. In my first consultation with the surgeon, I was struck by his total understanding and acceptance of my situation. He did not question me which was an immense relief, and when he examined me, he prodded my chest muscles and said, "Well that's all you, all that is mus-cle …" and then demonstrated the breast tissue he would remove and said, "And this is what shouldn't be there" … Never before had I felt such validation. He saw me as a man who simply should never have had breasts in the first place, and furthermore, he would remove them for me and create the most masculine chest he possibly could. He understood that top surgery was not about changing my female body into a male body: it was about removing the erroneous female bits from the body I should have had.
>
> (2020: 277)

My interviewees mostly struggled with the reality of their bodies either be-fore, during or post puberty. When this reality was unmanageable, either through their own or others' perceptions of it experienced by them, they turned to a more physical/medical/surgical solution in order to allay acute discomfort or depression. *Femaleness* was unwanted and more crucially *unfelt* by all the interviewees, to dif-ferent degrees and at different periods of their lives. These motivations align with the reasons for transition in the study that Littman (2021) carried out.

The Concrete Symbol

The importance of the capacity to symbolise and difficulties arising from a lack of this capacity, have been written about from the inception of psychoanalysis. In her paper 'Taking time: the tempo of psychoanalysis', Birksted-Breen (2012) discusses the temporal aspect that the analyst can forgo when patients show an absence of symbolic thinking. She suggests that in those situations a reliance on reverie and visual images can helpfully bridge the gap between the concrete and the symbolic so as to avoid an impasse. Impasse is understood by Birksted-Breen as lacking reverie as a 'third and temporal element' that can lead to the unchanging nature of concreteness for both patient and analyst.

In her paper she describes one analyst's struggle with her patient Jennifer's wish and drive to have plastic surgery for breast enlargement. The analyst under-stood this as an enactment of something lacking in the analysis and hence her own failure; the patient did not. The patient wished for and believed in the benefits of a concrete change to her body; the analyst was thinking symbolically and felt despair for the potential of the analysis. Their different languages created an impasse. Birksted-Breen describes the following:

> ... the problem rests on the fact that, while apparently upholding a symbolic mode of thinking, the analyst herself has slipped into concrete thinking. She believes that the plastic surgery means the literal and irreparable damage to the analysis and to any potential for thinking, as if the 'analytic breast' – that is, the analyst's capacity for thinking – will be literally destroyed by the surgeon's knife.
>
> (2012: 824)

Although this patient's wishes were not connected to transitioning from one gen-der to another, the impasse that the surgery engendered in the mind of the analyst is relevant. I mention this case because it highlights the bi-directional aspect of the impasse as being something stuck between patient and analyst. The analyst needs to be made aware of her concreteness before the impasse can be resolved. Ferro (1993) and Baranger et al. (1983) support the understanding of impasse as a 'couple related problem', in which the analyst can get entangled in their own one-dimensional thinking "which may masquerade as psychoanalytic theory when anx-iety that can't be faced is aroused" (Birksted-Breen, 2012: 825). Birksted-Breen advocates a mental attitude of 'taking time' and, the use of reverie that can facilitate the space for the potential for new ways of thinking to grow in the analyst's mind.

The Clinician's Conundrum

I have described pre and post transition situations from acute relief to acute regret. There is perhaps no right decision for the trans individual or the clinician who is trying to help them with their struggles. The ethical dimension of the work, particularly in specialist gender-identity services for children and adolescents, is riddled with complexity. Acting too quickly and watchful waiting can both be targeted as 'wrong' or unhelpful. As Wren (2019a) describes, "A focus on the clinical decision as the central one-off event, can offer a simplified dramatization of the ethical work" (Wren, 2019a: 217). She goes on to say that there is a danger that what might be deemed an ethical conflict for a clinician might replace a reluctance to accept a trans or gender diverse identity as valid. Wren advocates for young people's self-knowledge and their 'right to choose their own life course', although this can sometimes be at odds with professionals whose work is to seek out complexity. Wren is advocating respect and curiosity towards young people's own framing of their predicament (Wren, 2019a: 218).

Trans individuals can be deeply dissatisfied with healthcare systems both before and after transitioning. Post transitioning, and particularly for detransitioners, grievances about past experiences can veer towards claims of being fast-tracked with insufficient time to think, although slower thinking time is often very much unwanted at pre-transitioning stages, perhaps particularly for a younger age group.

The ethical tenets of well-being, self-interest, self-knowledge, autonomy, authority, authenticity amongst others that all exist in a particular period of history, shape the exterior as well as interior landscape of gender experience. It is possibly not by chance that GIDS at the Tavistock became a target for attack which might be less to do with individuals and the service, and more to do with a challenging cultural shift that the expansion of gender identity places on clinicians embracing ethical challenges in this field.

Psychoanalytic approaches to trans issues, whether this is the desire to transition or de-transition, can become the target of negative discourse. It is important that psychoanalysis is not side-lined as it has been so readily throughout its history. Although psychoanalysis is perceived as "an outlier in mental health treatment" (Osserman, 2024: 6), it can also have a reassuring presence with a temporality that is different to speeded up physical interventions. For it to be considered as a valuable resource in relation to trans issues, clinicians might need to adjust outdated attitudes that can be embedded unconsciously as well as consciously (Kloppenberg, 2022). Trans individuals might also need to allow the unconscious to have a place in non-pathologising explorations. Both clinician and patient need to grapple with the universal and ubiquitous unsettling nature of sex and gender, in all bodies. Kubie (1974) expressed this well: "The assumption whether tacit or overt that any human being can ever want to be only one sex to the exclusion of the other is psychoanalytically naïve and runs counter to all analytic experience" (Kubie, 1974: 11).

Hansbury (2017) has discussed the anxieties, confusion and distress that can be stirred up for clinicians who are confronted by trans patients:

> Until the twenty-first century, psychoanalysis remained fixed on determining what went wrong in the development of gender identities unanimously diagnosed as disordered. In the face of unthinkable anxiety, thinking about etiology can be a powerful defense.
>
> (Hansbury, 2017: 391)

This chapter has focussed on potential determinants for detransition as well as relevant testimonies and literature. This aspect of gender identity is ethically complex, not least because of the lack of data on the proportion of transitioners who detransition. The experience of detransitioning requires a capacity for reflection that is often painful after an active pathway has been sought, and can leave individuals with physical interventions that are irreversible and regretted, and that can affect fertility. Further debate and exploration is needed to aid understanding of what pathways could have been opened up by clinicians. In opening up detransitioning for exploration, it has not been my intention to posit detransitioning as *reason not to* transition. Many trans individuals do not regret their transitions and live with contentment, as in the experiences of my interviewees.

The term 'No Man's Land' is often associated with the First World War, as a description of an area of land between two enemy trench systems that is not controlled by either side. I have described difficulties within gender-identity struggles in relation to both transitioning and de-transitioning where it is immensely challenging for transitioned and detransitioned individuals and clinicians to find a territory that is free from injurious projections. I see the struggles with and towards gender identities as operating on both sides of a 'war zone'. The complexity of gender, especially pre and post transition, can invoke confused allegiances which inevitably affect clinicians, who can struggle to know how to align themselves internally and externally. It is easy for both trans individuals and clinicians to become caught in a zone between multiple fiefdoms. There is a need for a space that acknowledges the existence of both conscious and unconscious elements. This neutral zone is needed for and between trans individuals, between transitioners and detransitioners, between trans individuals and clinicians and between clinicians with varied approaches. Without it, a culture of conflict in which different 'sides' can too easily be perceived as enemies who need to be defeated, will continue to prevail.

Note

1 In the United States, a prevalent model for gender care is the 'Informed Consent Model'.

Bibliography

Alderman, B. (2016). *Symptom, symbol and the other of language: A Jungian interpretation of the linguistic turn*. Oxon. and New York: Routledge.

Bailly, S. (2023). The unconscious body image by Françoise Dolto and its links with the British Object Relations tradition. Paper presented at *Scientific Meeting, British Psychotherapy Foundation*, 11.5.2023.

Baranger, M., Baranger, W., & Mom, J. (1983). Process and non-process in analytic work. *International Journal of Psychoanalysis*, *64*, 1–15.

Beauchamp, T., & Childress, J. (2013). *Principles of biomedical ethics*. 7th ed. New York, NY; Oxford: Oxford University Press, 2013.

Bell-v-Tavistock (2020). Judicial Review, 1 December, 2020. Retrieved 29 July, 2020. https://www.judiciary.uk/wp-content/uploads/2020/12/Bell-v-Tavistock-Judgment.pdf

Bell-v-Tavistock (2021). Retrieved 15 April, 2024. https://www.judiciary.uk/wp-content/uploads/2022/07/Bell-v-Tavistock-summary-170921.pdf

Benjamin, J. (2004). Deconstructing femininity: Understanding "passivity" and the daughter position. *Annual of Psychoanalysis*, *32*, 45–57.

Bilek, J. (2018). Transgenderism is just big business dressed up in pretend civil rights clothes. https://thefederalist.com/2018/07/05/transgenderism-just-big-business-dressed-pretend-civil-rights-clothes/. Retrieved 16 January 2024.

Bion, W. R. (1962, 1984). *A theory of thinking, second thoughts*, chapter 9: 110–119. London: H. Karnac (Books).

Birksted-Breen, D. (2012). Taking time: The tempo of psychoanalysis. *International Journal of Psychoanalysis*, *93*, 819–835.

Botella, C., & Botella, S. (2005). *The work of psychic figurability*. London and New York: Routledge.

Bruhaker, R. (2016). As cited in Silber, L. (2019).

Butler, C., & Hutchinson, A. (2020). Debate: The pressing need for research and services for gender desisters/detransitioners. *Child and Adolescent Mental Health*, *25*(1), 45–47.

Cass Review (2024). Independent review of gender identity services for children and young people, file:///Users/serenaheller/Downloads/CassReview_Final.pdf. Retrieved 18 April, 2024.

Cavanagh, S. L. (2017). Transpsychoanalytics. *Transgender Studies Quarterly*, *4*, 326–357, Numbers 3–4, November 2017.

Chaplin, R. (2018). How to be both, by not being both: The articulation of psychic bisexuality within the analytic session. In R. J. Perelberg (Ed.), *Psychic bisexuality: A British French dialogue* (chapter 10, pp. 207–226). London & New York: Routledge.

Cohn, J. (2023). The Detransition Rate is Unknown. *Archives of Sexual Behavior* (2023) 52: 1937–1952. https://doi.org/10.1007/s10508-023-02623-5. Retrieved 26 October 2024.

Corbett, K. (2016). *A murder over a girl*. New York, NY: Henry Holt and Company. As cited in Silber, L. (2019).

de Vries, A. L. C., Doreleijers, T. A. H., Steensma, T. D., & Cohen-Kettenis, P. T. (2011). Psychiatric comorbidity in gender dysphoric adolescents. *Journal of Child Psychology and Psychiatry*, *52*, 1195–1202.

DETRANS Documentary. https://www.youtube.com/watch?v=3yvjFSX0TB0&t=858s PragerU 2023. Retrieved 23 April. 2024.

Detransitioning: She regrets transitioning from female to male https://www.youtube.com/watch?v=uOYKIpkueqM&t=2s. Retrieved 23 April, 2024.

Dolto, F. (2023). In S. Bailly (Ed.), *The unconscious body image. Introduction* (pp. 1–7), and chapter 2 (pp. 55–59). London & New York: Routledge.

Edwards-Leeper, L., & Spack, N. P. (2012). Psychological evaluation and medical treatment of transgender youth in an interdisciplinary "gender management service (GeMS)" in a major paediatric center. *Journal of Homosexuality*, *59*, 321–336.

Ehrensaft, D. (2017). Gender nonconforming youth: Current perspectives. *Adolescent Health, Medicine and Therapeutics, 8*, 57–67.

Entwistle, K. (2021). Debate: Reality check – Detransitioner's testimonies require us to rethink gender dysphoria, *Child and Adolescent Mental Health 26*, No. 1, 2021.

Expósito-Campos, P. (2021). A typology of gender detransition and its implications for healthcare providers. *Journal of Sex & Marital Therapy, 47*(3), 270–280.

Ferro, A. (1993). The impasse within a theory of the analytic field: Possible vertices of observation. *International Journal of Psychoanalysis, 74*, 917–929.

Figlio, K. (2024). Seminal masculinity, chapter 7, pp. 113–133; Incapacity and ambivalence in seminal masculinity, chapter 8, pp. 134–151, *Rethinking the psychoanalysis of masculinity, from toxic to seminal*. London & New York: Routledge.

Fonagy, P., & Target, M. (2007). The rooting of the mind in the body: New links between attachment theory and psychoanalytic thought. *Journal of the American Psychoanalytic Association, 55*, 411–456.

Freeman Sharpe, E. (1940, 1978). Mechanisms of dream formation, In *Dream analysis*, Chapter 2: 40–65. London: The Hogarth press and The Institute of Psychoanalysis (Original work published 1940)

GIDS (2020). Gender Identity Development Service, Referrals to GIDS, Financial Years 2015-2016 to 2019-2020. GIDS 2020 http://gids.nhs.uk/number-referrals Accessed 12 September 2023, site inactive 11 September 2024.

Griffin, L., Clyde, K., Byng, R., & Bewley, S. (2021). Sex, gender and gender identity: A re-evaluation of the evidence. *British Journal of Psychiatry Bulletin, 45*, 291–299.

Grindon, L. H. (1879). *Figurative language: Its origin and constitution*. London: James Spiers.

Hansbury, G. (2017). Unthinkable anxieties: Reading transphobic countertransferences in a century of psychoanalytic writing. *Transgender Studies Quarterly, 4*, Nos. 3–4, 384–404.

Harris, A. (2005). As cited in Silber, L. (2019).

Hertzmann, L., & Newbigin, J. (2020). A person beyond gender: A first-hand account. In L. Hertzmann, & J. Newbigin (Eds.), *Sexuality and gender now* (chapter 11, pp. 256–287). London: Routledge.

Holt, V., Skargerberg, E., & Dunsford, M. (2016). Young people with features of gender dysphoria: Demographics and associated difficulties. *Clinical Child Psychology and Psychiatry, 21*, 108–118.

Horney, K. (1926). The flight from womanhood: The masculinity-complex in women, as viewed by men and by women. *International Journal of Psychoanalysis, 7*, 324–339.

I Detransitioned: Here's what they will NEVER TELL YOU https://www.youtube.com/watch?v=OmsYKSiBZzU. Retrieved 23 April, 2024.

Jung, C. (1950). As cited in Marciano (2021).

Kaltiala-Heino, R., Sumia, M., Työläjärvi, M., & Lindberg, N. (2015). Two years of gender identity service for minors: Overrepresentation of natal girls with severe problems in adolescent development. *Child and Adolescent Psychiatry and Mental Health, 9*(1), 9.

Kloppenberg, B. (2022). What happens when a trans patient happens? *Journal of the American Psychoanalytic Association, 70*, 525–546.

Kubie, L. (1974). The drive to be become both sexes. *Psychoanalytic Quarterly, 43*, 349–426.

Lemma, A. (2022). Towards a psychoanalytic ethics-based practice with transgender individuals, chapter 5, pp. 89–106, *Transgender identities, a contemporary introduction*. London & New York: Routledge.

Lemma, A. (2023). Bioethical principles, chapter 2, pp. 31–62, *First principles; Applied ethics for psychoanalytic practice*. Oxford: Oxford University Press.

Lemma, A., & Savulescu, J. (2023). To be, or not to be? The role of the unconscious in transgender transitioning: Identity, autonomy and well-being. *Journal of Medical Ethics*, *49*, 65–72. (published online 30 July, 2021)

Levine, H. B. (2012). The colourless canvas: Representation, therapeutic action and the creation of mind. *International Journal of Psychoanalysis*, *93*, 606–629.

Littman, L. (2021). Individuals treated for gender dysphoria with medical and/or surgical transition who subsequently detransitioned: A survey of 100 detransitioners. *Archives of Sexual Behavior*, *50*, 3353–3369.

Livia (2019). *Detransition Advocacy Network event transcript*, as cited in Marciano 2021.

Lombardi, R. (2002). Primitive mental States and the body: A personal view of Armando B. Ferrari's concrete original object. *International Journal of Psycho-Analysis*, *83*(2), 363–381.

Lombardi, R. (2008). The body in the analytic session: Focusing on the body-mind link. *International Journal of Psychoanalysis*, *89*, 89–109.

Lombardi, R. (2017). The body in adolescence: Psychic isolation and physical symptoms. *Journal of Child Psychotherapy*, *43*, 134–137.

Mann, D. (1994). Castration desire. *British Journal of Psychotherapy*, *10*(4), 511–520.

Marchiano, L. (2021). Gender detransition: A case study. *Journal of Analytic Psychology*, *66*(4), 813–832.

Mitchell, J. (2023). Oedipal sexual difference, Chapter 8, pp. 173–186, *Fratriarchy, the sibling trauma and the law of the mother*. London & New York: Routledge.

No Way Back (2023). *No Way Back: The Reality of Gender Affirming Care*, Deplorable Films, www.DeplorableFilms.com

Osserman, J. (2024). Psychoanalysis and trans, a study of two psychosocial scenes. In S. Frosh, M. Vyrgioti, & J. Walsh (Eds.), *The Palgrave handbook of psychosocial studies*. Springer Nature, Cham, Switzerland: Palgrave Macmillan.

Patterson, L. (2018). Unconscious homophobia and the rise of the transgender movement. *Psychodynamic Practice, Individuals, Groups and Organisations*, *24*(1), 56–59.

Sapir, L. (YouTube) https://www.youtube.com/watch?v=3yvjFSX0TB0&t=858s. Retrieved 23 April, 2024.

Schwartz, D. (2012). Listening to children imagining gender: Observing the inflation of an idea. *Journal of Homosexuality*, *59*, 460–479.

Silber, L. (2019). Locating ruptures encrypted in gender: Developmental and clinical considerations. *Journal of Infant, Child and Adolescent Psychotherapy*, *18*(2), 134–154.

Winnicott, D. W. (1971, 1991). *Playing and reality*. London: Tavistock/Routledge.

Wren, B. (2019a). Ethical issues arising in the provision of medical interventions with gender variant children and adolescents. *Clinical Child Psychology and Psychiatry*, *24*(2), 203–222.

Wren, B. (2021). Diary, *London Review of Books*, 2 December, 2021, Vol. 43, No. 23.

Zucker, K. J. (2018). The myth of persistence: Response to "A critical commentary on follow-up studies and desistance theories about transgender and gender non-conforming children" by Temple Newhook et al. (2018). *International Journal of Transgenderism*, *19*, 231–245.

Zucker, K. J. (2019). Adolescents with gender dysphoria: Reflections on some contemporary clinical and research issues. *Archives of Sexual Behaviour*, *48*(7), 1983–1992.

Zucker, K. J. (2020). Debate: Different strokes for different folks. *Child and Adolescent Mental Health*, *25*(1), 36–37.

Conclusion

The conclusion reflects on the multiple strands of previous chapters. The social phenomenon of trans men, namely the move from femaleness to maleness, is discussed in the context of notably high numbers of referrals, and through a psychoanalytic lens. The centrality of gender in recent decades is explored and questioned; why does it take the form of a rebellion, and what is the meaning of gender protest? The valency in the culture that supports this social phenomenon is acknowledged. Working with gender identity can evoke defensiveness in clinicians as well as patients, as it is a landscape in flux. Ethical obstacles in relation to the timing of interventions are considered, as is the slippage from sex to gender as a category. Arguably, there is a need to 'unstraighten' some of the more rigid psychoanalytic approaches to gender, without losing basic psychoanalytic tenets. Gender transition is both a political and global movement, and a deeply personal endeavour; it cannot be detached from sexuality and desire, which links to the question of why femaleness is unwanted by so many. However, it is important to recognise that trans men are not a homogeneous group, and there is much variation amongst individual motivations.

A contemporary psychoanalytic understanding and approach to transitioning and de-transitioning requires a shift in epistemic understanding of clinical, medical, social and cultural structures over time, not least because it is a field of enquiry that is still emerging and one that puts forward unprecedented challenges. In the quest to 'unstraighten' psychoanalysis, I quote Ahmed who paraphrases Simone de Beauvoir: "one is not born but becomes straight" (Ahmed, 2006. 79). In the quest to unstraighten psychoanalytic ways of thinking that can be read as heteronormative, homophobic or transphobic, there is a need to adopt less rigidly straight modes of thinking and being. I am not advocating that psychoanalysis should abandon its central tenets, but more for it to absorb, register and acculturate itself to the climate of gender as it is lived now, in the early part of the 21st century. This might require a synthesis of conventional foundations with a move to more nuanced ways of thinking. Frosh (2017) comments on the complicated encounter between psychoanalysis and queer theory:

> ... despite the danger that each approach will defensively close itself off in the face of the other's critique, psychoanalysis and queer theory need to actively

DOI: 10.4324/9781032718613-8

needle each other and be destabilised from some other marginal place, or else they will each solidify still more into the kinds of orthodoxy that their own theoretical tenets would decry.

(Frosh, 2017: 390)

Clinicians who have not necessarily had to question their gender or how they know it, may struggle to identify with the extent of incongruence experienced when natal sex does not match felt gender. Psychoanalytic interpretations of gender incongruence have tended to veer towards the search for anomalies in personal history, rather than acceptance of the situation as it is presented. This can lead to formulations in which the individual is seen to be against themselves, positing natal sex as the enemy that cannot be reconciled with. For many trans individuals the post transition experience is one in which there is relief from the prior experience of being against oneself, and more of a move into oneself. Langer (2016) expresses it well: "Imagine your life has been lived out of tune and post hormone treatment, you suddenly have perfect pitch to play the instrument of your body" (Langer, 2016: 314).

My study of trans men is an attempt to look at a social movement and formulate a suggested theoretical understanding. This might resonate with individual experiences and offer potential new ways of thinking about them. It may also be unwelcome and rebuffed, if my understanding or proposed ideas feel alien and do not resonate.

Although I am encouraging evolution within contemporary psychoanalysis, aspects of Freud's writing lend themselves well to an understanding of trans identity today. Writing about the unconscious wish in dreams preceded his writing about sexuality in the *Three Essays* (1905), and it has been suggested (Haynal, 2009) that one led on to the other. The unconscious dreams and wishes of the trans men that I spoke to might have led them to a more conscious wish to transition. In the *Three Essays,* Freud suggested infants were born with sexual drives and polymorphous sexual impulses. The current multiplicity of gender identities and identifications might also come across as 'polymorphous gender impulses', indicative of a shift from sex to gender. Freud's so-called phallocentric thinking, the perception of 'a lack' for females in their sexual and Oedipal development, although much criticised, fits with some of the material I have written about. This lack can also be understood as an unmet need, that is as yet unrepresentable consciously, that finds its way into a gender presentation; gender can host affects that cannot be represented.

Biology was important to Freud, who started his career as a physician, and who throughout his life's work emphasised his belief in the biological substrates of behaviour; his wish was to "furnish a psychology that shall be a natural science" (Freud, 1950: 295). Biology and psychology come into conflict for the trans man, personally and socially. Gender as socially constructed moves away from gender essentialism as something innate, universal and immutable. Gender has become divorced from biology, and this divorce is both protracted and acrimonious. By recruiting psychoanalysis and the unconscious I suggest one possible way to bridge the binary between essentialist and constructionist approaches.

I hypothesise that the flight from femininity is to some extent embedded in the motivation to transition, more strongly at times than the wish, belief in or desire to be masculine or male. This denotes a wish for a more liminal space, less rigidly defined by man/woman, male/female, past/present. The core difficulty for most of my interviewees was their ambivalent identification with femininity and female-ness, and the strong sense of incongruence within themselves towards it. This necessitated a move away from womanhood that extended into the wish *not* to identify as female and gay. This could also be seen as internalised homophobia, as same-sex attraction as a lesbian appears to be unwanted as an identity. A (then) woman who is openly attracted to other women sexually might move towards a trans identity, as a safer domain than female homosexuality. By internalised homo-phobia I mean that societal or cultural disapproval might be absorbed, but also intrapsychically there is disapproval from within and a rejection of self as a lesbian. There might also be unconscious resistance towards the homoerotic aspect of early mother/daughter contact, in which passion was unrequited.

The sought identity was that of being a trans man, in which bisexuality or homosexuality was more acceptable. For a trans man, being gay appeared to be much more acceptable than an identity as an AFB (assigned female at birth) gay woman. Sometimes the object of desire (as in male or female) is maintained post-transition, but the orientation (from transmasculinity) towards this same object has altered; this showed that sometimes sexuality can transition along with gender. And also, that the inherent femaleness of lesbian desire was rejected. The orienting of oneself as male towards others, and the orienting of others towards the self as male was, understandably, extremely important for trans men. The success of this orienting is expressed by 'passing' as the gender one identifies as. This choice of word could imply that not passing is failing, that one can fail at or in one's gender. For a trans man the orientation towards a male partner would be seen as gay, and towards a female partner as straight. It can be perceived as confrontational to question the maintenance of a prior sexual orientation post-transition, as this reduces the current trans position into a transposition. This does not diminish the felt sense of maleness for trans men, but my interest in part lies in the understanding of how maleness might be set up against femaleness and female sexuality within the self.

For most of my interviewees the masculinity sought was not overtly or stereo-typically male; this implied that a form of bespoke masculinity as a trans man is preferable to inhabiting female masculinity or masculine femininity pre-transition. I discuss this in Chapter 4. The physicality of gender creates many painful difficul-ties, when the body does not corroborate the gender in mind. The mind is housed in a body, which not only changes with sexual development, but is inherently unfixed and uncertain. Many difficulties have arisen with attempts to pin down 'gender identity' as an entity that should adhere to externally defined prescriptive expecta-tions. This historic need for fixity has tended to expose gender theorists such as H. Benjamin, Money, Stoller and Kinsey to subsequent criticism.

A theme that I stress in my writing is the capacity to accept the reality of the difference between the sexes early and during the life cycle. Bion[1] (1967, 1984) stressed the significance and differences in *the infant's capacity to manage frustration*. Accepting reality necessarily requires a tolerance of frustration, and having to come to terms with both one's own limitations and the limitations in the external world, whether this is an infant waiting for the next feed, or coming to terms with being born a girl and not a boy. Trans identity brings into being the opportunity of *not having to renounce the sex that one is not*, or *foreclose on object choice*. It can be thought of as a hybrid of sex, sexuality and gender that is sometimes sought as a defence against primitive anxiety that threatens identity. This can be seen as 'identity as a defence against identity', not unlike Britton's notion of phantasy used as a defence against phantasies (1995: 87). Although I mention defences, I am not viewing trans identities as always and only ever defensive, they are also a way of managing or shaping identity that is threatened by an acute sense of dissonance.

Acceptance of reality is also a central factor (or aim) in psychoanalytic work: this includes the vicissitudes of patients' struggles to achieve this and their defences against it, as well as the defences that can get stirred up in clinicians. Both patients and clinicians have to recognise the reality in the room, and in each other's unconscious. This is the territory of transference and countertransference. In my chapter on temporality, I discuss the wish to revise developmental time into 'I am therefore I was' or 'I was what I am now'. This reversal can challenge the potential to understand causal chains in the developmental pathway of life. It can also invoke 'après-coup masculinity' for the trans man; by this I mean that it reverses 'then in now' to 'now in then'. It is, of course, not erroneous to wish to see the present as informing the past, or necessary to only see the present as informed by the past. Trans identities can challenge more conventional developmental trajectories and push at the boundaries of historicising what was into what is; 'après-coup' can become 'avant-coup'.

Money-Kyrle (1968: 691–698; 1971: 103–106) referred to 'the facts of life' that centre on recognition of differences that we all struggle to accept. These are: the goodness of the breast, the difference between the sexes, recognition of parental intercourse as a creative act, the difference between the generations and the reality of the passage of time. Lemma has suggested an additional fact of life: the inescapable fact of our embodied nature (2023: 811). The hatred of these 'facts' comes from the envy they can provoke and the threat to omnipotence. As a way to avert and deny these 'facts', a mythology is invented,[2] that functions to avoid facing our mortality and dependence on others. I have emphasised and expanded on the categories that Money-Kyrle cited in my thinking about gender identity. I suggest that gender (identity) has become one way to manage these 'facts of life' as it is sometimes, but not always, deployed to override psychic struggles that these unmanageable realities can evoke. This can be flipped into questioning whether the unmanageable realities of non-conforming gender identities can challenge a paradigm that does not meet its needs? I have advocated the need for movement in the minds and approaches of clinicians, who may need to open up new vistas of thinking that can accommodate trans-reality.

The continuous thread between infantile and adult sexuality (as advocated by Freud) can be questioned in trans gender identity, as a link to the past self can be unwanted. The drive to denounce chronological time or reverse it includes a wish to undo or arrest biological and physiological development along gender lines since birth, as (in some cases) natality or the assigned sex at birth is refuted. The *re-birth* aspect of gender transition can be seen to negate the reality of *the parents as a sexual and procreative couple* (the primal scene), as gender identity becomes *self-generated*; the sex at birth as conceived by one's parents is reconceived in the form of parthenogenesis. As Athena was born out of the head of Zeus, Metis was denied her position as a mother who gave birth to her daughter. Athena burst forth from the male psyche, rather than the female womb. Trans gender identity emanates from the psyche, it is conceived in the mind of individuals who can struggle with their identity. I have suggested that for some trans men, an unconscious matricidal wish can be embedded in the desire to transition. I posit this wish as supplementing the more traditional patricidal wish in the Oedipus complex.

My exploration has centred on how and why 'gender', especially that of young natal females has become so culturally central in recent decades. In my introduction, I asked why it takes the form of a rebellion and *what the gender protest is rebelling against?* An obvious answer to what it stands for, might be the liberty to be who one chooses to be and feels oneself to be, which raises the thorny ethical question of who has the authority to make decisions about medication (puberty blockers) that can affect teenagers' and pre-teens' future options, sometimes irreversibly. The difference between the sexes has become a political aspect of gender identity within the cultural landscape of the 21st century, with trans identity or trans rights often taking centre stage as one of the emblematic concerns of today's 'culture wars'.

The population born in the last 20 years does not necessarily know of a 'pre-transgender' time, in which gender identity was even more threatened. Access to social media forums lends those that are uncertain about aspects of their identity an online universe that can go unchallenged. This instant sense of belonging, or of sharing gender struggles, can in some instances risk the escalation of gender uncertainty into conviction that change is necessary, and in this respect can be thought of as having contagious elements for some individuals who can go on to regret the speed at which their transitions took place (Littman, 2021; No Way Back, 2023).

My interest has focussed on the move from femaleness to maleness, and within this focus I have discussed sex, sexuality, gender and identity across different psychoanalytic and academic schools of thought or disciplines. Identity (whether attached to gender or not) has, in recent decades, become central academically, politically and personally. This may be more pronounced for generation Y, Z & Alpha who have had more exposure to the digital world in terms of unprecedented online access; to a global recession; climate change and the Covid-19 Pandemic. Identity, our sense of ourselves, coheres around who and how we are psychosocially, and includes our relationship to and how we inhabit our bodies. It can apply to nationality, race and ethnicity and the legitimacy of being allowed to reside in another country, putting it at the centre of the politics and conflicts of immigration. Gender has become more central to identity, but it remains one facet amongst others. *Gender Without Identity* (Saketopoulou & Pellegrini, 2023) addresses the putative ontological status of identity and how identity is formed by intrusion from the other which can be experienced as traumatic. It can be hard to delink identity from gender (identity without gender) although the centrality of gender for individuals is hugely variable. It can be taken for granted or cause extreme despair.

In Juliet Mitchell's analysis of hysteria (Mitchell, 2000), she describes *saka*, an illness of the Taita people who live in the Coast province of Kenya. They acknowledge illnesses of the heart and of the head; the illness of *saka* is of the heart. It is described by the Taita people as an illness of 'wanting and wanting'. Taita women are largely dependent on men and have few privileges, and it is mainly these married women who become ill with *saka*. This takes the form of restlessness, anxiety or a self-hypnotic state; the sufferer can go into convulsions, lose consciousness and be in a trance like state. *Saka* can be triggered by a strong wish for something. One of the treatments for this illness is the *saka* dance, within which women adopt men's things or parts of their clothing that they use or wear. Mitchell describes the dance as one in which "gender ambiguity and fluidity is all-pervasive" (Mitchell, 2000: 2). This cathartic dance is an attempt to negotiate gender differences by allowing women to have some of the things that men have. The illness has hysterical qualities.

I have included the women who suffered from *saka* because there is something heart-breaking about their disappointment of finding themselves with less and less that leaves them 'wanting and wanting'. I make the leap from their trance to trans men, natally female, who also seem to be 'wanting and wanting' what they do not have, or 'unwanting and unwanting' what they do have. This wanting and unwanting can be understood to be so many things: to have been born male, to feel more at home in their female bodies that come to the fore during puberty, to manage the realities of difference between the sexes and generations, to accept their family dynamics whether mother/father, mother/daughter, father/daughter sister/sister or sister/brother, to fend off deep rooted psychological and bodily struggles such as depression, anxiety, self-harm, trauma and dysphoria, and mostly to inhabit an identity that feels authentic in body and mind. Freud asked the question "What does a woman want?" (Freud, 1925). Women and wanting has also been taken up by Benjamin (1988), who posits the idea that 'women want to want', and Elise who explored why 'women may not want to want' (2000: 126).

The *saka* dance with its rituals appeared to bring about some relief or catharsis for the unhappy women of Taita. Transitioning to the other sex and or gender is a complex contemporary dance for trans men. It can require much agile (conscious and unconscious) movement: psychic, physical, social, economic, hormonal, surgical, sexual, parental; and in relation to siblings, official recognition and a supportive peer group. A desired change in gender identity requires a momentous shift in both self and others. Sometimes this shift reverses in cases of de-transitioning, when the move from female to male or male to female gender identity has not provided the relief or solution that was sought, as I have discussed in Chapter 6.

Freud's dictum that the ego is first and foremost a bodily ego, that our early sensory experience is *necessarily bodily*, supports my writing about concreteness. Ferrari, as cited by Lombardi (2002), expands this notion via the 'Concrete Original Object', which correlates with transgender experience. The question seems to be not so much whether the conflict is in the mind or in the body, but *how to resolve the tension between them*: "events lying between the bodily and the psychic fact" (Lombardi, 2002: 363). Gozlan (2018) uses the term transsexuality, and describes the force of sexuality as carried within it but in a way that is not subdued or subsumed; it signifies an in-process, in-between and ephemeral subjective position that engages gender through the understanding and transformation of ourselves (2018: 3).

I consider *how gender begins to form* in the infant who is vulnerable to maternal and paternal influences before and after birth. In describing the pre-symbolic, I also describe the pre-gendered world. In some respect the influences of parental expectations and projections are ever-present in shaping the infant and toddler's gendering, or gendered projections. Fausto-Sterling (2012), a biologist and gender theorist, puts it well:

> The environmental trappings of gender, from the voices, faces, modes of holding and touching, dress, hair, and grooming, to the colours in the room, the toys offered and the baby clothing used, are ever present. From birth or before an infant absorbs them, commits them to memory, develops expectations about them, and receives bodily messages about their own sex and gender.
>
> (2012: 410)

I concur with Fausto-Sterling when she says that "... gender identity is *not a thing*, but a name given to a weaving together into a subjective self of aspects of the masculine and feminine" (my italics), (2012: 406). Freud did not refer to gender, but preferred to theorise about femininity and masculinity in women and men. It is also hard to name *as a thing* that which might destabilise gender identity, as it is multi-faceted and perhaps most recognisable when the experience of incongruence feels intolerable, an experience not always knowable or imaginable to outsiders.

Although struggles with gender identity have a valency that should not be underestimated, more data is emerging about the co-existence of other emotional difficulties in young people presenting with gender dysphoria. The gender framework can at times subsume other difficulties. Transitioning can bring forth immense relief but also an immense regret in varying proportions, and at varying stages of transition. Wren (2019), in her paper "Notes on a crisis of meaning in the care of gender diverse children" states that:

> It can be hard to disentangle the difficulties that are specifically gender-related from those that are associated with other developmental challenges, especially amongst those young people who present post-pubertally.
>
> (Wren, 2019: 192)

The struggles of an AFB young person who is unhappy and deeply uncomfortable with her natal gender are bound to break through with particular intensity during puberty, if they have not done so earlier. Experiences of puberty amongst the trans men that I spoke to or encountered in the literature varied; for some it was par for the course and for others it was intolerable. It is during puberty (and often earlier) that the wish to identify as trans can set in motion the pathway towards transition, when there is a felt need to arrest the development of secondary sex characteristics, that can feel so alien in their body. This includes the politically contentious questions about the appropriate age for medical intervention.

This resonates with the *saka* phenomenon of 'wanting and wanting' which often does not correspond with life as it is played out in reality. The *saka* illness plays out a hysterical attempt to manage the difference between the sexes, or more accurately the differences between how the sexes are treated and positioned socially. For the Taita women, this was a pronounced difference. The Taita women are reminiscent of The Furies in the Oresteia, that are described by Irigaray as "… women in revolt, rising up like revolutionary hysterics against the patriarchal power in the process of being established" (Irigaray, 1991: 37). The trans community might too feel that a revolution is necessary for their needs to be heard.

In an attempt to conceptualise what trans men might be seeking and wanting I explored non-genital masculinity, the trans phallus and après-coup masculinity. This masculine position does not necessitate a biological penis, it necessitates conviction and belief in a subjective maleness that is idiosyncratic, often supported by hormones and surgery. The quest is for a masculine social function, not necessarily a masculine sexual function. Preciado emphasises the power of pharmaceuticals, the 'technoscientific industry' on bodily needs; he brings in the notion of looking at the body 'from the outside in'. He implies that the solution to bodily needs can be so fast, that it is hard to know whether the need drives the solution or vice versa (Prozac for depression, Viagra for impotence, Testosterone for masculinity). This also applies to the technologies that support gender transition, and their accessibility. There are industries that thrive from the business of gender transition. Preciado refers to the industry as pharmacopornographic. He sees it as the *invention of a subject.*

The categories of sex and sexuality are necessarily challenged in writing about gender. As Brubaker states the very act of categorisation itself has been challenged, as the landscape of identity has become more complex (Brubaker, 2016: 41). These overlapping and yet distinct categories of gender, sex and sexuality have become dominant in relation to societal, cultural and biomedical ethics, as their meanings fracture and proliferate in equal measure. The ever-expanding variability of gender identity: 100 options on tumblr (tumblr, 2020) stretches pre-existing boundaries and parameters of masculinity and femininity, maleness and femaleness, man and woman, into an entirely new territory, or the invention of a new subjectivity. This new gender-territory is "unpoliced" (Hansbury, 2017: 1010), "fundamentally non-lexical" (Marcus, Marcus, Yaxte, & Marcus, 2015: 802), and "lays down a challenge to certain foundational logics" (Wren, 2019: 9). It challenges clinicians to both use a wide lens and adapt to this new territory. It is hard to think about gender outside "the pull of the present" (Schopf, 2005), which can overshadow what came before.

Trans individuals can feel marginalised, and indeed can easily become the target for projections that are rife with prejudice. Non-trans individuals can object to the pressures to comply. There can be tensions between the trans community and de-transitioners. These tensions can and have thrown gender identity into social war-zones. Trans activists struggle to defend their rights as individual citizens. There are warring factions between trans men, trans women and lesbians. It is a universe with its own language laws and linguistic taboos in which one can unknowingly break the rules. This communicates sensitiveness and defensiveness and can exacerbate the need to protect those *who are in* this community from *those outside it*. Those on the outside might also need protection from those on the inside. Implicit is a radical challenge to a prescription of sex/gender that is culturally expected. Perhaps what lies beneath the gender protest are the words: 'no-one but me can tell me who or how I am'. This is subjectively valid, but inevitably fraught with social and ethical obstacles.

It is destabilising for some clinicians, who might not question their own sex or gender, to have the categories of sex, sexuality and gender unmoored. Psychoanalysis has been and at times still is accused of 'measuring from the norm', and needs to be reminded that: "there can be no measurable norm without variance around it" (Fausto-Sterling 2012: 406 in reference to Corbett 1996, 2009). The explosion of gender identifications enacts a radical wish for *emancipation from constriction*. I believe that as psychoanalytic clinicians working with gender variability, a parallel emancipation is necessary. This involves a need to look deeply into our own gender identity or sexuality and loosen the hardened assumptions that might be carried both consciously and unconsciously. 'The age of consent' as it applies to the sexual act, now applies to the gender act too. I mean this in the context of the recent judicial review[3] about the age at which a young person is deemed to be able to consent to puberty blockers as a pathway towards gender transition. Maya Kaye (Kaye, M. 2021), who was born male and transitioned to female, and identified in 2021 as transsexual, spoke openly and movingly about how there was no stopping her at the time of transitioning several years before. Following much therapy, she believed that if she'd had 'real' therapy at the time of having surgeries, she might not have had so much surgery and when speaking in 2021 felt that something was missing from her body that should have been there. Maya Kaye's capacity to mourn her masculinity and maleness many years after her transition is both heartening and disheartening. She is reflective and brave about opening her thoughts to the public. More recently Maya, now identifying as Sam, chose to detransition and feels more at peace following this decision. He speaks candidly about this decision and experience. (Kaye, S. 2024)

The binary of two sexes is the source of much protest: why only two? The act of transitioning has also been thought of as subscribing to a gender binary: the wish to be a man or a woman, but not the one assigned at birth. Wren (2019) raises and acknowledges many questions that arise in relation to early physical intervention:

> We do question whether early physical intervention is emancipatory for every-one who requests it, as for some young people it may side-step a later adjust-ment to the body as-it-is and disrupt pathways to same-sex sexuality. We are also conscious of the way early medical intervention may re-inscribe binary gender conformity by encouraging steps towards rendering trans experience and trans bodies invisible.
>
> (Wren, 2019: 195)

In non-binary gender identity, the rebellion appears to be against the binary, the unwanted premise that there are two biological sexes with specific chromo-somes. The protest against man and woman incorporates a more unconscious pro-test against a pro-creative sexual couple (the primary scene). Although there is variation from the heteronormative in gay or trans parenting, the sperm still has to come from a man and the ova from a woman, whether the fertilisation is inside or outside the body.

There has been a linguistic, societal and cultural transition or slippage from sex to gender in recent decades as the concept of gender can subsume the biological certainty of sex. I refer to the linguistic aspect in my introduction (De Graaf & Carmichael, 2018). The force of gender threatens to supersede the certainty of sex as a category, although these do not have to be oppositional, but have become so in some discourses. Biological sex, if mentioned or referred to, can threaten and offend trans individuals, as it can be seen to undermine their legitimacy as indi-vidual citizens with 'gender identity rights'. Clearly the context of where and how this comes about is crucial. It is an ongoing debate in relation to fairness in sport participation.

The conflict for the trans man and pre-transition female is *the gap between the desired state and reality*, and it is often a painful journey to negotiate. As Westen (1997) said, when discrepancies arise, it can lead to an altering of the 'reality per-ception' so as to achieve the wished for goal state. The gender that is felt in mind, is (usually) the 'reality state' for a trans man, in spite of the body's imposition of a different reality state. The goal will usually manifest in 'passing' as the gender one identifies as. Passing necessarily recruits the other's perception, how I want you to see me, requires generosity in acceptance of trans reality. Others are invited in to this universe, one that has its own language requirements. It flips the generational norm of a parent teaching their child to speak. The public, that stand in for the par-ents, need to learn how to speak the language of gender or the children will leave home.

Transgender identity poses an ongoing theoretical, ethical and clinical chal-lenge to psychoanalysis, *but not an impasse*. A breakdown of defences is not just a requirement for the patient, both clinician and patient are exposed to anxieties that need to be felt and confronted. The double bind is double sided: a trans patient is likely to want to protect (rather than confront) their defences or anxieties in relation to their gender identity choices and so might a clinician wish to defend their freedom to use psychoanalytic methods, or hold onto previously held beliefs and theoretical positions. In order for psychoanalysis to have a better and broader understanding of gender identity, it is important for there not to be a *fixed desired state* in the approach of the clinician towards the patient. I referred to this in the introduction as 'unstraightening'.

The trans men that I interviewed were content with their gender identity, and their body modifications (hormonal and surgical) had brought them relief, even more so four years on from the initial interviews. For them, mourning was not necessitated by misgivings about their transition, but perhaps more in relation to their struggles during puberty and subsequently in establishing a gendered identity that aligned with their felt sense of self.

The capacity to reflect or mourn the gender that has been relinquished, is usually only possible after the transition has occurred, when it is experienced as not having provided the wished for solution to psychic conflict and social integration; and if it has provided this, there is still a history to be mourned. The drive or mindset to transition can be unstoppable, as the space for reflection is not yet accessible (Chiland, 2000; D'Angelo, 2020; Lemma, 2012; Oppenheimer, 1991; Quinodoz, 1998; Kaye, 2021, 2024). Careful monitoring of countertransference is likely to help the clinician experience, manage and untangle projections both from and towards the patient, as well as "primitive gender terror" (Saketopoulou, 2015 in Hansbury, 2017: 1018). A necessary component of the work for a clinician is to feel pulled right into the patient's gender conflict, and be willing to be in a place that can feel unmoored.

The terms 'gender' and 'identity', are at once combined and separate. Gender forms a major part of one's identity in the world, much more so when there are intense feelings of incongruence between body and mind. Although the experience of finding a gender identity that enables the body to cohere with what is felt in mind can bring immense relief, it can also leave underlying struggles unresolved or displaced as gender identity becomes the goal state.[4] It can also become the victim or site of abuse, as (female to male) detransitioners[5] speak about femaleness as that which was *blamed, attacked and irreversibly altered* in the body. This can also happen in reverse, in instances of male to female transition.

Gender identity is *self-generated*, and can bypass the 'laws' of nature, biology, physiology, chromosomes and endocrinology. It disorders and reorders the status quo of prior relationships, it moulds and shapes a new landscape, one that dissents fundamentally from that which was there before. In this context gender identity alters temporality, and re-translates reality by inventing an individually generated subjectivity. The gender protest can be seen as a protest against nature, science and the so-called facts of life (Money-Kyrle) that can shape aspects of reality. Although it could be argued that reality is immutable, in the arena of gender identity it has a subjectivity that is idiosyncratic. At the same time, it is a manifestation of an individual struggle with the complexity of (sexual) identity that necessarily involves a relational aim and object which Freud recognised in 1905.

The substantial growth in referrals to Gender Identity Services, particularly by AFB individuals, has sometimes been referred to as a 'psychic epidemic'.[6] For an epidemic to take hold, there needs to be a valency in the culture at the time, that supports it. Social media inevitably plays a large part in the social phenomenon of gender dysphoria (that can include elements of dysmorphia) in the 20th and 21st centuries, as do doctors, surgeons, pharmacists, clinicians, patients and parents. In her writing about modern epidemics, Showalter (1997) asserts somewhat cynically that: "Hysterical epidemics require at least three ingredients: physician-enthusiasts and theorists; unhappy, vulnerable patients; and supportive cultural environments". She goes on to advocate the redefining of hysteria as a universal response to emotional conflict (1997: 17). This is not to say that all individual experiences of gender dysphoria (which are on a vast spectrum of variance) necessarily emanate from hysteria, although hysteria in essence means that the body is expressing (somatising) emotional unease that is usually unconscious. Hysteria is defined by Yarom as the struggle between the sexes as enacted in the body. She finds hysteria, once separated from its history, a useful part of the language needed for understanding unconscious difficulties in relation to sexuality and gender (Yarom, 2005: 13). This has resonance for trans identities.

The gender revolution,[7] and within it the transgender movement, has achieved in years what has taken decades for other movements (women's, gay and lesbian rights) to accomplish. The sociologist Michael Biggs suggests that this has been possible not least because of funding from pharmaceutical companies, medical providers and a few wealthy individuals (Biggs, 2018[8]). This sheds light on the complex industry of gender, the weight of the movement, and the many factors that shape it. Hausman (1995) noticed that technologies influenced the taxonomy of transsexualism, and that feminists have written about gender as facticity, a self-evident category of analysis that is independent from sex. These considerations do not undermine the poignancy or validity of the multi-faceted or 'polymorphously diverse'[9] nature of gender identity, an area rife with prejudice and controversy, but provide important context.

Self-generation, or what might be termed 'the generation of the self', is occurring within a specific culture and time in history. Trans gender is both an influential and political global movement, but also a private, personal and individual movement. Many subscribe to the former as part of their trans identity, but many do not, and go about their lives discreetly and privately. I hope this book might contribute to an understanding of sexual and gender identity by recognising that unconscious elements are at play, in all bodies, not only individuals who identify as trans.

The subject of female to male transition that I address in this book is not one that allows a conclusion, and in my writing I have tried to explore mostly unconscious aspects of trans men's gender identity, as these are embodied physically and psychically.

The increasing number of natal females who are driven to transition opens questions about societal and cultural expectations, and the weight of this burden upon them, as well as the weight of the demand from individuals on their families and health services.[10] The same might be said for the burdens of individuals who are assigned male at birth, although that is not the focus of this book. Gender cannot be segregated from sexuality and desire that form a subject and their identity. I have not approached this writing from a position of certainty, knowledge or authority, but as a psychoanalytic clinician who is adopting a "cerebrally pessimist, nervously optimist" (Deleuze, 1981, in Bacon, 1985: 11) approach to the complex subject area of gender identity.

In my thinking about trans men, I offer psychoanalytic formulations that might be helpful in extending the understanding of unconscious drives within female to male transition; and more expansively in relation to what it means to be born from a body and into a body that has to be borne. I do not view trans men as a homogeneous group, and it is important for my work not to be read as such. My ideas developed from a broad range of psychoanalytic theory and the lived experience of trans men, from interviews, literature and to a lesser extent online sites; my formulations are not designed to be read as literal, conscious or manifest pronouncements on any trans individual.

Notes

1 Bion stressed the difference between the infant's capacity to evade or modify frustration in relation to evacuative modes of relating or an apparatus for thinking (1967, 1984: 112).
2 Steiner (2018) introduced the 'Garden of Eden Illusion' as a defensive retreat from the reality of time.
3 A judicial review took place on 1.12.20 (Bell-v-Tavistock, 2020, Judicial Review) about the practice of Tavistock GIDS to prescribe puberty-suppressing drugs to persons under the age of 18 who experience gender dysphoria. The outcome was that a child under 16, may only consent to the use of medication intended to suppress puberty where he or she is competent to understand the nature of the treatment; and that it is highly unlikely that a child under 13 would be competent to give consent. In September 2021 (Bell-v-Tavistock, 2021), the Court of Appeal overturned the High Court's judgement, specifying that it is for doctors, not the courts, to decide on the capacity of young people to consent to medical treatment.
4 Westen wrote about goal states through life that can encounter conflict between desire and reality, this can lead to an alteration of the reality perception in order to achieve the wished for goal state (1997: 531–536).
5 www.4thwavenow.com
6 Marchiano, L. (2017). Jung's use of this term is cited by Marchiano in: 'Outbreak: On Transgender Teens and Psychic Epidemics', *Psychological Perspectives, 60*, 345.
7 'Gender Revolution' was on the cover of National Geographic, January 2017 Issue.
8 Biggs, M. Associate Professor of Sociology, University of Oxford, conducts research into social movements and collective protests.
9 The phrase 'polymorphous diverse' was used by Schwartz, A. (1998).
10 The Gender Identity Development Service at the Tavistock was closed down in March 2024.

Bibliography

Ahmed, S. (2006). Introduction: Find your way (pp. 1–24) and Sexual orientation (Chapter 2, pp. 65–108). *Queer phenomenology*, Durham & London: Duke University Press.

Bacon, F. (1985). *Francis Bacon*, Tate Gallery, Web of Images, Dawn Ades pp. 8–23, London: Tate Gallery &Thames and Hudson.

Bell-v-Tavistock. (December 1, 2020). Judicial review. Retrieved July 29, 2020, from https://www.judiciary.uk/wp-content/uploads/2020/12/Bell-v-Tavistock-Judgment.pdf

Bell-v-Tavistock Judgment. (2021). Bell-v-Tavistock Judgment. Retrieved April 15, 2024, from https://www.judiciary.uk/wp-content/uploads/2022/07/Bell-v-Tavistock-summary-170921.pdf

Benjamin, J. (1988). *The bonds of love: Psychoanalysis, feminism and the problem of domination*. New York: Pantheon Books.

Biggs, M. (May 25, 2018). *The Open Society Foundations & the Transgender Movement*. Retrieved July 29, 2021, from https://4thwavenow.com/2018/05/25/the-open-society-foundations-the-transgender-movement/

Bion, W. R. (1967, 1984). A theory of thinking, chapter 9, pp. 110–119, *Second Thoughts*, London & New York: Karnac.

Britton, R. (1995). Reality and unreality in phantasy and fiction. In E. Spector Person, P. Fonagy, & S. A. Figueira (Eds.), *On Freud's 'Creative writers and day-dreaming'* (pp. 82–106). New Haven and London: Yale University Press.

Brubaker, R. (2016). *Trans: Race and gender in an age of unsettled identities*. New Jersey, USA: Princeton University Press

Chiland, C. (2000). The psychoanalyst and the transsexual patient. *International Journal of Psychoanalysis, 81*, 21–35.

Corbett, K. (1996). Homosexual boyhood: Notes on girlyboys. *Gender and Psychoanalysis, 1*, 429–461.

Corbett, K. (2009). *Boyhoods: Rethinking masculinities*. New Haven & London: Yale University Press.

D'Angelo, R. (2020). The man I am trying to be is not me. *International Journal of Psychoanalysis, 101*(5), 951–970.

De Graaf, N. M., & Carmichael, P. (2018). Reflections on emerging trends in clinical work with gender diverse children and adolescents. *Clinical Child Psychology & Psychiatry, 24*(2), 353–364.

Elise, D. (2000). Women and desire: Why women may *not* want to want. *Studies in Gender and Sexuality, 1*(2), 125–145.

Fausto-Sterling, A. (2012). The dynamic development of gender variability. *Journal of Homosexuality, 59*, 398–421.

Freud, S. (1905). Three essays on the theory of sexuality. In *Standard Edition* (Vol. 7, pp. 123–243). London: Hogarth Press.

Freud, S. (1925). Some psychical consequences of the anatomical distinction between the sexes. In *Standard Edition* (Vol. 19, pp. 248–258). London: Hogarth Press.

Freud, S. (1950). Project for a scientific psychology. In *Standard Edition* (Vol. 1, pp. 295–397), London: Hogarth Press.

Frosh, S. (2017). A plague on both your houses. In N. Giffney & E. Watson (Eds.), *Clinical encounters in sexuality* (pp. 385–390). Earth, Milky Way: Punctum Books.

Gozlan, O. (2018). Introduction. In O. Gozlan (Ed.), *Current critical debates in the field of transsexual studies, in transition* (pp. 1–12). London & New York: Routledge.

Hansbury, G. (2017). Unthinkable anxieties: Reading Transphobic countertransferences in a century of psychoanalytic writing. *Transgender Studies Quarterly, 4*, 384–404.

Hausman, B. (1995). *Changing sex: Transsexualism, technology, and the idea of gender*. Durham, NC: Duke University Press.

Haynal, A. E. (2009). Sexuality: A conceptual and historical essay. In P. Fonagy, R. Krause, & M. Leuzinger-Bohleber (Eds.), *Identity, gender and sexuality* (Chapter 2, pp. 21–32). London: Karnac Books. (Original publication 2006 The International Psychoanalytic Association).

Irigaray, L. (1991). *The Irigaray reader*. In M. Whitford (Ed.). Oxford: Blackwell.

Kaye, M. (2021). Dead naming, denial and detransition. Retrieved September 4, 2021, from https://www.youtube.com/watch?v=iy1csC7gyYA

Kaye, M. (2021). A fascination with the feminine. A transsexual view. Retrieved September 4, 2021, from https://www.youtube.com/watch?v=Thpxye9ZnNs

Kaye, S. (2024). Detransitioning after 25 years. From self-centredness to surrender. Retrieved September 12, 2024. https://www.youtube.com/watch?v=TJw36g5oyk0

Langer, S. J. (2016). Trans bodies and the failure of mirrors. *Studies in Gender and Sexuality*, *17*(4), 306–316.

Lemma, A. (2012). Research off the couch: Re-visiting the transsexual conundrum. *Psychoanalytic Psychotherapy*, *26*(4), 263–281.

Lemma, A. (2023). The missing: Exploring the use of photographs in "working through" the natal body with transgender youth. *International Journal of Psychoanalysis*, *104*(5), 809–828.

Littman, L. (2021). Individuals treated for gender dysphoria with medical and/or surgical transition who subsequently detransitioned: A survey of 100 detransitioners. *Archives of Sexual Behavior*, *50*, 3353–3369.

Lombardi, R. (2002). Primitive mental States and the body: A personal view of Armando B. Ferrari's concrete original object. *International Journal of Psycho-Analysis*, *83*(2), 363–381.

Marciano, L. (2017). Outbreak: On transgender teens and psychic epidemics. *Psychological Perspectives*, *60*, 345–366.

Marcus, L., Marcus, K., Yaxte, S. M., & Marcus, K. (2015). Genderqueer: One family's experience with gender variance. *Psychoanalytic Inquiry*, *35*(8), 795–808.

Mitchell, J. (2000). Hysteria. In *Mad men and Medusas*: Reclaiming hysteria (Chapter 1, pp. 1–42). London: Penguin Books.

Money-Kyrle, R. E. (1968). Cognitive development. *International Journal of Psychoanalysis*, *49*, 691–698.

Money-Kyrle, R. E. (1971). The aim of psychoanalysis. *International Journal Psycho-Analysis*, *52*, 103–106.

No Way Back. (2023). *No Way Back: The Reality of Gender Affirming Care*. Deplorable Films, www.DeplorableFilms.com

Oppenheimer, A. (1991). The wish for a sex change: A challenge to psychoanalysis? *International Journal of Psychoanalysis*, *72*, 221–231.

Quinodoz, D. (1998). Termination of a Fe/Male transsexual patient's analysis: An example of general validity. *International Journal of Psychoanalysis*, *83*, 783–798.

Saketopoulou, A., & Pellegrini, A. (2023). *Gender without identity*. New York: The Unconscious in Translation.

Schopf, W. (September 1, 2005) as cited in Shermer, M. (2005). Retrieved February 1, 2021, from www.skeptic.com; https://michaelshermer.com/sciam-columns/rumsfelds-wisdom/

Showalter, E. (1997). Defining hysteria. In *Hystories, hysterical epidemics and modern culture* (Chapter 2, pp. 14–29). London: Picador.

Steiner, J. (2018). Time and the garden of Eden illusion. *International Journal of Psychoanalysis*, *99*(6), 1274–1287.

Schwartz, A. (1998). *Sexual subjects: Lesbians, gender and psychoanalysis*. London: Routledge.

tumblr. (2020). Common non binary genders. https://genderfluidsupport.tumblr.com/gender

Westen, D. (1997). Towards a clinically and empirically sound theory of motivation. *International Journal of Psychoanalysis*, *78*, 521–548.

Wren, B. (2019). Notes on a crisis of meaning in the care of gender diverse children. In L. Herzmann & J. Newbigin (Eds.), *Sexuality and gender now: Moving beyond heteronormativity* (Chapter 4, pp. 189–212). London & New York: Routledge.

Yarom, N. (2005). A "matrix of hysteria": The struggle between the sexes as enacted in the body, in *Matrix of hysteria: Psychoanalysis of the struggle between the sexes as enacted in the body* (Chapter 1, pp. 13–18). London & New York: Routledge.

Index

For Product Safety Concerns and Information please contact our EU
representative GPSR@taylorandfrancis.com
Taylor & Francis Verlag GmbH, Kaufingerstraße 24, 80331 München, Germany

www.ingramcontent.com/pod-product-compliance
Lightning Source LLC
Chambersburg PA
CBHW050607280326
41932CB00016B/2951